The Insider's Guide to Graduate Degrees in Creative Writing

The Insider's Guide to Graduate Degrees in Creative Writing

SETH ABRAMSON

BLOOMSBURY ACADEMIC
LONDON • NEW YORK • OXFORD • NEW DELHI • SYDNEY

BLOOMSBURY ACADEMIC
Bloomsbury Publishing Plc
50 Bedford Square, London, WC1B 3DP, UK

BLOOMSBURY, BLOOMSBURY ACADEMIC and the Diana logo are
trademarks of Bloomsbury Publishing Plc

First published in Great Britain 2018

A catalogue record for this book is available from the British Library.

A catalog record for this book is available from the Library of Congress.

ISBN: HB: 978-1-3500-0041-4
PB: 978-1-3500-0040-7
ePDF: 978-1-3500-0043-8
eBook: 978-1-3500-0042-1

Typeset by Deanta Global Publishing Services, Chennai, India
Printed and bound in Great Britain

To find out more about our authors and books visit www.bloomsbury.com
and sign up for our newsletters.

CONTENTS

Introduction

There are as many ways of living the writing life as there are writers. Tonight in America there is an aspiring novelist who wants nothing more than to have her work read by local book clubs around the country, and another who'd secretly rather be writing genre fiction than the literary fiction graduate-school admissions committees value. There's a fiction-writer who hopes one day to be a screenwriter, and another enchanted by the sort of "alt-lit" fiction that more commonly gets sold in comic book boutiques than bookstores. Tonight there's a poet who expects to publish with single-proprietor indie presses for all his writing years, and another who wants to establish a stable relationship with a university press as soon as possible. While some of these poets and fiction-writers hope to one day teach at a university or work at a publishing house, others can think of no greater nightmare than to find themselves at the head of a classroom or holed up in an office in New York City. And all of these imagined authors might see their ambitions change radically over the next months, years, and decades.

The decision about whether to apply to a graduate creative writing program is not, despite what some say, a decision that will determine your future as a writer. While a small number of graduate creative writing programs are particularly adept at finding agents for their aspiring novelists and indie publishers for their aspiring poets, well over 95 percent of graduate creative writing programs have no such track record to speak of. Just so, while the data tells us that somewhere between a third and a half of creative writing master of fine arts (MFA) applicants would like to teach creative writing upon graduation, it also tells us that less than 1 percent of MFA-holders will ever get the chance to do so full-time. None of this means that those with an MFA in creative writing won't go on to do extraordinary things within and without creative writing—including publish widely, teach others how to write, and generally lead satisfying writing lives—it's just that, if we look at the data collected in the discipline over the last decade, one's decision about where to attend graduate school, or whether to attend graduate school at all, is only a small piece of the picture.

One reason for this is that graduate programs in creative writing—and you're going to hear me say this a lot—are *not* professional degree programs. They are fine arts programs. While prospective employers would rather see more education on a job applicant's resume than less, it's not clear that the MFA moves the ball very much as a job market chit. And while the MFA is held by a number of people now working as literary agents and publishers, little in the degree itself particularly prepares one for those occupations. Likewise, while we increasingly see MFA-holders applying to doctoral programs in the humanities rather than the fine arts, most acknowledge this as a detour from, rather than a continuation of, their creative writing education—and as you may have heard, the job market for humanities PhDs is pretty bleak at the moment.

All of this helps explain, I hope, the central premise of this book: that in choosing a graduate program in creative writing, three simple considerations should dominate above all others. First, have you developed appropriate expectations for your graduate creative writing program before applying to one? Second, have you identified which aspects of a prospective program—whether it's the program's location, faculty, curriculum, or student body—will be the most significant to your program experience? Third, have you done all you can to ensure that nothing about the program is likely to cause you lasting harm? This last consideration is key to avoiding crippling student loan debt, living in a place or situation in which you feel unwelcome or uninspired, or spending your postgraduate years with questions about your writing that arise not from within you but from elements of your program that inadvertently discouraged rather than encouraged you.

With these considerations in mind, this book aims to give you a thorough and unvarnished introduction to graduate creative writing programs. The information you'll find here comes from the very best sources available: first, the largest stock of hard data about graduate creative writing programs ever assembled; second, FAQ sections developed with the assistance of the largest permanent community of graduate creative writing applicants in the world; and third, the hard-won experience of a well-published author who writes in all three major genres of creative writing, has attended both the smallest and one of the largest MFA programs in the country, and has taught creative writing at three flagship public universities. The hope is that, by putting these disparate resources between the covers of a single book, we're giving you a one-stop compendium of everything you need to know before you apply to graduate creative writing programs, while you're applying to them, and even once you've matriculated.

This book is called *The Insider's Guide to Graduate Degrees in Creative Writing* for a good reason: because it's focused exclusively on *your* well-being as an applicant—not on the interests of the programs you will be applying to or on creative writing as a discipline. One of the reasons little of the data creative writing applicants crave was available for the first 75 years of graduate writing degrees is that these programs, along with their official trade organization—the Association of Writers & Writing Programs, or AWP—controlled the conversation about access to data. It is only within the last decade that advocates for creative writing applicants have insisted that applicants have access to critical admissions, funding, and curricular data whether or not the programs want it to be released. So if you find in this book some impolitic assessments of creative writing workshops or conventional wisdom about applying to MFA or PhD programs in creative writing that you've never heard before, that's because this book is designed especially for you, the applicant—and always chooses truth-telling over crowd-pleasing. Not all of the news you read in this book will please you, but I can promise you it is offered to empower you as you make important life decisions in the years ahead.

With all that in mind, I should say that there are three things you won't find in this book. And I promise you in advance you won't miss them. The first is testimonials from anyone paid to advocate for (or who would personally benefit from advocating for) a given graduate creative writing program. While it might seem natural to want to hear directly from faculty and students at individual programs, a decade of research into the sort of advice interviews of this sort produce tells us the following: people like, and recommend, whatever it is they already know, and where possible will encourage aspiring authors to make all the same decisions they did. There's nothing nefarious about that inclination, by the way. It's simply that others' decisions may be entirely wrong for you. That's why I promise to give you wide-ranging insights into applying to graduate creative writing programs, but never a landing strip of blinking red lights pointing you in one program's direction over another. You know better than me, and better than anyone employed by or studying in any of the creative writing programs discussed in this book, exactly what you need from a graduate creative writing program. What we'll do here is ensure that you know all the questions you should be asking on that score, and have access to all the hard data that could help answer those questions.

A second thing you won't find here are "overall" assessments of any program. In fact, no assessment of that sort has ever been done in the discipline, nor will it ever be. And there's a good reason for that: it's impossible to say definitively what makes a program superlative, or which aspects of a program's culture and curriculum are most important. Those judgments naturally vary from applicant to applicant. That's why even the much-discussed *U.S. News & World Report* "rankings" of creative writing programs compiled in 1996 only assessed programs by one measure: how current creative writing faculty members rated the overall "reputations" of individual programs. "Reputation" wasn't defined, and respondents were given no guidance on that score other than being precluded from rating their own programs. An "overall quality" assessment it was not.

Not surprisingly, the *U.S. News & World Report* found that the oldest programs in the nation, as well as the programs with the largest faculties—therefore, the ones with the largest networks of professional associations throughout the discipline—performed the best in this single-category analysis. And that may be why the magazine stopped ranking graduate creative writing programs over two decades ago. Even at their very best, education rankings can only measure one narrow program feature at a time.

In 1993 and in 2007, two publications—the *Dictionary of Literary Biography* and *The Atlantic*—tried to assess programs using the personal opinions of a single individual. The results there, too, were predictable. One person's opinion is never anything more.

Instead of seeking to approximate a program's "overall" reputation using a numeric scale, or asking a reporter to visit a few programs and then rank 250 of them, this book uses hard data to let you draw your own conclusions about individual program features.

Want to know which programs offer the best funding, have the best student-faculty ratio, are most selective in their admissions, and place the most graduates in college teaching positions and postgraduate fellowships? This book can tell you that. But what it can't tell you, and won't try to tell you, is how much weight you should put on any of these assessments and what they do or don't say about the overall quality of a program. Wealthier applicants may well worry less about financial aid; nontraditional students concerned about the didacticism of professors younger than they are may not focus as much on programs' student-faculty ratios; those with no intention of teaching creative writing or attending a postgraduate fellowship may well skip those metrics altogether.

For most applicants, none of these measures, taken individually, are sufficient. What they do, instead, is begin to paint a picture about what life at individual programs might be like. Would the high cost of living and sparse funding at Program A require you to take on a side job in-program, thereby eating into your writing hours? Does a low acceptance rate at a program held in high esteem by well-researched applicants really mean that program attracts the strongest candidates? Is it better to be in a two- or three-year program? How about a program that allows writers in different genres to take classes together, as opposed to one that doesn't? These distinctions, and dozens more that we'll discuss, are for you to make, not me. But I can say with confidence that this book contains the information you need to make assessments on these and other questions.

A third and final thing this book does not hope to do, and indeed could never do, is ensure that you'll have a good experience at any graduate creative writing program you may attend. What I've found, interviewing thousands of creative writing program applicants, students, and alumni over the past decade, is that what you get out of a program depends most significantly on what expectations you went in with and how you behaved once you got there. If your expectation for your program or, more broadly, your understanding of what graduate education in creative writing can and can't do, is misguided, your chance of finishing a program dissatisfied skyrockets. On the other hand, if you use this book to develop a reasonable sense of what attending an MFA or PhD in creative writing looks like, your odds of one meeting your expectations are high.

The chapters of this book track with the process creative writing MFA and PhD applicants take from the moment they begin considering graduate programs to the first time they reflect seriously on their program several weeks into the first semester there. At times you'll find me giving you options on how to think about a step in the process; at other times I'll be giving you hard data and urging you to take, on account of that data, certain things about the application process as a given. For instance, we're going to have a long, multifaceted conversation about how one might philosophize the operation and utility of the conventional creative writing workshop. Our purpose will be not just to prepare you for the cornerstone pedagogy of every graduate creative writing program, but to discuss how this knowledge, when retrofitted, helps you choose the best program for you in the first instance. On a few occasions, I'll give you an unambiguous warning based on years of hard data—for instance, about the postgraduate job market. As we go along, I know you'll distinguish between items that are up for debate and those that are statistical certainties. (All the same, I'll probably point out the distinction on occasion.)

If you're reading this book, one thing I know about you is that you're very serious about writing. Which means you're very serious about living the life of a working writer. And I can promise you—from years of experience—it's a wild ride whether you apply to any of the programs discussed in this book or not. While I may not be a conventional sort of tour guide as we consider the grand maxims and statistical minutiae of creative writing, I do hope you'll come to see me as a concerned and caring acquaintance who very much wants you to take whatever first step in your journey is right for you.

CHAPTER ONE

A Brief History of Creative Writing Programs

If you're like me, you spent your college years studying a major whose history as an academic discipline no one ever taught you. For me, the subject was English, and while I loved studying literature, I'll admit I never had any deeper understanding of English *as a discipline* than this one: English majors read books and analyze them. This was more than enough information for me to have about the disciplinary history of English as an undergraduate subject. As long as I was willing to read a stack of books and then write a large number of painstakingly boring essays analyzing them, I was fine.

Graduate school is different. When you apply to graduate school in a discipline, you're committing much of your life to the study and practice of one subject. If you take out loans for school, your future financial well-being is tied to your graduate degree; if you go on the job market, employers assess your qualification for a position based in part on the highest degree you obtained. Friends and family construe the subject in which you obtained your highest degree as emblematic of your skills and interests—or else wonder bemusedly why you wasted years after college on a subject you never think about or practice anymore. So as graduate school is a serious commitment to an area of study, understanding something about the history of your chosen field is essential.

In the case of creative writing, understanding even a bit of the history of the discipline offers a wealth of knowledge about what you can be—and maybe should be—looking for in a graduate creative writing program. The hundreds of creative writing degree programs operating today often deviate substantially from what historically was the purpose and scope of such curricula. For some of you, these deviations will seem a blessing; for others, only a program linked up with the history of the discipline will do.

A popular misconception about creative writing degree programs is that their core pedagogical component—the creative writing workshop—spontaneously appeared in Iowa City, Iowa, in the form of the Iowa Writers' Workshop, sometime in the mid-1930s. In fact, the workshop pedagogy ("pedagogy" meaning, here, "teaching method") first appeared at Harvard University in the early 1880s, when a group of self-professed radicals in that school's composition program began taking significant license with the homework they assigned to their students and the classroom activities they permitted.

Whereas prior to 1880 an advanced composition class saw its students do little more than write response essays to a small roster of predictable "themes"—almost all of which had to do with civics and ethics—beginning in 1880 many Harvard undergrads were permitted by their professors to select their *own* daily writing topics. Moreover, these professors allowed their students to write "imaginatively" if they desired. Many students chose to write what we'd now think of as creative nonfiction or flash fiction. Some wrote fables. Within a few years, the advanced composition courses at Harvard that gave students this leeway were among the most popular classes at the university.

It's worth understanding that at this point in the history of "creative writing" an academic discipline by that name did not exist. In fact, the term "creative writing" didn't enter the national lexicon until the late 1920s. Nor was "composition" a separate area of academic inquiry; both it and what we now think of as "creative writing" were part of the study of English—then, unlike now, one of the most popular fields of study in higher education. Harvard professors' reimagining of English through new writing pedagogies was in a sense the birth of both composition studies and creative writing as disciplines.

At the time, however, the idea was simply that English students should be doing more than merely reading and analyzing literature. Harvard's educational pioneers believed English students should be "creative readers" as well as "creative writers"—to use two terms that first appeared in a speech by Ralph Waldo Emerson in 1820—and therefore should at once speak well, write well, critique well, problem-solve well, and *imagine* well. The young men attending Harvard's single-sex educational program in the 1880s thought of their advanced composition courses as opportunities to learn how to be a "citizen of the world." Literature was a piece of that, yes, but so was civics, so was history and political science, and so was what they thought of as "imaginative writing."

It wasn't just that late-nineteenth-century Harvard undergraduates taking select advanced composition courses wrote "imaginatively" almost as often as they wrote critically, it's that the work they produced was critiqued weekly by their classmates in a classroom activity that would today look to us very much like "workshopping." First, a student would read a classmate's imaginative work aloud to the class; next, an assigned student would deliver an introduction and overview of the work; finally, the whole class would discuss the work, and not just as to its technical proficiency but also its *aesthetics* (a term I use here to mean "personal writing style"). Because this basic setup also featured assigned readings in poetry and fiction, we can say that Harvard's advanced composition classrooms in the 1880s looked a lot like the writing workshops of today.

The purpose of Harvard students' imaginative writing was, even then, very clear: it was an attempt to undercut the then-tiny "canon" of acceptable American literature. By asking students to spend almost as much time critiquing one another's original work as responding to work that had already been published, Harvard professors like Barrett Wendell not only exposed students to writing that may have seemed more relevant than, for instance, the five or six American poets whose work was then considered suitable for a classroom, but also broadened the range of topics that students could discuss in class. For instance, if the so-called "Fireside Poets" who then dominated the American verse canon were all in favor of early marriage, in Wendell's courses students could discuss peer-written texts in which the prospect of ever getting married at all was disparaged.

If this sounds to you like a radical democratization of American academia, it was. The earliest instances of what we now term "creative writing pedagogy" were strident attempts to change what could and could not be talked about in English literature classrooms—both as to the texts considered appropriate reading and the themes that were fair game for discussion. Even more than this, these Harvard educators' privileging of student-written work celebrated students' tendency to write *idiosyncratically*. It celebrated deviations from, rather than rote adherence to, the conventional writing style then seen in textbook-published poems and stories. From its outset, then, what we now know as "creative writing" was a rebellion against the American canon, conventional academic discourse, and even some of the longstanding fundamentals of English-language writing.

The "Harvard model" for advanced writing instruction spread like wildfire during the 1890s and early 1900s. As had been the case at Harvard in the 1880s, the model was used in both undergraduate and graduate classrooms. Increasingly, colleges and universities developed courses in which students could focus specifically on "verse-writing" or "versification"—as the study of poetry writing was then called—as well as playwriting or "the short story." And educators began to more aggressively encourage students to explore their own unique perspectives on the world, often emphasizing the inclusion of the towns and cities in which each student had been born and raised.

Because many early undergraduate courses in creative writing were founded at universities in the Midwest, creative writing instruction manifested as a cultural revolution as well as an academic one. Traditionally, the undergraduate texts of the mid- to late nineteenth century had been written by American intellectuals living on the East Coast; with the expansion of imaginative writing pedagogies in the 1890s and early 1900s, suddenly students at University of Nebraska at Lincoln and University of Montana in Missoula were being encouraged to write on topics of particular interest to those born and raised in those regions of the country. If this all sounds rather obvious now, realize that at the time the view that great American literature could focus on current events in the small towns of America's Midwestern and Mountain regions was a minority opinion.

By the time the first terminal graduate degree in creative writing was established—a "Master of Fine Arts" that the University of Iowa began offering in 1936—the basic structure of creative writing study at the university level had already been established. Iowa's primary innovation, then, both when it started awarding the MFA in 1936 and when it formally opened the "Iowa Writers' Workshop" in 1942, was to pull creative writing instruction even *further* from conventional education in English. For instance, at the Writers' Workshop one was almost as likely to have a classroom session held outside a classroom as inside it; one-on-one meetings with professors in their offices became as important to the learning process as in-class student discussions; and especially talented students could be admitted to graduate study just by showing up in Iowa City and presenting a faculty member with a reasonably strong manuscript in poetry or fiction. Moreover, the Workshop was an early adopter of the idea that working writers with little or no scholarly background and little or no prior teaching experience can, on occasion, make fine role models for aspiring poets and writers.

The surprising thing about the University of Iowa's decision to begin awarding terminal degrees in creative writing is that, in many respects, it was a failure. A quarter-century after the Writers' Workshop began awarding MFA degrees, not a single college or university in the world had followed suit. A handful of institutions had created creative writing MA programs—considerably more academic than the MFA, and intended partly as preparation for doctoral study in English literature—but the idea that there should be a discrete discipline called "creative writing" and that it deserved a terminal degree was not, in fact, a popular one. At the start of the 1960s the nation's handful of undergraduate and graduate creative writing programs flew in the face of the abiding reality in higher education: creative writing was most definitely a subfield of English.

It was in the 1960s and 1970s that English as a discipline essentially blew up. Creative writing, composition studies, communications, women's studies, and African American studies made their final breaks from it, leaving English as a field of inquiry significantly diminished in size and scope. To composition studies went much of the civics and nearly all of the writing instruction; to communications went any emphasis on the use of technology to communicate; to women's studies and African American studies went the most robust analyses of the literature and critical theory attached to those topics; and to creative writing went systematized in-class critiques and a narrow band of writing instruction, as well as the opportunity for largely unguided imaginative writing practices. "English" retained reading, conventional critical analysis, and—to the displeasure of many an undergraduate and graduate English student—a broad swath of critical theory. What happened to the problem-solving, the history and political science, and the encouragement of students to be "citizens of the world"? No one really knows.

The fracturing of English study in the 1960s and 1970s, which was mostly due to administrative and professorial in-fighting within English departments, did not, I'd submit, benefit English departments. It significantly diminished English by turning what had once been a host of vibrant subdisciplines into separate disciplines.

Another important development of the 1960s—which has only reached full flower in our present decade—was the popularization of *non*institutional workshops. One of the best-known workshops of the 1960s wasn't an academic program, actually, but New York City's "Umbra Workshop," an unaffiliated workshop founded in 1961 and geared toward the literary aspirations of the city's African American authors. While the first noninstitutional workshops, such as those at Middlebury's annual Bread Loaf Writers' Conference, had been founded decades before, it wasn't until the 1960s that it became clear that workshops could empower entire literary subcommunities just as much as individual authors. Today, we find local nonacademic workshops in towns and cities across America, as well as urban writing centers focused on the advancement of local communities and subcommunities. From the tradition of Bread Loaf has sprung a small network of summer writing conferences that writers pay to attend, and the internet has brought with it myriad opportunities for writers to workshop their poetry or fiction for free with strangers from around the world. So while the 1960s did see other schools finally take up the "Iowa model" of awarding terminal degrees for student-authored creative theses, it also proved that workshopping needn't be limited to tuition-driven institutional spaces.

Composition studies and communications responded better to the strife within English in the 1960s and 1970s than did English or creative writing. Both disciplines developed robust pedagogies and their own body of critical theory, as well as expanding their inquiries into civics-minded topics like literacy (composition studies) and digital-age cultural studies (communications). Whereas English has now been mired in deconstructive critical theory for around 70 years—longer than any cultural paradigm has ever had hold of any academic sphere—composition studies and communications have embraced digital-age paradigms that point toward a more optimistic, "post-postmodern" worldview. During this same period, women's studies and African American studies, joined by peer disciplines such as Asian-American studies and queer studies, have found exciting ways to draw knowledge from a range of academic fields.

Meanwhile, English has puttered on largely as before, though concurrent with the "boom" in graduate creative writing programs in the 1980s and 1990s it began to alienate creative writers by communicating to them, in ways large and small, public and private, passive-aggressive and aggressive, that they weren't welcome in the discipline anymore. English has thus become more resolutely a space for the study of literature rather than writing, and for critique rather than imaginative inquiry. And to the extent that many English departments have failed to register the decline of the book and the rise of multimedia and transmedia art—a development communications has benefited from enormously—they have come to suffer the enrollment shortfalls we read about today.

The sad truth is that creative writing did even less than English in the 1980s and 1990s to develop itself. With the boom in undergraduate and graduate creative writing programs during these two decades, creative writing arguably had no present need to evolve or obligation to reinvent itself. Students wanted creative writing courses—that much was clear—so why should the discipline amend what it had done in the 1930s?

From a certain view, one could argue this conservative stance was warranted. From the late 1990s onward, the field of terminal-degree programs in the literary arts had expanded faster than the terminal degrees of any other academic discipline—including all the hard sciences, all the social sciences, and all the other humanities. So even as the humanities have seen declining enrollments nearly across the board, creative writing has been one of its biggest success stories. There are now graduate creative writing programs in every corner of the country, and at times they even exhibit a sort of diversity: they're all different sizes and durations; they have differing views on cross-genre study; and many have slightly variant prerequisites and curricular requirements.

From another view, the discipline is stagnant—something you need to understand if you're going to graduate school to study it. For instance, today's creative writing workshops tend to be narrower than the workshops of the 1880s. Whereas those workshops were a shot across the bow of the then-dominant literary canon, today's workshops encourage students to think deductively rather than inductively about writing, beginning with a rather vague collective consensus about what "mastery" looks like on the page and then implicitly asking students to replicate that presumption. Whereas the early creative writing workshops were focused on students' ability to engage critically and creatively with the issues of the day, workshop-generated lyric-narrative poetry in 2018 more commonly operates in what is called the "post-confessional" mode—full of ironic and carefully obscured self-revelations—while "literary fiction" as a rule dedicates itself to intimate settings rather than grandiose ones. Whereas advanced composition at Harvard was fundamentally cross-disciplinary, the curricular insularity of today's creative writing programs make it less likely students will collaborate with those in other disciplines or engage new technologies in their work.

Harvard undergraduates in the 1880s benefited from an English department whose "citizen of the world" philosophy encouraged the development of problem-solving skills and a "poetics" of engagement (a writer's "poetics" is her idiosyncratic relationship with language, genre, self-identity, and culture, as well as her sense of what her chosen literary genre can accomplish in the world that no other manner of self-expression can). Today's workshops focus disproportionately on "aesthetics"—matters of "craft" and style—and much less on poetics or problem-solving. Wendell and his peers wanted their students to consider why we write, how writing engages our environment, and how writing profoundly edits us and those around us rather than the other way around. The workshop pedagogy now in use demands authors be silent in class when their work is discussed, and rarely asks them to vocalize and dialogue through their development as writers or consider what it means for any of us to have and perform for an audience.

In the 2000s, a small group of creative writing instructors developed what we now call "critical creative writing pedagogy" and an attached subdiscipline known as creative writing studies. Critical creative writing pedagogy and creative writing studies ask of the workshop and its advocates questions that, ideally, would have been asked in the 1930s: What are the most *effective* and *inspiring*, rather than merely the *existing*, ways of teaching creative writing? Should we deep-six conventional writing workshops?

Should we fundamentally alter how the creative writing classroom is organized, and its curriculum, and even what we denominate "creative writing" in the first instance? What role can new technologies play in the creative writing classroom, and are there boldly experimental approaches to writing and writing instruction that certain students may respond to more than the current ones? Creative writing studies scholars ask also about the instruction we give aspiring authors on *how to workshop* and *what to expect from a workshop*. They help us redefine what it means to find and develop an audience.

Nothing now happening in creative writing studies replaces the core elements of creative writing instruction—regularized writing and critique and the production of a substantial project at the end of a several-year course of study—but much is happening that could gradually change what it means to be a graduate creative writing student.

One major shift in graduate creative writing study over the last twenty years is the introduction of "low-residency" graduate creative writing programs. While a handful of these were founded prior to 2000, an incredible fact is that half of the new graduate creative writing programs founded since 2000 are low-residency programs. These programs turn conventional creative writing instruction on its head by redirecting focus to the mentor-mentee relationship, sizable reading lists, self-starting writing practices, and the use of technology to communicate with other members of the program. While low-residency students attend two "residencies" annually during which they participate in workshops and lectures the likes of which a full-residency student would recognize, there's no doubt the low-residency model is a "revolution" within writing instruction.

In the 2010s, we've seen the very beginnings of another sort of revolution: full-residency programs that are "themed," cross-disciplinary, or in some other way targeted toward students with something other than an interest in conventional lyric-narrative poetry or literary fiction. Unfortunately, as many of these programs are new and/or located at art schools—which historically offer much less student funding than flagship public universities—it's still the case that the most affordable full-residency option for the overwhelming majority of applicants is a conventional creative writing program.

Interestingly, despite being the nation's most popular creative writing program, the Iowa Writers' Workshop continues to be an outlier in many respects. Whereas most programs assign students letter grades, the Writers' Workshop does not; the Workshop also doesn't take attendance, operates in a separate physical plant from the rest of its host university, and exclusively offers academic courses taught by nonscholars. It forbids cross-genre study. Its ad-hoc funding scheme differentially funds incoming students, and sometimes on the oddest of bases, too—indeed, I know someone who attended Iowa on a skiing scholarship. It's also more willing than most programs to pay for admitted students to make site visits prematriculation, admit students who are widely published or already hold an MFA, and encourage authors whose work is self-admittedly strange.

I mention all this to underscore that if there's an "archetypal" creative writing program, it is neither the Iowa Writers' Workshop, nor any low-residency program, nor any cross-disciplinary art-school program or "themed" program. Rather, the archetypal graduate creative writing program requires a mix of workshops and academic courses; assigns grades; takes attendance; refuses to pay for site visits by admitted students; encourages some cross-genre study; favors conventional lyric-narrative poetry and literary fiction; and has a standardized scheme for funding its students—usually by way of offering a minimal percentage teaching assistantships with full tuition remission.

This last point brings us to the most profound change we've seen in graduate creative writing programs this century: an increase in the number of "fully funded" programs. A "fully funded" program is one that offers full tuition remission and a livable stipend to all students, whether or not all students receive identical funding packages. At the turn of the century, only a small number of graduate creative writing programs were fully funded. Today—in part because the increased availability of funding data has made applicants more selective about where they're willing to matriculate—so many full-residency programs are fully funded that no applicant should feel *obligated* to apply to or attend a creative writing MFA or PhD program unfunded. This dramatic rise in the number of fully funded programs has also solidified the position of the creative writing MFA as a "coterminal" degree in the field alongside the creative writing PhD; in the United States, most terminal degrees are fully funded, so the rarity of finding a fully funded MFA program in the 1970s, 1980s, and 1990s called into question whether the MFA really was a "proper" terminal degree.

Having said that, in just the last few years the terminality of the MFA has come under something of a shadow. While the total number of doctoral creative writing programs—PhD programs that MFA students can apply to postgraduation to continue workshopping and prepare another book-length project—hasn't changed much over the last thirty years, the value of the degree is higher now than it ever has been. The short explanation for this is that MFA programs have become so numerous and so popular that it's becoming harder and harder for creative writers to distinguish themselves, to the extent they feel they must, on the basis of their master's-degree alma mater. This is a particularly significant development for MFA graduates who hope to teach full-time at the university level after graduation. Increasingly, colleges and universities are choosing to hire creative writers with doctorates. This is partly because these students have more teaching and (often) publishing experience, and partly because academia has long considered the PhD the gold standard for incoming faculty. Nonwriters on a creative writing faculty search committee invariably respond better to candidates with a PhD.

As you can tell from all of the aforementioned reasons, this is an unusual time to be applying to graduate creative writing programs. More and more creative writing instruction is happening online; more and more programs are fully funding their students; and more and more students are looking to attend not just two or three years of graduate study in creative writing but more like six or seven. All of which means that acceptance rates are dropping dramatically even as unfunded programs struggle to find students they can be genuinely excited about. Due to the influx of low-residency programs, which often cater to nontraditional students, the average age of an MFA matriculant is slowly rising. And technology plays a large role in their instruction. Significant pedagogical innovations are almost certainly taking place within individual classrooms, though since many programs' promotional materials lag behind the times, we haven't heard yet about many of them. Programs are more aware than ever before that they are being assessed in areas like student funding, postgraduate placement, and student-faculty ratio, even as there's too little evidence these programs are reorienting themselves to cater to students working in multimedia, transmedia, multidisciplinary, multigenre, or cross-genre modalities.

In short, the field is in flux and its future will take it in one of two very different directions: either millennial applicants will increasingly find the workshop pedagogy and the sort of literature most favored by it irrelevant to their own worldviews, and creative writing programs will have to, after many years of stagnation, *dramatically* rethink their presumptions; or, equally possible, the field will continue to expand without much innovation at all, as more and more young Americans decide they want to memorialize their artistic inclinations through the dedicated study of literary art. If the discipline can more broadly embrace multimedia, experimental writing, dynamic pedagogies, across-the-board "full funding," and aggressive career counseling, I think the first future is the more likely of the two. If the discipline maintains its eighty-year-old conventional wisdoms—"pick a program for its faculty"; "choose a genre and stick with it"; "write for the page, not the stage"; and so on—I think it will suffer the same fate English study has suffered over the past few decades. It'll decline, and with no evident endpoint in sight.

FREQUENTLY ASKED QUESTIONS: A BRIEF HISTORY OF CREATIVE WRITING PROGRAMS

Q1: So how is all this knowledge helpful to me in choosing a program right now?
A1: What I hope this brief history of creative writing programs helps establish for you is what you can and can't expect from such programs— or from the discipline generally—at this point in its evolution. If you're a multimedia artist, an experimental writer, someone who can't attend a graduate creative writing program without full funding, someone who needs each classroom session you attend to be dramatically different than the one before or after it, or someone who thinks an MFA is a sufficient qualification to get you a teaching job postgraduation, this history should have given you some pause. Likewise, if you're expecting the professors you study under in your program to be reflexive about classroom pedagogy, or incredibly flexible in their aesthetic approach to your chosen genre, you might be disappointed. If you think an MFA program will help you answer the big questions—"Why do I write?" "What makes my writing

invaluable to my culture?" "What does it mean to have an audience?" "What does it mean to boldly experiment in the literary arts?" "What is the utility to all this self-expression?" "Who does my writing help, and who or what does it change?"—you may want to think again.

In the next chapter, I talk about how to decide whether or not now is the time for you to apply to a graduate creative writing program, or whether you should apply to one at all.

Q2: You sound a bit cynical about graduate creative writing programs. Why is that?

A2: In more than a thousand interviews and discussions with prospective, current, and former graduate students in creative writing, one refrain I've heard over and over from the latter two groups is that they did not enjoy their program experience. I get this response from about half of those I talk to, which is a startlingly high percentage given that some of them went into over $100,000 of student loan debt for their degrees.

My point is that a good reference guide doesn't just shove you out the door with more information than you had to start with, it also encourages you to think critically about which door is the right one for you. The main reason so many creative writing graduate students are dissatisfied isn't because of some terminal defect in the discipline they chose to study, though of course the discipline has a great deal of work to do on itself to become all it possibly can be. No, most of these men and women are unhappy because they went into their program with certain expectations and those expectations weren't met. My hope for this book is that it will help you to be more realistic about the adventure you're embarking upon without becoming jaded, too, in the process.

Q3: You talked about graduate creative writing programs in this history, but not about undergraduate creative writing programs. Are there differences between the two?

A3: Absolutely. On the surface, undergraduate creative writing programs tend to look a lot like graduate creative writing programs—largely because both use the workshop pedagogy almost exclusively—but the differences between the two are profound.

Undergraduate creative writers tend to hail from many different academic departments, may well have read very little published creative writing preworkshop, often have not yet selected a genre of choice, and have little expectation of reaching a large audience with their work in the near term, and so their emphasis is almost entirely on self-expression.

(Continued)

Because they've not yet learned the basic mechanics of the major genres of creative writing, they're less likely to try—or ever be asked—to subvert those conventions. One result of this is that undergraduate creative writers tend to be more aesthetically conservative than graduate-level creative writers. This means they rarely work in multimedia or across genres, have a somewhat narrower sense of what can or should be considered "poetry" or "fiction," and are not just shy about performing their work but have given little thought thus far as to how one finds an audience for one's writing. One fallout from this rudimentary understanding of *audience* is that undergraduate creative writers are more likely than other creative writers to respond to the work of their peers emotionally rather engage with it critically. Acting as a "peer mentor"—trying to see the ambition of your peers through *their* eyes, not your own, and advising them accordingly—is usually not an option at all, as the undergraduate creative writer just doesn't have the writing or reading experience to fulfill that role.

For these reasons, undergraduate workshops often study multiple genres during the course of the semester, focus on basic craft in each genre, rarely ask students to innovate with form, permit students to respond "affectively" (i.e., emotionally) to the work of peers, and avoid "big topics" like audience, medium, and "personal poetics."

I'd like to say that graduate creative writing workshops are a different beast, but they're not. In fact, the reason so many creative writing MFA and PhD alumni express frustration about their experiences is not that these experiences failed to replicate their undergraduate experience but that they *did* and *shouldn't* have. Undergraduates are expected to commit themselves only to the expectations of their course syllabi and their own artistic instincts; graduate students are charged with something quite different: committing themselves to art and the life of an artist. This means graduate school is supposed to be a time and place in which workshopping and literary discourse generally are reinvented. Students and professors should expect more of themselves and their time in class. When those expectations aren't met, it colors the experience for students and, dare I say it, their professors, too. I discuss all these topics much more in Chapter 10.

Q4: So that's the MFA and PhD. What's the deal with creative writing MA programs?

A4: Nonterminal creative writing MA programs were first developed in the late 1940s as an alternative to the "Iowa model"—that is, MFA as the terminal degree in the burgeoning field of "creative writing." Ostensibly these programs were better suited to aspiring poets and writers who thought they might want to go on to do a PhD in English, English literature, or literary studies (three terms for one discipline). They had their heyday at the tail end of the last century, and are now dramatically declining in number as the MFA continues its meteoric rise in popularity. There are a small number of fully funded MA programs in creative writing, and undergraduates who are not having luck gaining admission to an MFA program sometimes apply to these so they can spend a year or two more perfecting their creative portfolios. Because the MA is nonterminal, one can apply to MFA programs—or, for that matter, PhD programs in creative writing—upon graduation. As you might expect, the same conventional wisdom I'll offer regarding MFA programs applies with equal or greater force to MA programs: do not go into substantial debt for a creative writing MA. Indeed, because the degree is nonterminal, even "de minimis" (very minor) debt may not be worthwhile. It is possible creative writing MA programs will disappear in the next two decades, given how popular the MFA is and how hard it's become for MA programs to find well-qualified applicants.

Q5: How can I reconnect with the cousins of creative writing— composition studies, English, communications, and interdisciplinary disciplines like women's studies and African American studies—in an MFA program? And would doing that benefit me?
A5: One reason English used to be such a popular major is that it was *encompassing*. And one reason creative writing now disappoints so many who study it at the graduate level is that it is exceedingly limited in scope—both inside and outside the classroom. I hope reading this brief history of the discipline will help you see that it's not too late for creative writers to reconnect with their peers in closely related departments, and that in fact a graduate creative writing program can be the perfect place to do just that.

A major difference between undergraduate and graduate creative writing programs is that in the latter you are expected to be a self-starter. Well-conceived graduate-level creative writing curricula are impressively flexible. They allow you to more or less design your own course of study, which means they give you ample room to take courses outside your genre of choice and even outside the program. They give you little enough homework, and require of you few enough in-class hours, that

(*Continued*)

you have ample time to attend lectures and social events attended by students at the school who are *not* literary artists. They foster close enough relationships between students and professors that you can ask a professor to supervise you on an unconventional—say multimedia, transmedia, or cross-genre—creative thesis. Most of all, they're defined by a "hands-off" attitude toward your creative development. That means that if you speak up for yourself, you'll find ways to radically personalize your program experience.

It is too rarely observed that some of our best poets and writers are those with a strong interest in, and expertise drawn from, a discipline *other* than creative writing. One thing I hope the brief history I've offered above underscores is that it's only recently that people have begun to think of creative writing as belonging to its own discipline—and thus far it hasn't done nearly as much with that opportunity as it could have. What this might indicate to you is that, until the discipline is more fully formed and more reflexive about its evolution, it's up to you to use your graduate creative writing program experience to become a "citizen of the world."

And all that means is treating creative writing as a skill-set that must draw from many knowledge bases and collaborations to be as dynamically meaningful as it can be.

Q6: It often seems like the history of graduate creative writing programs is the history of six or seven "famous" programs. Is this a reasonable understanding of things?
A6: The small cadre of programs that receive a disproportionate percentage of the media coverage surrounding creative writing MFA programs would like you to think so. And I don't blame them. Certain creative writing programs have established a strong reputation in the discipline, and sometimes these reputations are well deserved. It's understandable that some hope to promulgate a telling of the discipline's history that features their own stories and that of the institutions to which they are attached. There are even many scholarly books that take this view; they encourage us to believe that if we understand the experiences of students at a handful of "prestigious" programs, and perhaps the biographies of a few famous writing instructors, we'll have a good handle on what creative writing is. To a certain extent I've fanned that flame here by focusing on Harvard in the nineteenth century and the University of Iowa in the twentieth.

But the truth of the matter is much more complicated. Some of the most well-known creative programs achieved that status simply by virtue of being older than any of the others, which means they've had more time to develop a reputation, be written about, hire famous faculty as adjuncts, place students in jobs and fellowships, organize their promotional materials, appear in all the creative writing program rankings ever published, and graduate alumni who go on to publish well-received books in their genre.

There's another cadre of creative writing programs that aren't as old but are monstrously *big*. They put so many alumni into the world it's hard not to discuss them.

Q7: If I decide I don't want to get an MFA, or find I can't get into one, or matriculate at one and then later decide not to finish it, does that mean I'm not a "real writer"?

A7: Absolutely not! The MFA is in no way whatsoever mandatory for a poet or writer. Only apply to and attend one if you earnestly believe that it will aid your writing.

CHAPTER TWO

Applying to Creative Writing Programs

The decision to apply to graduate creative writing programs should not be an easy one. Not every aspiring poet or writer benefits from workshopping their work, and not every artist will thrive within an intimate community of fellow writers. Many who would apply for a Master of Fine Arts in creative writing are not well positioned to take on the significant student debt such degrees sometimes produce. Even those in a position to finance a nonprofessional graduate degree may find that the ideal time for them to attend such a program is five or ten years later than they'd originally thought.

I don't make these observations to startle you, but rather to ensure that you do not conflate the purchase of this book with the decision to apply to a graduate creative writing program right away. For many of you this may well be the right decision, but this book begins with the assumption that what you most want, now, is to learn everything you can about this type of graduate degree. Hopefully by the time you've finished this book you'll be ready to start—rather than finish—a robust decision-making process.

As you read this guide, my hope is that you'll learn not only about MFA and PhD programs in creative writing, but also about what it means to be a committed poet or writer living and working in a university community. For as much as you won't find any such instruction in the promotional materials of a graduate creative writing program, the fact remains that the decision about whether or not to apply to these programs is in many ways a decision about how to live a life—and live well—as a literary artist.

When Tom Kealey published *The Creative Writing MFA Handbook* in 2005, it was the first comprehensive guidebook for applicants to graduate creative writing programs. At the time, Tom said that he saw himself as a "bus driver" taking prospective program applicants on a "tour" of the various graduate degree options in the field. I'll admit from the outset that my ambition is a bit different. What I hope to do in this book is show you how the story of graduate creative writing programs, and hard data relating to those who apply to and attend such programs, are relevant to you not just as a potential applicant but as an artist who hopes to grow in your craft, imaginative faculties, and literary ambitions.

The truth is that the "graduate creative writing program" as we know it today is a fairly recent phenomenon and so, not surprisingly, its kinks are still being worked out. Just thirty years ago there were only a few dozen graduate creative writing programs in the world, and those that did exist were identical to one another in their primary mode of instruction: the creative writing workshop. These programs brought together a small number of aspiring poets or writers in a classroom and asked them to read and comment on one another's work. To be honest, at the time there wasn't much more to the degree than that. Sure, students would also read some published work in their chosen genre, and spend some time socially with their peers and perhaps even their professors, but in the end the simple fact was that students were learning how to write creatively by discussing unpublished and published literary work with other writers. And since most of the published work they were reading was fairly conventional in its aspirations, most of the unpublished work they themselves produced (or read, when their peers produced it) was likewise conventional. Little to no research had been done on the efficacy of the workshop method, and certainly there had been no study of how creative writing programs might affect American fiction and poetry long-term. Much was taken on faith; undergraduate creative writers sought more time to write creatively postgraduation, and colleges and universities were—for a fee—very happy to oblige.

Have things changed dramatically since graduate creative writing programs hit a "boom" in the late 1980s and early 1990s? The answer is yes and no. It continues to be the case that certain modes of writing—the lyric narrative in poetry, so-called "literary fiction" in fiction, and the memoir in nonfiction—continue to be the order of the day in most graduate creative writing workshops. Students still tend to focus on just a single genre, to read much more unpublished than published work in workshop, and to focus on the mechanics of their genre more than the reasons why we write in the first place.

On the other hand, with so many more graduate creative writing programs today than thirty years ago, there are many more options for applicants in terms of program size, duration, location, student-faculty ratio, and curricular prerequisites. Whereas in 1988 only a handful of programs provided full tuition remission and a livable stipend for all their students, now more than fifty do. A small number of programs have even begun to experiment with new pedagogies, such as doing away with conventional genre designations or (on the other end of the curricular spectrum) providing a supportive learning environment for students committed to highly specialized creative endeavors.

Another thing that's changed, though it's too rarely discussed, is that with so many undergraduates having the opportunity to workshop while still in college, and therefore producing ever stronger work for their graduate-school application portfolios, graduate creative writing programs have become much harder to get into on the front end and full-time teaching jobs much harder to find postgraduation. There also appears to be an epidemic of disillusionment among graduate-school poets and writers, who by the time they finish their degrees have spent so many years running everything they write through the consensus-driven processes of the workshop that they wonder whether they have any interesting authorial idiosyncrasies left. As they become bored with the sameness of the writing they read, they become bored, too, with their own work. As we'll discuss more a little later on, if there are two things the conventional writing workshop struggles to reward, it's formal complexity and imaginative audacity.

But let's say you're not the sort who's likely to become disillusioned with institutional instruction in creative writing. What can this book offer you? The simple answer is that this book was written from a presumption that was, for many years, considered heresy to discuss openly in the American literary community: that certain features and benefits of a writing program can be *quantified*. In fact, this book presumes that much of what goes into a graduate writing degree can be quantified no differently than is the case annually with, say, law schools or medical schools.

This hard data—information about acceptance rates, class sizes, program duration, student-faculty ratios, postgraduate placements, and other key indicators of how and whether a writing program is offering a valuable service to aspiring authors—should be part of your decision about where to apply and where to attend. But because hard data is only a small piece of a much larger puzzle, this book will go well beyond the numbers in helping you decide your next move as a potential applicant.

FREQUENTLY ASKED QUESTIONS: APPLYING TO CREATIVE WRITING PROGRAMS

Q1: Will you discuss genres of creative writing besides fiction, poetry, and nonfiction?
A1: While I'll occasionally mention MFA programs in screenwriting, playwriting, young-adult fiction, genre fiction, and literary translation, this book focuses mostly on the three "major" genres of creative writing. One reason for this is that the history and current situation of screenwriting and playwriting programs differs markedly from programs in what we've conventionally called "creative writing"—in part because screenwriting programs are often housed in film departments and playwriting programs in theatre or drama departments. While a growing number of "conventional" creative writing programs are adding tracks in screenwriting, playwriting, or one of the other specialized prose tracks I just mentioned, this isn't yet a major trend in the discipline (though I'll note that playwriting and the broader category of "dramatic writing" are well outpacing the other genres in this regard). Suffice to say there are more than 75 MFA programs in playwriting in the United States and about that number of graduate writing programs in screenwriting or, as it's sometimes called, "writing for stage and screen."

Q2: Why are so many graduate creative writing program websites so unhelpful?
A2: Graduate creative writing programs have been around for over 75 years, and internet use became widespread over two decades ago. So it's reasonable to wonder why so many websites in the field are so bad— worse than what the graduate-school applicants in other disciplines must

contend with. As you'll already know if you started to look for programs online before purchasing this book, on creative writing program websites you rarely find dead links to faculty biographies, faculty publications, or event descriptions involving faculty appearances. Visiting faculty receive the same "live-link" treatment, as do alumni who went on to publish books. Links to coursework requirements will also be accessible and at least rudimentarily legible; it makes things much easier for program faculty in the medium and long term if applicants know what will be required of them before they arrive. If you want to know how well a program is funded, however, that link, if there is one, is sometimes dead—or it sends you far away from the program's website, to a usually unhelpful, university-wide graduate-school portal. If you want to know your chances of getting a generous funding package if admitted to the program, that information is unavailable on 70 percent of program websites. Information concerning a program's selectivity—such as data on how many people apply to the program annually or are admitted annually—will be unavailable on 90 percent of program websites. Virtually no website will tell you about your healthcare options and costs, your student fees and their possible waivers, or any stipends attached to program assistantships. You won't be able to tell, from most program websites, how big the program is, and with half of them you'll need a calculator to even determine how long it takes to complete the program. If, with good reason, you want a listing of full- versus part-time faculty, you can't have it.

I wish I could to tell you that these oversights are accidental—merely the result of programs being run by artists who may not be very tech-savvy. But the real history of graduate creative writing programs' promotional materials in the digital age is that, beginning in 2009, programs were on notice that their online promotional materials would be the basis for the national assessments you find in guides like this one. In response, some programs *removed* information from their website that they thought would make you less likely to apply to them. Some—very few—*added* information they felt was beneficial, while keeping offline contrary or disheartening data. A clear majority did nothing at all, and their websites are as hard to navigate today as a decade ago.

Like you, national surveys of graduate creative writing programs can only work from available information. Neither applicants nor guides like this one can properly assess programs that hide their information, whether willfully or negligently. Nondisclosure hurts programs, this much

(Continued)

is clear; but if the programs are not convinced of this, they'll continue providing you with the quality of promotional materials you're now seeing as you hunt around for a program. Do I think you should infer something about the administrative culture of those programs that have not created a usable website since the advent of the World Wide Web? Sadly, I do. I think you can expect that the best-run programs, with the most thoughtful and fastidious administrators, offer you the most informative websites. Certainly, that's been my experience over the years.

Q3: So, should I do an MFA or PhD in creative writing?

A3: A great many poets and writers go through the months-long process of applying to graduate creative writing programs, matriculate at the program of their choice, and get through a semester or two of weekly workshopping before they ask a question that by all rights you should be asking yourself right now: why do I write? Don't be the aspiring literary artist who waits until they've made an irrevocable life choice before asking that question. Ask that question today, and keep asking it over the next few days and weeks.

Some of you reading this will have a ready answer to this question: because I enjoy it, of course! And that's a good, indeed unimpeachable reason. Creative writing is an endeavor one should only undertake because it brings pleasure, as only one of every ten or twenty thousand working writers can survive off the income their craft brings in. If you don't love writing generally and, as importantly, the unique works you produce, you should stop writing. Frankly, that's just about the *only* good reason to stop writing.

Within the overarching justification of personal satisfaction there are many subjustifications that might point one toward or away from applying to a graduate program in creative writing. For instance, if you write exclusively for yourself—for your own pleasure and no one else's—you may find that institutionalized writing instruction doesn't do much to advance or extend that satisfaction. A good deal of institutional writing instruction is about learning how to write for others, and that sort of knowledge doesn't always, for obvious reasons, enhance one's own enjoyment of the writing process. Likewise, having your most intimate self-expressions harped on weekly by peers you may or may not like or admire is unlikely to deepen the pleasure you feel in putting down on paper your most complex thoughts, emotions, and experiences.

But perhaps you *do* expect to write for others for the rest of your life—and hope, moreover, to make a ton of money doing it. You may be an aspiring fantasy author angling to be the next J. K. Rowling, or a poet seeking to emulate some of the great versifiers of the late twentieth century by teaching full-time at the university level. You may have lived a life of such rich and varied dimensions that you suspect there's not just one but four or five great memoirs in the offing for you. If these archetypes sound like you, let me issue a gentle warning that any mid-career poet or writer would give to any early-career peer: do not become a writer for the money or for the promise of a steady job down the line. Both of these ends are illusory inasmuch as they *could* happen but, to a near-certainty, will not. As I discuss more later on, no poet makes a living from writing poetry alone, and less than 1 percent of creative writing MFA graduates will ever teach full-time at the university level. While particularly sought-after memoirists and novelists do sometimes live off the proceeds of their labors, this is the extraordinary rather than the typical case: for every novelist who "makes it" as a full-time author, hundreds do not.

If you're like most poets and writers, though, what motivates you is not money or fame, nor even mere self-satisfaction, but something rather more amorphous: the desire to master an art you love. In fact, this is exactly what many of the first graduate creative writing programs were developed to help students accomplish. Inasmuch as writing workshops tend to focus on the mechanics ("craft") of writing in the three major genres, the aspiring author whose goal is the "mastery" of such craft is a perfect fit for graduate study in creative writing. And in many such instances, it works out exactly that way: students come out of graduate creative writing programs with a stronger sense of craft, and a better ability to execute within their chosen genre, than they had going in.

The concept of "mastery" is worth some additional consideration here, however. As I know from having taught creative writing to scores of undergraduates, mastering the mechanics of a genre means first mastering the basic compositional gestures that make poetry poetry, fiction fiction, and nonfiction nonfiction. Some students master these basics as undergraduates; others are still working on them even as they attend a graduate program in creative writing. And there are even those who, despite receiving an MFA in creative writing, continue to struggle with the basics of craft in their chosen genre their entire writing lives. There's nothing wrong with any of these scenarios, by the way: many a poet or writer has enjoyed a moderately successful publishing career having mastered only the basics of craft and—at that—only intermittently.

(Continued)

But all this is why the question of "mastery," and your own opinion on it, is so important. If mastering basic craft in a single genre of creative writing, and then replicating that craft regularly in order to enjoy a lengthy publishing career, sounds good to you, a graduate creative writing program may be the very best way to do that of any method yet devised. But if your hope is to master basic craft and then move on to advanced and even *expert* craft—the latter being particularly difficult to teach or even discuss because it is made up, finally, of the ingenious formal and imaginative idiosyncrasies devised by individual authors—the evidence of graduate creative writing programs' utility is more muddled. The reason many of the most memorably strange poets and writers never attended an MFA or PhD program in creative writing is that regular workshopping can gradually disincline you to take risks in your writing. Some regular workshoppers, despite the insistent didacticism, resist this devolution in creative control; others aren't as lucky.

I realize this all this sounds a bit morbid. Why can't a book on applying to graduate creative writing programs just presume that you *know what you're doing* in considering such programs and get on with it? The answer is that if this book were about applying to *undergraduate* colleges and universities, you'd be exactly right. But applying to graduate school is a different matter altogether. It's no coincidence, for instance, that many undergraduates who love to read, write, and argue naturally end up in law school; and it's equally predictable, given that legal practice is about so much more than just reading, writing, and arguing, that law should have one of the highest attrition rates of any profession. The same goes for creative writing. Loving to write is not in itself a justification for going to graduate school for two to four years to do so. So I'd be doing you a disservice if I didn't push back a bit on whatever inclinations brought you to purchase this book in the first place. It's possible the utility of this advice won't be apparent now, but one day it may be. In the last decade I've talked with thousands of applicants to, students of, and graduates from MFA and PhD programs in creative writing, and as I've mentioned, about half either regret their decision to attend one of these programs or feel ambivalent about having done so. I want you to be—if you do end up applying to a graduate program in creative writing—in the other half.

Q4: So what are some worse—and better—reasons to apply to these programs?
A4: Let's start with some of the better reasons. Nearly all of the good reasons to go to graduate school for creative writing fall under one of two

categories: *time* and *space*. Because MFA programs in creative writing last from two to four years, and PhD programs in creative writing—which you really only apply to if you've already done an MFA program in the subject—can last up to six years, there's no question that graduate study in creative writing gives you plenty of time to improve your writing. This is critical because, as many poets and writers have found out far too late, it can be difficult to simultaneously commit yourself to your writing and *also* other obligations like a full-time job, family, or lengthy academic program in a different field. To be a writer of distinction requires not just thousands of hours of reading and writing over many years, but also countless hours spent *thinking about* reading and writing. Many would argue, and I'm in this group, that succeeding as a writer also requires sustained attention, for many years, to those aspects of human behavior and the human condition that others fail to see. If it sounds like I'm saying that graduate creative writing programs are useful in part because they allow you to briefly lose yourself in the life of the mind, that's because I am. And as long as you don't stay resident in that space too long—two to six years should do it—you'll see improvement in your imaginative faculties because of it.

Advocates for graduate creative writing programs also talk a lot about *space*, which in this case is a more abstract concept than *time*. The sort of programs we're discussing here often have bare-bones curricula that allow you to focus only on your writing and areas of inquiry related to your writing; they bring you into the classroom rarely enough that you can spend most of your time reading and writing if you choose; they put you in the way of professors who, if they're doing their jobs, enter congenially into *your* headspace to assist you rather than demanding that you read, write, and study on *their* terms. But pursuing and then having a graduate degree in creative writing is also a way for you to mentally clear space in your life for the fact that *you are a writer*. It encourages you to self-identify this way and to live daily with that self-identification.

One final note on space: it's not all about clearing away the morass of other obligations and preoccupations; it's just as much about building from the ground up a new space in which to live and work as a writer. While graduate creative writing programs are overrated as hubs for literary networking (only a few programs assist their students substantially with this, as we'll discuss later) they're underrated as places to meet people who will meaningfully populate your world for the rest of your life. I can't tell you how many poets and writers of my acquaintance still consider

(Continued)

their grad-school peers their first and best readers for new work. And the support poets and writers can offer one another when the going gets rough—as it surely will—is of incalculable value.

Having said all this, I'll admit that the reasons *not* to attend a graduate creative writing program are larger in number and more varied in scope. I'll skip over the ones we've already discussed to focus on five additional considerations for any potential applicant. But keep in mind that, as noted, there's unlikely to be writing-related money or full-time employment waiting at the end of a graduate program in creative writing.

That aside, I want to say, first and foremost, that you should not matriculate at a graduate creative writing program simply because you don't know what else to do. I promise you that that road leads to an end you won't enjoy. Rather, attend a graduate creative writing program when you've reached the point in your writing life at which writing regularly, being around other writers, and conversing about writing daily feels necessary to your continued development. That time might come in your mid-twenties or mid-thirties, or it may not arrive until much later than that. Remember that, because the MFA and PhD in creative writing are nonprofessional programs, you can attend a program of this sort at any age and suffer no financial penalty for having waited to go.

Some aspiring poets and writers worry that waiting to go to graduate school in creative writing will cost them the opportunity to network their way into a book deal. For poets, whose publishing organs are generally independent operations with editorial processes favoring individuals known to the editor, there's some truth to this; the poets you meet in your graduate poetry program are disproportionately likely to end up your editors as well, even if around half of new poetry books are published by university presses reading their submissions blind. For aspiring novelists and memoirists, though, the networking justification for attending a graduate program in creative writing is a bit more complicated. There are about ten fiction- and nonfiction-writing programs—out of about 250 nationally—that do a reasonably good job connecting young authors with prospective agents, but even these can do little more than make introductions. The rest is up to you. Meanwhile, there are about 240 programs that don't do even this much.

This next admonition is perhaps the most controversial. You should not choose or attend a program on the basis of a fondness for the writing of one of its professors. There are many reasons for this, but here are the best five: the relationship between being a good writer and a good teacher is dubious at best; a good teacher teaches you how to be the best version of you as an author that you can possibly be, not an emulation of them or their work, so it's often preferable to study with those whose work you do *not* wish to emulate; the more popular a professor, the more likely they are to be on sabbatical when you arrive, or to move to another institution, or to teach courses you may not be able to get into when you want to; professors who are also extremely successful authors may well have less free time to dedicate to mentorship, socializing, and course preparation than their less well-known peers; and admission to an institution doesn't necessarily mean that your portfolio was enjoyed by all members of a program's faculty equally—so you may arrive at your program only to find that your favorite author is more interested in taking other program students under their wing.

Ideally, you'd be able to find out in advance of applying to programs which faculty members at each program enjoy a strong reputation as teachers. While joining an online group catering to graduate-school applicants in creative writing might help you uncover this information, you won't be able to get all the information you need and what you do get will undoubtedly be anecdotal. Just so, making a site visit to a program you're particularly interested in is useful if you have the money to do it, but valuable in assessing faculty only if they let you sit in on a class—which they may or may not let you do. For these reasons, the current "conventional wisdom" says that one shouldn't pick a graduate creative writing program on the basis of the writing acumen of its faculty.

Certain organizations, like the Association of Writers & Writing Programs, urge applicants to research program faculties to determine whether a given faculty, broadly speaking, shares your aesthetics. This is good advice. While you ought not make a critical life decision based upon your admiration for a single celebrity you've never met or seen teach, you also don't want to be at a program whose faculty has little personal investment in the sort of work you aim to write. That said, any program that is selective in its admissions and decides to admit you is obviously interested in your literary vision, so to some extent the question of "aesthetic fit" takes care of itself during the admissions process.

A related consideration, for many applicants, is the tone and tenor of writing programs' instructional methods. If you write primarily to please yourself, or if you're inclined to please others but can't follow others' direction in trying to do so, graduate study in creative writing may not be for you. The fact is, at an MFA or PhD program in creative writing there

(*Continued*)

will be a lot of people advising you —sometimes telling you—what to do with your talents. If that doesn't sound like a welcome prospect, take that fact into consideration when choosing whether to apply to any of the programs in this book.

I've hinted at the fifth admonition already, but it needs to be stated as clearly as possible that you must not matriculate at a graduate creative writing program if you'll have to go into substantial debt to do so. When I say that graduate creative writing programs are "nonprofessional" programs, I mean that they do not *in themselves* prepare you to enter any professional field or fully qualify you for a full-time job. That's another way of saying you'll have a tough time paying back your student loans postgraduation unless you find work in a field other than creative writing.

Q5: Isn't it the case that any professor who writes in a way I like can teach me how to write in that way?
A5: The honest answer is "no." Having knowledge about how to write helps make one an artist; what makes one a teacher—a *very* different profession—is having the ability to transmit that knowledge. The best literary artists are masters of expressing themselves through poetry and prose, but a great many of these masters are neither particularly interested in nor particularly adept at transmitting what they know to others. And this includes many such persons who ultimately decided, for financial or other personal reasons, to become professors. And keep in mind that teaching well is about much more than transmitting one's knowledge. A good professor is patient, temperate, articulate, engaging, tireless, a good listener, and a good reader of others' work. Many a professor who otherwise might be able to transfer their knowledge to others has fallen flat in the classroom because they lacked the personal qualities that the best mentors possess.

But these observations, as critical as they are, pale in comparison to a second one: you are not attending a graduate creative writing program to be taught how to write like someone else—even a literary hero. You are attending a graduate creative writing program to find professors and peers who can so intuitively and expansively understand who *you* are as a poet or writer that they can help you be the best, most authentically idiosyncratic author you can be. To the extent others in your creative writing MFA or PhD community are willing to help you, what they are helping you do is create literature only you, and no one else, would be able to (or dare to) write. When you pick a program because you wish to emulate someone who teaches there, the best advice anyone can give you at that point is to save your money and simply buy as many books by that author as possible. Take copious notes on their strategies, perhaps as part of a study group with others similarly intrigued by this author, and then write a hundred imitations (i.e., works written "in the style or manner") of this author you all admire. You will, without the need for a graduate creative writing program, soon manage to produce work that looks like this other author's writing. And what you will find, if you show this work to agents, is that no one will take it because they'll call it "derivative." And it will be.

A good creative writing professor has little enough ego when it comes to writing that they can draw from a vast storehouse of literary knowledge *only* those artifacts that will be relevant and helpful to *you*. While at the undergraduate level we might expect professors to be a bit more didactic, an MFA or PhD program in creative writing is a terminal-degree course of study for poets and writers already confident enough in their craft to have a sense of what they want to do. If you're thinking of applying to such a program with the sole intention of letting others—faculty or otherwise—tell you what to do, do not apply to a graduate creative writing program. Wait until you're more certain of yourself. The reason I often say that the best graduate creative writing program experiences are those in which a student learns more from her peers than her professors is because this is almost tautologically true: students who are receptive to the inspirations of a community rather the prescriptions of a single mentor are the ones ready to be immersed in a graduate-school-level community of poets and writers. Authors still looking to be firmly led by others are not yet ready for graduate school in the discipline of creative writing. By the same token, when graduate creative writing workshops fail it is often because the participants are treating their classroom time as an undergraduate would—looking for validation and instruction—rather than as a graduate student must. Graduate students are self-motivated, self-directed, and are *inspired* by the perspectives and techniques of others, rather than co-opted by them.

Q6: Am I too old for an MFA?
A6: Almost certainly not. According to polling, the median age of an incoming student at a full-residency creative writing MFA program is 27, which means you'll find plenty of students who've just graduated from college there, but also many who are in their thirties or forties. Meanwhile, the median age of a student at a *low*-residency MFA program in creative

(*Continued*)

writing is 37, which tells you that student ages at such programs run the gamut. While admittedly we see few students over fifty at full-residency programs, there are many such writers now studying in low-residency programs. And the reason for the dearth of older writers at full-residency programs isn't primarily due to any age bias in the admissions process, but self-selection: older writers are less likely to feel like they can up and move to a college or university campus for two to four years.

Are there some faculty members slightly less interested in working with older applicants as opposed to younger ones? Unfortunately, yes—there are some. They worry that older authors may be less open to instruction, by virtue of being more set in their writing practices. A less commonly heard and even more unfair self-justification from such professors is that older students have briefer writing careers in front of them, and therefore there's less opportunity for a professor's instruction to be deeply meaningful to their future work. As some part of what drives any poet or writer to think they can teach other poets and writers is vanity, we do come across professors who take such a proprietary interest in their students that they want new mentees who will be writing for a half-century more. As you can imagine, I don't in any sense condone these views.

So are you too old for an MFA? No. Though older applicants may have to work a bit harder to get admitted to certain programs, ultimately your writing is what counts.

Q7: Wait a minute—is there any chance I'm too *young* for an MFA?
A7: Yes. In fact, there's a much better chance you're too *young* to attend an MFA in creative writing than too old. And yes, some of that has to do with maturity; not every twenty-two-year-old is ready for the self-directed curricula we find at graduate schools, and my interviews with creative writing MFA and PhD alumni reveal that a program's youngest students are more likely to opine, years on, that they spent their program years feeling unguided and directionless. That's as much a program's fault as it is anyone else's, of course. Programs should be ready to handle students of all ages—they should put their professors through workshops on the differences between twenty-two-year-old students and forty-year-old ones—but they're not and they don't.

For our purposes, however, the most important sort of maturity is the maturity one develops as a writer. Until one has been writing for at least five years, one is more likely than others to make key errors like confusing critique (whether yours of others or others' of you) with personal insult; confusing a workshop with a soapbox from which you can declaim your strongly held views on writing, rather than treating class as an open-ended discussion among equals; being either too much or too little open to suggestion in the editing process; and feeling shy enough about your status as a writer that you fail to fully engage your peers and professors as a committed literary artist. These are just a few examples of how attending an MFA in creative writing too soon can cause you to draw less from the experience than you otherwise would. And this is exacerbated by most early-career authors' lack of understanding of the publishing world; many young MFA students have outsized expectations for the networking that takes place in-program, the importance of publishing often and early, and the likelihood that a student's first poetry or fiction manuscript is really the one they should seek to publish.

I say all this having been both a straight-from-college graduate student—I began law school, I can now safely say "unwisely," at twenty-one—and a nontraditional one, inasmuch as I showed up at my first-ever creative writing workshop when I was thirty. So all of the mistakes I describe in my answer to this question and the preceding one are mistakes I've made myself. But trust me when I say that my answers are informed not just by experience but years of speaking with graduate creative writing students of all ages.

Q8: Can I take longer than usual to finish my MFA, or attend my program part-time?

A8: Chapter 18 offers a nonexhaustive list of programs that allow part-time, evening, or weekend attendance. Most programs will allow you to take much longer than the usual timeframe to finish your degree—usually up to twice the program's listed duration. Many programs offer details about such options in their online promotional materials.

Q9: What if I write genre fiction, slam poetry, transmedia memoirs, or "weird stuff"?

A9: I'd like to say that the idiosyncratic nature of your work bears no relation to whether or not you get into a program, but that's not true. And as series editor for *Best American Experimental Writing*, you can imagine that not only are my own authorial inclinations "experimental" in nature but so too are my tastes as a reader, editor, and publisher.

But the universe of graduate creative writing programs is something else altogether. Broadly speaking, it is hostile to experimentation in fiction, moderately hostile to it in poetry, and variably hostile to it—it really depends upon the program—in nonfiction.

(*Continued*)

The reasons for this aesthetic conservatism are not particularly nefarious, either. The "workshop" pedagogy has always placed mastery of *craft* at its center, and for that reason more than 99 percent of full-residency fiction-writing programs teach (and thus accept from applicants) exclusively literary fiction. Even those who somehow gain entrance to an MFA program in fiction writing using a genre-fiction or cross-genre portfolio are gently steered toward literary fiction once in-program. Literary fiction, which largely emphasizes realism over fabulism and is more conspicuously rule-bound than other subgenres of fiction, may well be your cup of tea. If it isn't, there are a handful of low-residency programs that let you write genre fiction (e.g., fantasy, science fiction, mystery, horror, thriller, western, and romance) and a few full-residency programs that encourage students to experiment formally—but in both instances you'll find your slate of available programs to be in the single digits. This is partly a product of the times. Thirty years on we can expect to see more diversity in graduate-school writing. We're just not there yet.

Another thing the overwhelming majority of creative writing programs don't do well, and to their credit don't *claim* to do well, is teach students how to perform their work or author it in multimedia and transmedia environments. The discipline of creative writing, chained as it is to the creative writing workshop, leaves little room for instructors to work on students' performance skills or help them develop a facility with other media besides the printed page. So if the printed page isn't your bag, or if you think your work operates best on the stage or in televisual or immersive reality, a graduate program in creative writing may not be for you. You might look, instead, at programs like Duke University's MFA in Experimental and Documentary Arts, CalArts' interdisciplinary writing MFA, Brown University's Digital Language Arts track, or the PhD in Intermedia Writing, Art, and Performance at the University of Colorado at Boulder. Or consider a graduate program in another art (e.g., film, the material arts, or theatre).

Q10: So I'm out of luck if I don't write lyric poetry, literary fiction, or staid memoirs?
A10: Not exactly. While it's true that if you don't write the sort of work that 99 percent of graduate creative writing programs are equipped to foster and applaud, you may have to do more pre-application research than your peers—maybe temper your expectations during the application process, too—you may find a small slate of programs open to the sort of work you're interested in (or work in the *neighborhood* of the work you'd

most like to write, for instance postmodern lyric poetry, genre fiction with strong "literary" elements, or transmedia memoirs with substantial "page" components). You may have a piece of work that isn't perfectly representative of your interests but suitable for an MFA portfolio. Whatever approach you take to resolving any distance between what you'd prefer to write and what the programs you prefer would prefer you write, realize that graduate-school application processes are too time-consuming, emotionally taxing, and expensive for you to send your creative portfolio to programs unlikely to value it.

Q11: What if I want or need to commute to my program daily from a great distance?
A11: Administratively speaking, this is fine. Many programs do not offer on-campus housing to students and only a fraction of working poets and writers would take them up on the offer if they did. But I'd point you to some of the previous question responses, which underscore that one of the benefits of attending a writing program is getting a chance to build a lifelong community of fellow travelers. Students who commute to class or in some other way excuse themselves from their program community for long periods of time are less likely to reap this benefit from their program experience. That said, life is complicated—if for work, family, financial, or other reasons you can commute to your program's location but can't live there, do what you've got to do. Just try your best to engage robustly with your professors and peers during the hours you're on-site.

Always remember that the opportunity to attend a graduate creative writing program is also an opportunity to take advantage of the panoply of opportunities a college or university can offer. So there's a great benefit to be gained by only attending a graduate creative writing program when you can fully devote your time to it.

Q12: What if I only want to work with one faculty member at a school I'm applying to?
A12: If that's your view—and it's a common one—you might be setting yourself up for disappointment. As I discussed earlier for Q5, if you're applying to graduate school solely to work with a single author you've never met or taken a class with, that's a lot of time and resources to gamble on a guess. Don't let an imagined mentor-mentee relationship that might not come to fruition be your raison d'être for graduate study in creative writing.

(*Continued*)

Q13: What if I write in several genres?

A13: Most programs will let you apply in multiple genres if you pay multiple application fees, but of course you'll only be admitted in—and write your thesis in—a single genre. While in-program, most will allow you take at least one workshop, sometimes more, in genres other than the one in which you were admitted. In fact, a few programs even require it. See Chapter 18 for a lengthy list of programs offering cross-genre study.

Why do some programs prohibit cross-genre study? It goes back to the idea of "mastery" we discussed earlier. Creative writing programs bill themselves as places to hone your craft in a single genre in part because their implicit mission statement is to guide a student toward mastery in poetry, fiction, or nonfiction. As a matter of principle, some feel this view requires a concurrent one: that any time one spends working in a second genre is time one *should* spend on the genre in which one hopes to be a master.

If that sounds a bit narrow to you, it should. In many respects, "genre" is an artificial construct; moreover, the future of creative writing may well lie not just in multi- and transmedia work but work that fuses and profoundly alters many genres.

Q14: I plan to get into a program as a "stealth" candidate— submitting a portfolio that's conventional, then letting my freak flag fly once I'm in-program. Thoughts?

A14: Applicants discuss this application strategy a lot more often than you'd think. Many applicants who consider themselves "experimental writers" suspect that a graduate program in creative writing might not be a good fit for them—for the reasons we've discussed already—but want the time and space to write, and the funding, that a graduate creative writing program can provide. I can't and won't advise you to falsify your ambitions on a graduate-school application, of course, and will note that when you show up at any institution under false pretenses you tend to be treated accordingly by the institution as soon as your true designs are caught out. That said, I want to emphasize that programs try to be flexible with students whose ambitions evolve over the course of their studies. I think there are very few graduate creative writing programs that would disallow a student from trying to bring a multimedia artwork into a workshop or from incorporating transmedia elements into a thesis. Would the faculty members presented with such an idea be well equipped to aid or evaluate it? Possibly not. Might your peers snicker and think you're trying too hard? Sure. But you're a writer—be a writer. Do what you must do to become the sort of inventive, courageous author any graduate creative writing program that admits you should want you to be.

Q15: Can I still apply to an MFA if I've already published a lot in my chosen genre?
A15: Yes. In fact, some (albeit not many) programs look for "indicia of future success" *pre*-admission. This doesn't mean prior publication is a prerequisite for applying to MFA programs in creative writing—it most definitely is *not*—just that having placed work in magazines might be a minor asset in applying to some of the top MFA programs. These programs have alumni who publish frequently, but may hope to further distinguish themselves from their peers by hosting poets and writers who publish while on campus.

That said, it's easy to have too much of a good thing. Publishing widely in literary magazines before applying to an MFA program is one thing; publishing multiple books before applying is quite another. While I don't think there's any number of prior magazine publications that would noticeably weaken a graduate-school application—and as noted, that sort of CV might be helpful at gaining admission to certain schools— even a single prior book publication is pushing your luck at a majority of programs.

Keep in mind that if you have published a great deal before matriculating, you should feel free to stow that fact away for the entirety of your program. You attend a program to learn, and to act like a learner, even as you wish to be treated as a peer by your peers and even your professors. But being treated like a peer means acting like a professional—and more often than not acting like a professional means waiting for others to mention your accomplishments rather than broadcasting them yourself.

Q16: Should I apply straight from undergrad, or take time off to do something else?
A16: My advice—and it's only that—is the latter. You don't want your graduate-school experience to feel like an extension of your undergraduate creative writing program. It really isn't, and shouldn't be. You also might find, in your immediate postgraduate years, that you're not quite ready to do an MFA program, or even decide it's not right for you at all. Many undergraduates apply to graduate school straight from college out of

(Continued)

fear rather than longing. I should know; it's at least part of the reason I ended up in law school. So I speak from experience in saying fear of the unknown—not having a job lined up, a place to live, a long-term goal—isn't a good reason to apply to grad school.

Q17: Should I do a one-year MFA?

A17: If all you need is a credential—for instance, if you've already published one or more books but can't get a teaching job because you don't have a terminal degree—sure. Otherwise, I would be wary of programs like this. Time and space to write are the key reasons to apply to an MFA program, and a one-year program offers an insufficient amount of either. The moment you show up at a one-year MFA, you must already start thinking about what you'll be doing the following year, and perhaps beginning to look at applications for that opportunity. That's a difficult environment in which to try to write.

Q18: How many schools should I apply to? How do I create an application list?

A18: This will partly be a function of how much money you have—as application fees add up, and sending transcripts and standardized test scores also costs money—but there must also be an element of strategy to your application list. While you shouldn't apply to any program you wouldn't be willing to attend, you also must be careful to avoid *only* applying to "reach" programs with yield-exclusive acceptance rates under 5 percent. Even if your professors have told you your work is superlative, and even if you believe one of your recommenders has strong connections to several of the programs you're applying to, your chances of admission to any one program are statistically quite low.

Typically, I recommend that applicants start with the question of *location*. Where are you willing to spend the next two or three years of your life? What environments might inspire you to do your best work without unduly distracting you from the difficult task of writing regularly? What locations could you afford to live in on a likely meager stipend? Keep in mind that answering these questions takes some research; I'd advise against making judgments about locations based on rumor, innuendo, even anecdotes. If you think a program might interest you, do your own online research to get a sense of what its on- and off-campus culture is like. Many places you've never thought of living in before are actually quite lovely, and many of those places, not for nothing, are in the interior of the United States—something I mention because, based on my interviews, coastal-dwelling authors are often loath to move away from whatever coast they're on.

If you're not dead set on attending a program next year, apply to however many schools you'd be genuinely excited to attend (assuming you can afford the application fees, transcript fees, GRE and score-reporting fees, and so on). Should you not get in anywhere, which is likely when one only applies to "dream" programs, you'll have the consolation of knowing you can always apply again. There's just no rush to do an MFA.

If, however, you've got to get yourself into a program as soon as possible—for whatever reason—you'll want to apply to twelve to fifteen programs. More than that, you'll need to make sure the programs you apply to represent a range of schools in their selectivity, funding, popularity, and location. If you apply to twelve to fifteen "dream" schools the hard math isn't, in fact, that much different from applying to six to eight such schools.

If you apply to twelve to fifteen schools, make sure at least six are "dream" schools. That way you'll know you gave it a shot at a decent number of schools you really would be very excited to attend. Another six to eight schools should feature both moderate selectivity and moderate funding, as there's not much purpose in applying to a school that offers no one full funding unless you're independently wealthy. A final two schools might include a local nonselective program, assuming you like it and they have a few funding packages which, if you got one, would make the whole thing manageable. But again, don't rush to accept any offer of admission you're not truly excited about.

Q19: What questions should I ask of a current student at a program I'm considering?

A19: If you were directed to the student by the program, you can ask whatever you like but I'd be very cautious about taking their answers at face value. Programs select ambassadors who they believe will speak highly of the program no matter what, and what you're really looking for in a situation like this is radical candor. If you've located the student yourself, first and foremost you should ask them what the atmosphere and culture within the program are like. Do students hang out together after workshops? Are workshops constructive or destructive? How available are professors outside of normal class hours? Does the program sponsor a real *community*—readings, lectures, social gatherings, and so on—or does it feel like everyone comes together only for class? I think

(*Continued*)

the most telling question, however, is the broadest one: if you could do everything over, would you still attend this program? The answer to this question will tell you a lot.

Once admitted, many MFA applicants ask current students about housing, fees, transportation, cohort demographics, opportunities for cross-genre study, credit requirements, opportunities for summer employment, and the quality of local cuisine. In speaking with program coordinators or directors, applicants generally ask questions that only this person is well suited to answer. Needless to say, there's no need to ask questions of program administrators or students if you don't really have any questions.

Q20: I discovered a typo in my statement of purpose/creative portfolio. Is that bad?

A20: Yes. While no one gets into or is denied by an MFA program *exclusively* because of their statement of purpose—unless you admit to some really bad behavior—there really should be absolutely no typos in yours. And that goes double for your creative portfolio. Programs assume you've read it over so many times the chance of a typo is virtually nil.

Q21: A work that I put in my portfolio has just been published. Do I tell the programs?

A21: No. Your portfolio is judged on its own merits, not on whether it's been published.

Q22: A recommender forgot to send his/her recommendation. Will my application be read?

A22: Almost certainly yes. Programs don't want to miss out on a great writer due to an error made by a third party. Just get the recommendation to them as quickly as you can.

Q23: Do programs conduct phone or in-person interviews?

A23: Almost none do. On occasion you'll come across a program that asks for a phone interview. If this happens, expect that their interest is simply in getting to know you as a person. Be yourself. They'll probably ask about your reading and writing interests and what inspires you to write. Don't expect a pop quiz; expect a friendly conversation.

Q24: I just applied to a number of creative writing programs. When will I hear back?

A24: The earliest reporting programs report in late January and early February, while the latest reporting programs send out letters in the first week of April. Many programs send out acceptances and rejections around the same time each year, so check the prior year's "MFA Draft" Facebook group to get a sense of when a program makes decisions.

Q25: Is it okay to email a program to ask when it plans to send out acceptances?
A25: No.

Q26: When do *most* programs report their acceptances, rejections, and waitlists?
A26: Most programs will notify you between mid-February and mid-March.

Q27: How are acceptances communicated?
A27: Some programs call, some send an email, some send a letter, others have you check your application status via a website. There's no standard format for an MFA acceptance, though I'd say that in recent years a phone call followed by a formal letter has become the most common approach for notifying an applicant of admission.

Q28: Where can I find out about programs' acceptances and rejections in real time?
A28: Check "GradCafe" and the "MFA Draft" Facebook group for your application year.

Q29: I'm admitted! How can I get in touch with others admitted to the same program?
A29: Put out a call on your application year's Facebook group (e.g., "MFA Draft '19"). You'll usually find at least one person considering the same program. If you decide to matriculate, you may get an email list of your cohort from your program coordinator.

Q30: If a school gives me a deadline to accept their offer, will they ever extend it?
A30: If they really want you, they will. Or, if they're lukewarm about your work but responded more favorably to your writing than to that of the person who would replace you in the cohort, they will. A small number of programs refuse to move deadlines as a matter of policy, but even so, whether you know that a program allows extensions or not, it never hurts to ask (assuming you do so politely). The worst they can do is say no.

(Continued)

Q31: Can I defer an offer of acceptance?

A31: At some programs, you can; at others, you can't. Usually you'll have to contact the program to find out what their policy is. Most programs don't announce any policy at all on their website, perhaps to discourage anyone from asking. Before you make any phone calls, though, keep in mind that deferring for a year can create an invisible rift between you and the faculty of the program you were admitted to, as in their view they admitted you for *this* year and now you're asking for—as it were—an *additional* favor. I've also heard rare stories of deferrals not being honored, perhaps because students don't always honor them in return (choosing instead to attend a different program in the following year). Indeed, another reason some programs disallow deferrals and all programs mistrust them is that many students who defer reapply to other programs the next year—a clear ethical violation. My advice? Do not defer, or even attempt to defer, unless your situation is such an obvious emergency that any faculty member with a conscience would understand the necessity of you waiting a year to matriculate.

Having said that, if a program *desperately* wants you to attend, they may allow you to defer and even tell you that it's all right if you apply to other programs the following year.

Q32: I got decent funding at a school I'm lukewarm about. Should I go, or reapply?

A32: All things being equal? The latter. Unless there are special circumstances requiring that you be in school right now, a second maxim besides "don't go into substantial debt for an MFA" is "don't attend any program you're not excited to attend." You can always keep working on your portfolio in the hope of getting into a top-choice school later on.

Q33: I've been accepted to a program I won't be attending. How do I decline my spot?

A33: Send a brief, polite letter to the program coordinator or director. They may or may not write back. Don't be surprised—or take it personally—if they don't. Program coordinators are very busy around application time. Do try to reject offers as soon as you know you won't be taking them; it's an enormous service to your fellow applicants, who may well be on waitlists at some of the schools whose offers you're declining.

Q34: What happens if I get put on a waitlist?

A34: You wait. It's awful. The good news is that hundreds and hundreds of aspiring poets and writers go through the same thing every year. The one mistake you want to avoid is regularly checking in with the program to see where you are on their list; have confidence that they'll contact you if or when it's your turn. Besides, not every program ranks their waitlist—some decide who's next on the list only when they know for certain they've got to dip into their pool of waitlisted candidates. The only exception to the general rule about not calling programs that have waitlisted you is if you have another outstanding offer and are facing down a deadline to accept or reject it. In that case, it's reasonable to send a polite email explaining your situation and asking if the program coordinator has any sense of how likely your admission off the waitlist is. Essentially, you're asking them where you are on their waitlist without saying so explicitly. They'll either encourage you to hang on or encourage you to take any outstanding offer you have—which is their way of telling you how far down the waitlist you are. Sometimes they'll say exactly where you are on their list, but unfortunately you can't count on this.

Q35: What if mid-April comes and I'm waiting for a response from my top choice? Can I accept another offer and rescind my acceptance if accepted at my "dream" school?
A35: This definitely does happen. My advice is to be honest: either ask for an extension at the school that's already accepted you or, if they won't grant one, accept their offer and let them know that you're still on the waitlist at another school. Presumably, you've been in contact with the school you've been waitlisted at and have some sense of when they're going to give you a decision. Pass that information on to the school whose offer you've accepted. Once you've communicated your acceptance and received a response, you can remove yourself from any other waitlists— as if you know you prefer a school you said "yes" to over schools you were waitlisted at, you shouldn't stay on those waitlists.

Having said that, if you get the sense from a program that they're going to rescind their offer if you remain on any other program's waitlist, just accept the first program's offer and remain on your "dream" program's waitlist anyway. It's entirely possible that that waitlisting will never become an acceptance, and if it *does*, you can feel as though you had a right—because you paid to apply to that school—to not have removed yourself from their waitlist until you knew for certain that they wouldn't accept you. If the first school can't understand that that's your right, then it's they who are in the wrong, not you. But again, to the extent you feel you've been given the space to do this, be as honest as possible. Only

(Continued)

resort to acting in bad faith if the program you're dealing with has already done so first. I think that, objectively, that's the fairest approach to this sort of situation.

Q36: How long is it possible to remain on a waitlist?

A36: A long time. I've spoken to several applicants who were taken off a waitlist a few weeks before they matriculated. Needless to say, you can query the program well before this, but don't be surprised if they tell you that they won't officially close their waitlist until July or August. This situation is particular to programs that don't fund many students; fully funded programs can usually close their waitlists by April or early May.

Q37: Will programs that reject me give me feedback on my creative portfolio if I ask?

A37: No.

Q38: If I apply in multiple cycles, should I change my statement of purpose and/or my recommenders?

A38: Chances are that your rejections were based on your creative portfolio, not your statement of purpose or recommendations, so unless you have real reason to doubt the strength of the recommendations or find glaring errors of judgment in the content of your statement of purpose, all of these documents can be resubmitted.

CHAPTER THREE

Application Requirements

So you've decided that now is the right time for you to apply to a graduate creative writing program. The next question you'll have to ask is whether you're *ready* to apply. While the application process for graduate creative writing programs isn't terribly complicated, it can be time-consuming, expensive, and a bit overwhelming due to all the options before you—so it's best to start planning your applications as soon as possible. Application deadlines tend to be in the late fall and early winter, but to do this thing right you're going to want to begin preparing at the start of the preceding summer.

The most important element in your MFA application—by far—is your creative portfolio. Conventional wisdom holds that more than 95 percent of the admissions decision is made on the basis of your creative work. While you'll spend a good deal of time on the rest of your application, there's little chance your other materials will significantly add to the odds of your admission to a program, and only a slight chance they'll materially damage them. Our goal in this chapter, therefore, is to make sure you make as few errors as possible and eliminate any foreseeable and wholly unnecessary frustrations.

Because the core of your application is your creative portfolio, it goes without saying that you should spend the bulk of your preparation time on this. In fact, unless you've reached a point at which you're *extremely* confident about your writing sample, you should wait to apply to programs. There's no point spending scores of hours working on the ancillary parts of your application when the part that really matters isn't up to snuff. Remember that because MFA programs are not professional programs—meaning, an MFA can't by itself land you a full-time, long-term job or make you money in the short term—there's no particular rush to apply. As we've seen, the median age of an incoming creative writing MFA student is 27. Five years post-college may seem like a long time to wait to apply, but it's the amount of time most writers find they need before they can put together a writing sample likely to gain them admission to a strong writing program.

Keep in mind, as you prepare, review, and seek feedback on your writing sample, that acceptance rates to graduate creative writing programs are in many instances as low as for medical schools and top law schools. Unfortunately for you, whereas aspiring doctors and attorneys can look at their GPAs and standardized test scores and quickly work out their chances of admission to a given program, faculty assessment of a writing sample is necessarily subjective. You could write a sample so stellar that a New York City trade press would publish it immediately, then for some byzantine reason see it land, owing only to your bad fortune, in the lap of a faculty member inclined to dislike it. On the other side of the coin, you could put together a slapdash "experimental" excerpt that has little thought behind it but for some reason tickles the fancy of a faculty reader. The topics you select for your poetry or prose might for reasons you could never fathom particularly intrigue or disgust your audience. This means that you should never take rejection from a program personally—as subjective factors may have carried the day.

So if your writing sample is so important, but if it's also subject to the unknown whims of its assessors, how do you know when it's ready? Some will tell you that the key is getting as much feedback as you possibly can, and there's some truth to that. Certainly, you won't want to submit anything that hasn't been looked at by some readers whose judgment you trust. On the other hand, you mustn't let the integrity of your writing be compromised by edits-by-committee or excessive assistance from more experienced authors; there's no point in gaining admission to a program on the strength of a sample that doesn't actually represent the sort of work you want to do in-program. If you submit work that's arguably much better than you're really capable of, you'll spend your years in-program feeling like your professors are disappointed in you—which they might be, in that instance. Likewise, if your sample is so overedited that it loses its essential character as an artwork only you, with your unique skills and perspective, could create, you could wind up getting rejected by a program not because it wasn't interested in *your* writing but was unmoved by the writing of your *editors*.

The best advice is to spend enough time on each of the works in your writing sample that you can honestly say to yourself that the sample constitutes your best possible work product. Some selective requests for feedback can help you make this assessment— particularly when your readers are familiar with your work generally—but don't overdo it. And remember that when I say "best possible work product" I mean by your standards, not someone else's. Your best possible work product may well be unusual in certain ways, and that's okay; creative writing professors would rather not be bored into retirement by reading the same sort of work semester after semester. That said, you must make sure anything you submit exhibits exemplary craft. This telegraphs that faculty won't need to waste instructional time teaching you the basics; it confirms, too, that you're competent enough to catch basic errors by your classmates if necessary.

Another very important component in your application, though it runs a distant second to your writing sample, is your personal statement (sometimes called a "statement of purpose"). This matters to the committee in part because it helps ensure you have basic writing skills, and in part because it offers a glimpse of how you think.

The reality, of course, is that no one can understand you, nor can you adequately encapsulate who you are and wish to be, in a few hundred words. It's for this reason that you're better off viewing your personal statement as an opportunity to *mess up* your application rather than put it over the top. The list of major errors that applicants are almost preternaturally inclined to make in their personal statements is quite long, but here are just a few: exhibiting arrogance; appearing flippant or excessively jocular; confessing to past (or ongoing) crimes; discussing drug use or juvenile delinquencies; discussing mental health issues of any variety; fawning excessively over the work of faculty members (or, especially bad, a single faculty member); talking about past MFA applications, or other current MFA applications; discussing past failures that might reflect poorly on your character, rather than focusing on challenges since overcome that enabled you to advance your writing; drawing your creative interests too narrowly or too broadly; speaking ill of any poet or writer, living or deceased; expressing more interest in a second genre than the one you're applying in; failing to fix typos in the text; using poor grammar or low (slang or vulgar) diction; appearing overly eager to publish; in any way casting yourself as "unteachable" by implying you have deeply entrenched writing habits, practices, or instincts no education could roust you from; or discussing existing personal entanglements (for instance, complex family matters or an ongoing romantic relationship) that increase the likelihood you won't finish the program or will be perpetually distracted in workshop. These are a few examples of personal statement no-nos; hopefully they underscore that the personal statement is your opportunity to emphasize, and not undermine, the hard work you put into your portfolio.

A good personal statement is warm, articulate, professional in temperament, and harmless in content. It tells your reader enough about you for them to want to get to know you, but little enough that they're unlikely to form a negative perception of your personality and social skills. It emphasizes your desire to excel in your writing but also your equal desire to be an actively engaged mentee, peer, student, and community member. Your goal is to have readers think to themselves, "This person seems nice, and might well be interesting to be around." You're not auditioning for "superstar student" or "tortured artist" or "renegade author"; you're not trying to flatter anyone or misstate your interests. Avoid any big mistakes and produce a document that approximates but doesn't caricature who you are as a person and writer, and you'll be just fine.

The third-most important element of your application—though under certain circumstances it could be the second-most important—is your recommendations. Because this book throws caution to the wind and tells you how things are rather than how they *should* be, I'll tell you that if you apply to a program at which a faculty member is a good friend of your primary recommender it *can* give you a big advantage. Faculty writers are, after all, working artists, so the emotional attachments they've developed with peers over the years remain meaningful to them even when they're in the midst of a formal admissions process. Likewise, working poets and writers inhabit a sometimes surprisingly hierarchical subcommunity in which there are "celebrities" of a sort. If one of your recommenders is well known, you can expect some readers will take note. This won't get you into a program, but it may get your work a closer read.

All of which is to say that you should pick your recommenders carefully, but don't be despondent if you don't have recommenders who are recent professors, working writers, or in any sense famous. Remember that a recommendation is like anything else in your application that isn't your writing sample: it can help you a little bit or hurt you a lot. Even the slightest criticism of your work or your personality in a recommendation letter can be devastating, if only because faculty admissions committees are accustomed to reading recommendations that are relentlessly and even implausibly positive. So even more important than choosing a recommender who knows someone at a program you're applying to or is a public figure within their subfield is choosing someone who admires and believes in you. That's right: it's better to have your third-grade teacher write about seeing you as a second son or daughter than to ask a recent Pulitzer Prize–winning author to write a lukewarm letter about you. I'm serious.

Many applicants will find that recommendation letters are the toughest part of the application process. Why? Because they're the one part you don't at all control. Once you've gotten a recommender's agreement to write a letter on your behalf, you are, to some extent, at the mercy of their goodwill and diligence. It will be your responsibility to stay on top of the deadlines for letter submissions, as you can be certain your recommenders have a lot of other things going on and will—I repeat, *will*—let you down in one way or another. (Okay, maybe some won't, but you'll be better off assuming at least one person who agreed to write a letter for you will be flaky about it.)

The other reason recommendation letters can be frustrating is that you usually don't get to see them before they're submitted, which means you don't have any way of knowing whether they're likely to help or hurt your candidacy. One protection here against the unexpected is to include, in your request for a recommendation letter, a little bit of information about why you're asking this person in particular to write a recommendation and what they might remember about you and your work. Professors see so many students come and go that you can't assume they will remember you. While professors are always preferred as recommenders, if you find yourself needing to ask someone outside academia and/or the literary community to write a letter for you, they may need some additional information about your writing and "you as a writer." Be willing to volunteer some information about yourself and your ambitions up front, and be clear that you can send along any additional information (including your writing sample or other exemplars of your writing) should they wish to see it. Most of all, remember to start the process of securing recommenders as early as you reasonably can; you don't want a recommender's unexpected flakiness to send your whole application process into a death spiral days before a set of important deadlines.

Were you to ask me whether any element of your creative writing application matters besides your writing sample, personal statement, and recommendations, I'd likely say no. Those components of your application make up about 98 percent of what your readers care about. Unfortunately, those readers—a group mostly or wholly comprising working poets and writers—will be constrained by administrators and other university bureaucrats into caring about a few other things. Or, rather, "caring," as these are elements that must be in your application but won't be factors in the selection process.

First among these, of course, is the application itself. It communicates some basic facts about you to the committee, and I suppose that in a close call between two candidates a faculty reader might be distantly interested by your academic background, activities you were involved in during your college years, or (more likely, to be candid) some demographic information about you that confirms that beyond being a superlative artist you'd also bring some much-needed diversity of perspective to campus. These things will matter a bit more if you're an older applicant; there are stories of faculty committees becoming enamored with an applicant due to life experiences they've had that have nothing to do with the arts. By the same token, there are occasions in which a particularly strong undergraduate pedigree will interest a faculty reader because they know how rigorous a given undergraduate creative writing program happens to be.

The most anxiety-inducing component of your MFA or PhD applications will be the GPA requirements, standardized testing requirements, and—in some instances—the post-admission foreign language requirements. Tackling the last of these first, the good news is that few programs have in-program foreign language requirements, so if the idea of taking a basic reading comprehension exam in a language you've studied in the past, or two classes in a new foreign language, is particularly daunting to you, you can skip such programs altogether.

As for GPA requirements and standardized test scores, you should know that these are requested by MFA programs not because they care about them but because the graduate schools to which MFA programs are generally attached almost universally do. Most colleges' and universities' graduate schools have minimum GPA and GRE standards, so MFA programs must collect this data—and sometimes even deny students admission because of it—though they do not find it relevant to your chances of being a successful poet, novelist, or memoirist. At most graduate creative writing programs, the minimum GPA that the graduate school is willing to accept is a 3.0 (i.e., a "B" average).

Having said that, there are exceptions to every rule and limits to the forbearance an admissions committee can show. If your college transcript shows failed courses or a number of very low grades—below a C—it may communicate that you're not ready for graduate study and cannot be relied upon to stay in the program through graduation.

Applicants ask more questions about application requirements than all other topics combined, so here's a correspondingly long list of FAQs on this expansive subject.

FREQUENTLY ASKED QUESTIONS: APPLICATION REQUIREMENTS

Q1: Can I send a portfolio that's longer or shorter than what a program requests?
A1: Don't do this. Trust me.

Q2: Should I include a range of writing styles in my portfolio?
A2: Send whatever you earnestly consider your best and most representative work. Don't try to game the system by sending work you think will please a particular faculty member, or which shows "range" at the expense of demonstrating technical excellence. Skip all that and send the work you most want to represent you at the time you apply.

(Continued)

Q3: My writing sample includes some offensive material. Should I send it anyway?

A3: Think carefully before doing this. If you're certain the material is artistically justified, *and* that the work is your strongest and most representative, *and* that there's no other work equally strong and representative to replace it, *and* you're willing to have your application denied because you chose this hill to die on—well, you get the picture.

Q4: Will the admissions committee read my whole sample, or just the beginning? In other words, should I focus on poems/stories that start strong, even if they end weak?

A4: No one is admitted to their top-choice program with a writing sample that's uneven. All finalists for admission to a given program will have their sample read in full, so if you're only comfortable with part of yours, it means it's not yet ready to be submitted.

Q5: What font-size and typeface should I use for my sample?

A5: Use one of the most common typefaces (for instance, Times New Roman) and 12-point font unless a program requests otherwise. Generally, you want the work—not your presentation of it—to do the talking. Anything other than that communicates to the committee, rightly or wrongly, that you fear your work won't stand on its own.

Q6: Is it all right if my writing sample contains no previously published work?

A6: Absolutely! While prior publication of your sample at an established literary venue with strong editorial oversight may suggest your sample is of the style and content that will find a generally favorable reception at certain MFA programs, that's very different from saying that the mere fact of its prior publication is an asset to your application.

Q7: I'm applying to fewer programs to save money on application fees. Good idea?

A7: Not really. Only allow an application fee to keep you from applying to a program if you really can't afford it. While application fees range from free to over $100, in the end it's important that you apply to every program you're interested in. So start saving up early, as many applicants apply to over a dozen programs and application fees pile up.

Q8: Should I take the GRE General Test?

A8: Yes. You really limit your application options if you don't, and the field of graduate creative writing programs is already competitive enough without anyone inadvertently making things harder on themselves.

Chapter 18 has a list of programs (including many fully funded ones) that require the General Test. Having said that, there's no compelling reason to study and pay for the GRE Subject Test in English. Virtually no one requires it, and if your "dream" school is one of the handful that do, you'll surely have scoured their website carefully enough to have found out about that requirement well in advance.

Q9: Okay, I should take the GRE General Test. What if I'm really, really bad at math?
A9: It may not be as much of a problem as you think. MFA programs don't themselves much care about the GRE, only requiring it because their host universities' graduate-school administrators demand they do. But MFA programs make admission decisions, not graduate-school administrators, and while MFA programs may have to run any acceptances past their graduate school they will likely argue that only your analytical writing and verbal reasoning scores should matter, given the program you're applying to. That said, you might need to top a relatively low overall-score bar to be admitted. But because that bar is low, I urge applicants to take the GRE if (a) they have the money to do so, (b) would like to attend a program that asks for GRE scores, and (c) they're willing to study *just* enough to get a low but not prohibitively bad score on the quantitative reasoning section of the test. Many programs will either say on their website what their minimum GRE score is or—more often—you'll find this information on the graduate-school website for the university in question. If your "dream school" requires the GRE and you receive a score too low for admission, you might ask them if GRE waivers are possible or whether the GRE can be retaken prematriculation or while in-program.

Q10: Do I send transcripts from all of the schools I attended, including community colleges?
A10: Yes, though if all your community college grades appear as transferred courses on your BA transcript and are designated as such, just the BA transcript should be fine.

Q11: Do MFA programs care what my undergraduate major was?
A11: No.

Q12: Do programs care about my undergraduate GPA? Can it help me get admitted?
A12: It definitely won't be what gets you into a program. As to whether the programs care, they care only if your GPA is so low that it suggests

(Continued)

you can't handle academic coursework in English (they may look more at grades in English than your overall GPA). But as with the GRE, there may be graduate-school baselines you must contend with.

Q13: Should I tailor my portfolio to what I think is each program's overall aesthetic?

A13: Almost certainly not. That sort of thing is impossible to guess at, even if it *feels* knowable. Just send your best work—work that represents your abilities and interests.

Q14: Should I only include previously published work in my fiction portfolio?

A14: It doesn't matter if the work you're sending was previously published, unless you so trust the judgment of the editor who published it that the mere fact of its publication confirms for you that this is your very best work. Otherwise, make your own judgment.

Q15: I sent an email to a program and never heard back. How often does this happen?

A15: All the time. Every year we hear stories of programs that don't reply to emails, reply months late, or reject the same applicant twice. Many programs are understaffed, and unprepared to deal with a deluge of queries. So only email in an emergency; otherwise, seek an answer from other applicants or a program's promotional materials. You don't want to bug a program to the point you're unlikely to gain acceptance, however strong your writing, because they worry you might be more trouble than your writing is worth. These people may well be future peers and faculty—so act accordingly.

CHAPTER FOUR

Cohort

"Cohort" is one of the primary application drivers in the field of creative writing. Many poets and writers are unwilling to apply to programs whose student bodies they suspect are homogenous. As a result, many programs—particularly in the Midwest and South—receive fewer applications than they otherwise might. The demographics issue tends to focus, in creative writing, on five categories of student identity: race, ethnicity, sexual orientation, gender identity, and, to a lesser extent, religion. Age, too, is a topic of concern, but as I discussed it in Chapter 2, I'll focus on these five other indicators.

You may notice that "gender" doesn't appear in the list of indicators just outlined. There's a good reason for that: according to the available hard data, many more women than men apply to graduate creative writing programs and more women than men are admitted. For all that there is rightly much discussion about whether self-identified male and female writers receive equal treatment from literary institutions once they've graduated from an MFA or PhD in creative writing, we have no data thus far suggesting that there is gender discrimination in the admissions process for these types of programs, nor that any program is insufficiently heterogeneous as to gender. Certainly, some of the smaller programs may on occasion matriculate an all-male or all-female cohort, but there's no evidence that such gender demographics are anything but aberrational.

There *is* anecdotal evidence suggesting that many programs struggle to achieve racial, ethnic, sexual orientation, gender identity, and religious diversity in their classes. Some of this struggle originates with applicants' application decisions, which is why we discuss this topic in this book rather than leaving it to social scientists or others who research and write on systemic prejudice. Based on many interviews with and discussions involving writers of color, transgender writers, and Muslim writers, there is reason to believe many applicants from these communities refuse to apply to certain programs.

Concerns about cohort are usually expressed as a function of local demographics or hard data on populations. Poets and writers identifying as nonwhite, nonstraight, and/or non-Christian/Jewish often report concern about attending graduate creative writing programs in the South or, to a lesser extent, the Midwest. They often report concern, more broadly, about attending programs that are not located in urban centers, on the assumption that the larger an urban center is, the more likely it is to have a diverse population.

It is not for this book to describe, explain, defend, or otherwise deconstruct the apprehensions of individual applicants. What I can do is make general observations on the "cohort" question that might shed some light on individual applicants' deliberations.

First, and most importantly, applicants of all backgrounds should be prepared to socialize outside their program of study. This may seem self-evident, but as graduate creative writing programs are notoriously insular it is not, in fact, self-evident to many. Because MFA and PhD programs in creative writing are in some respects artists' communes, it is easy to develop a "commune" mentality in which one considers all persons to be either "inside" or "outside" the community. Certainly, graduate creative writing students share a love of writing, and in many cases a curriculum that rarely intersects with that of other graduate students at the same university, so it's easy to feel your graduate creative writing program is an island with no boats coming into, or embarking from, its harbor. That sense of isolation can be exhilarating or alienating, depending upon your personality; those who've never before been immersed in a creative community may find in their cohort all the social engagement they need, whereas others who've experienced the complications of such communities firsthand may come to see it as stifling. Obviously there's no right or wrong answer on this score.

But the ways in which creative writing programs insulate students from the rest of their host university or discourage students from intellectually cross-pollinating outside the classroom can deter students who need to look outside the program for social and intellectual stimulation. This is why, when poets and writers applying to graduate school in creative writing ask me the extent to which they should consider the likely demographics of their cohort, I hesitate to answer. I just don't know how much or how little any individual applicant will need to rely on their cohort for society, nor the extent to which any given applicant is made unhappy by inhabiting a community whose members to a great extent don't look like them. So what I say, instead, is something I know to be true: all graduate creative writing students benefit from making full use of being on a college or university campus. That means seeking out friendships and even artistic collaborations with those outside your program, and doing your utmost to attend lectures and other events sponsored by groups other than your writing program.

Early on in this book, I noted that "time and space" are the key reasons to attend a graduate creative writing program. I said that one must mindfully build up both rather than relying on your program to do that for you. Here's where that admonition comes most clearly into play: if you only make time and space in your life for students within your program, you are underresourcing your imagination and robbing yourself of the diverse resources any institution of higher learning is likely to offer you. If you spend every week hanging out at the local "poet's bar" or "fiction-writer's bar" you will miss the chance to see where the college's or university's art historians, engineers, and astrophysicists are congregating. You miss a chance to imbue your writing with the vitality that comes from diverse experiences as well as diverse company. And while you might not expect—or welcome—a book on applying to graduate creative writing programs giving you this sort of advice, keep in mind that I say this to you because hundreds of current and former creative writing students have said it to me. This advice arises in part from my own experience, it's true, but far more importantly from theirs.

A second observation about cohort is one which, of all the observations I'll make in this book, graduate creative writing programs may find the most disturbing. I submit here that the workshop pedagogy *implicitly encourages demographic homogeneity.*

That's a big claim—and one that's critically important to those of you worried about the demographics at your programs of choice—so I want to spend some time with it. It arises from complaints I've heard about undergraduate and graduate creative writing workshops from nonwhite, nonstraight, and non-Christian/ Jewish poets and writers. The most common complaint holds that writing program homogeneity is dangerous because it leads to bad workshopping experiences for minority students. The bad workshopping experience most commonly described to me, and for that matter most commonly written about in literary and popular magazines, is one in which a white workshop participant makes undue presumptions about—or puts specious restrictions upon— the literary work of a nonwhite, nonstraight, or non-Christian/ Jewish peer.

What sort of classroom environment would defuse such situations before they arise? The answer is one in which authors are invited to discuss their ambitions and writing processes *before* peers adjudicate their work; one in which workshop participants are trained in how to critique literature to the benefit of its writer rather than its reader; and one in which students ask questions of their peers before they hear comments on their work. In essence, the answer is a classroom in which discourse across all artificial boundaries is encouraged rather than hindered. Of course, the conventional creative writing workshop permits none of this: students are trained never to speak of what animated a given piece of writing, nor to ask questions of peers whose work they are reading, nor to treat the ability to critique as a learned skill in itself rather than one any person of sense would naturally possess before walking into a workshop. Conventional creative writing pedagogy encourages silencing, presumptuousness, and critical hubris.

Most workshops also spend little time on the question of *audience*—that is, the extent to which an author should consider her audience when writing. Many of the "bad workshop" anecdotes I hear, whether they involve disputes across racial, ethnic, gender, and other demographic lines or not, are founded in this foundational question. If a work, no matter its genre, comes authentically from your own perspective, experience, and values, should that automatically protect it from critique—even ignorant critique— from readers with different perspectives, experiences, and values (indeed, even provincial ones)? Certainly, when your book of poetry or fiction is sold online or in stores you won't have an opportunity to engage readers directly with an explanation of why their reading of your work is, in some sense, limited or disappointing.

And indeed this is creative writing's response, as a discipline, to some of the complaints about its processes that I've aired here. Why, most creative writing professors will ask, should I allow you any different sort of audience in this workshop than you can expect to receive among the consumers in a bookstore? And so the question becomes, if you know your book will be read by people lacking your knowledge and worldview, is the correct response to change your content, style, expectations, writing processes, agent, marketing, or some combination of these?

I don't have an answer to these questions. I can only say that bad workshop experiences are instructive in ways that are also hurtful, and that to the extent conventional creative writing pedagogy inadvertently encourages such pain it also, maybe equally inadvertently, encourages such an education in what it means to be an author that perhaps some portion of that pain is worthwhile. (And I say this from hard experience.) So while I can say with confidence that every creative writing student should want to study in a diverse workshop, within a diverse program, and within a diverse college or university community, I can also say that one benefits as much from ignorant criticism as enlightened criticism, as much from empty praise as considered praise. How so? Because all four of these reactions to literary work are common, and the best authors learn to distinguish between the four by being regularly subjected to all of them. The reactions of your readers *matter*—to a point. Deciding where that point is, and what you're willing to do or not do to get there, is what finally makes you a writer.

By the same token, your ability to engage with work you find objectionable is its own education, if not for its author than for you as someone still learning how to discuss complex literary topics with incisiveness and grace. I often say that one learns far more from one's workshop cohort than one does from one's professors, and that's true if we understand the learning that happens in a workshop to be as much about what it means to be a writer and reader as about the particulars of "craft." You may learn little about craft from your peers—who are, after all, approximately as experienced as you—but you'll learn all you need to know about being a conscientious writer, critic, and reader from engaging with their work. It is they who confront you with questions of audience and authorial ethos; the thorny social obstacles to honest critique; the intractability of our own literary biases; and, above all, what it means to inhabit a cloistered community of creatives, many of whom are striving for the same sort of writing life as you are.

I can tell you that across untold workshops, I learned more about the writer, critic, editor, and reader I do *not* want to be from my workshop peers than I ever did from my professors. I don't intend this as a criticism of my classmates, either; I learned as much about what I didn't want to do from peers whose work I *admired* as I did from peers whose work was less compelling to me. In every chasm that suddenly opens between you and a classmate—whether it's a dispute over process, style, content, philosophy, or even core values—lies the sort of intelligence most working authors would envy accruing. Once you leave your writing program, it becomes much more difficult to get feedback on your work in real time. Your access to your readers' thought processes and innate biases is so limited that you begin to long for the access you once had in workshop. Only when we cease to wonder altogether what anyone makes of our work, or become complacent that the response will be exactly as we hope it will be, do we cease to advance our understanding of what it means to be a writer in the world.

FREQUENTLY ASKED QUESTIONS: COHORT

Q1: Can I get demographic data from the programs I want to apply to before I apply?

A1: Only if you visit the program and take a real-time census. Generally speaking, programs won't release this data to nonadmitted students and only rarely—perhaps with some hostility or suspicion—to admitted students. Your best bet, if this data is critical to your application decision, is to track down current students or recent alumni.

Having said that, program administrators are not monsters. While they won't often speak to mere applicants and are unlikely to release sensitive data about student demographics, once admitted to a program you should feel free to candidly express any concerns you have to whichever program liaison you've been communicating with. Often they'll be able to put your fears to rest by speaking broadly of their student body or the college/university's host location. If they themselves are a minority poet or writer, they'll be able to speak from firsthand experience. If not, they may be willing to put you in touch with someone whose program experience could be analogous to yours.

Q2: Lacking any demographic data, should I avoid programs located in certain regions?
A2: No—"avoid" is far too strong a word when we're discussing drawing conclusions about a location you've not yet visited. But what I will say is that you should do your homework, investigating program locations by talking to members of programs' current or recent student cohorts if you can or, failing that, finding people whose experiences you think might be relevant to your own who've traveled to or lived in the locations you're researching. If you hate college towns, by all means don't apply to any programs located in one; but the list of college towns that are racially and ethnically diverse, or known to be particularly welcoming to LGBTQI+ individuals, is actually rather long. And it includes many towns in which MFA or PhD programs in creative writing are located.

Q3: How much weight should I give viral program lists ("Most _____-Friendly MFAs")?
A3: An assessment is only as strong as its methodology, though because graduate creative writing programs are historically—and notoriously—opaque to their applicants, we often have to make do with compelling and well-researched but nevertheless unscientific methodologies. I understand and deeply appreciate the intentions of those who generate this type of list; they're trying to offer a service to their fellow applicants, and they're doing it with open hearts and without compensation. And some of the lists produced in this context are useful reference tools for applicants. What I worry about with these assessments is not the motivations behind them but their tendency to oversimplify. Those oversimplifications could end up costing you a lot of money, a situation most of you reading this guidebook purchased it—in part—to avoid.

Take, for instance, a listing of "queer-friendly MFA programs" that you might come across online. I've encountered a few lists like these, and all of them, I'll say, are facially sensible—they look and sound like the sort of listing you'd expect them to be, with listings of towns/cities (mostly cities) that are known to be home to large LGBTQI+ populations. Other entries on the list are clearly programs with LGBTQI+ professors. The theory behind such entries is only partially convincing: does the fact that San Francisco, a city of nearly a million people, has a very large LGBTQI+ community mean that your San Francisco–located MFA program of

(*Continued*)

twelve poets and writers will be welcoming to poets and writers who are not straight? Not necessarily, though I suspect the theory behind putting San Francisco programs on such a list is that if you are an LGBTQI+ poet or writer and you find the atmosphere in your graduate creative writing program hostile, you can quickly shift your attention to creating a social network that's outside the program but still within San Francisco. Fair enough. But it begs the question, does the same theory work in reverse? Can an MFA located in a town or city with a fairly small LGBTQI+ population be experienced as welcoming if your incoming cohort at a program located in that town or city is itself diverse and/or particularly welcoming to LGBTQI+ authors? I don't claim to be able to answer this question for you, but it's worth thinking about. The question of how much socializing you expect to do within and without your program and its host university is a key one in figuring out both how much a cohort matters to you *and* what experience you might anticipate at a given program.

What about terming a program "queer-friendly" simply because it has a single LGBTQI+ faculty member? On this subject, my opinion is a bit more fully formed. It's dangerous to select any program because of a single faculty member, as they might not be on faculty by the time you arrive, might go on a sabbatical or become a visiting faculty member elsewhere for a significant portion of your program experience, or simply might not connect with you on a personal level, whatever shared experiences you may have. The fact is, I've talked with over a thousand MFA students and alumni over the last decade and have heard only the rare anecdote of any faculty member—whatever their demographic and subject position—exhibiting animus to a student on the basis of race, ethnicity, sexual orientation, religion, disability status, nationality, or any other subject position. To be clear, I don't in any sense suggest that hateful conduct doesn't occur, simply that the MFA applicant community is now so large, so centralized on Facebook, and so candid in its discussions that you're likely to hear straight away if a given faculty member is acting inappropriately toward any of his or her students. What you will much more commonly find is LGBTQI+ students saying that their straight professors couldn't have been more welcoming, supportive, and dedicated to their students. So I'd hate for anyone reading this to put limits on their application list on the basis of this program or that one having more than a certain number of LGBTQI+—or African American, Latinx, Jewish, noncitizen, transgender, and so on—faculty members.

While program administrators will rarely give out MFA students' contact info to applicants as opposed to admitted students—in fact they can't legally do this unless they've asked a student, and a student has agreed, to act as a liaison to prospective students—if you're deeply concerned about a given program's environment, see if you can get a contact person at each of the programs you're interested in to put you in touch with a current student. To be clear, you take a real risk of annoying the administrator when you do this, so look first on social media (both within MFA-applicant Facebook groups and without) to see whether any current students will talk to you, or whether the in-program environment at the school in question has already been a topic of conversation. First-hand accounts, however subjective they'll undoubtedly be, will be far more useful to you than assessments based exclusively on tallies of current faculty.

Having said all this, if you're deeply concerned about these issues and can't get information from a current or former student, you can certainly use the faculty roster and your knowledge of a program's host location as a very rough—possibly inaccurate—guess about a program's atmosphere and culture. But be warned: limiting yourself to programs that meet requirements of this sort could cost you a great deal of money in the long run, and could cause you to miss out on an excellent program experience at a program better suited to you in many other ways. Continue reading this chapter for more information on the intersection between a program's cohort and a program's cost.

Q4: So—bluntly—can I expect my writing program to be racially or ethnically diverse?
A4: Not really. Data suggest about 75 percent of graduate creative writing students nationally are white, though this figure is likely higher in the Midwest and South and lower at MFA programs on the coasts. (To be clear, we're speaking of averages; there are noncoastal programs every bit as diverse as programs in New York City and Los Angeles.) One of the ongoing struggles within the discipline of creative writing is that many of its institutions are overwhelmingly white. This poses a problem for all poets and writers, of course, but particularly for applicants of any background hoping to attend a diverse program—as you can't know in advance what the demographic composition of your cohort will be. This may be why some nonwhite applicants look for faculties that have a number of nonwhite members; the thinking here—entirely sensible— is that one *can* determine the racial or ethnic composition of a faculty, whether or not one can as to one's cohort.

(*Continued*)

Q5: Is there anything wrong with drafting an application list based, in substantial part, on one's perception of which programs are most welcoming to minority authors?

A5: There may be, and not simply because any such perception would necessarily be a guess—and with years of your life and untold dollars hanging in the balance, that's a lot to chance on a guess. No, the much more important issue is that, by and large, MFA programs in large cities are less well-funded than programs in medium-size cities, small cities, college towns, or rural towns. Because many of those looking for diverse student and faculty cohorts look first at graduate programs in large urban centers, they end up never looking at, or applying to, most of the nation's best-funded creative writing programs. The result—and there's anecdotal evidence to support this—is that nonwhite and/or nonstraight poets and writers are more likely to go into substantial student debt than are their straight white peers. That's a deeply concerning situation for a discipline already dealing with a lack of diversity. Indeed, if this trend continues, it could dissuade nonwhite and/or nonstraight authors from pursuing graduate creative writing degrees, which would exacerbate the discipline's already sizable and troubling demographic disparities.

The easiest solution to this problem would be for more MFA programs in large urban centers to fully fund their students, but this is unlikely to happen for precisely the reasons we're discussing here—because more applicants want to pursue an MFA in a large urban center than any other type of setting. So programs in large urban settings can fill their annual cohorts despite not offering as much money to their students, on average, as programs in smaller population centers. Soon enough, it all becomes a vicious circle.

A second solution would be for graduate creative writing programs to actively recruit nonwhite and/or nonstraight poets and writers, perhaps by hiring more nonwhite and/or nonstraight faculty, developing new student-applicant liaison positions, updating their websites to speak more about their host locations, or any number of other initiatives. Some programs are already starting to take these measures, but far more must be done.

Q6: I've heard that romantic liaisons are a real danger to small cohorts. Is this true?

A6: Yes. I'd suggest you do everything in your power to avoid romantic entanglements with classmates. Your entire cohort will thank you. I can't describe how awkward it is when two of a very small number of workshop participants have previously been romantically involved. Sounds like a far-fetched scenario? I promise you, it's really not.

Q7: I just had my first workshop and I'm feeling "imposter syndrome." What do I do?
A7: At this stage in your writing life, essential "writerly" traits like persistence, courage, audacity, imagination, dynamism, reflexivity, and dedication are more important than "polish." You'll often come across writers in your workshops more "polished" than you, and perhaps some will actually be further along in their skill development in a more than superficial way. But every student accepted to an MFA was accepted for a reason; the faculty saw something in you and is willing to be patient in watching it emerge. Every writer has fecund and fallow periods, so if you're not thrilled with what you're writing now, go back to the texts that inspire you most, immerse yourself in them, and slowly work your way toward that inevitable future period when your work really shines.

CHAPTER FIVE

Selectivity

It's common practice for graduate programs in popular fields of study to publish their acceptance rates so that potential applicants can gauge their chances of admission in advance. Applicants to law, medical, engineering, business, and other professional degree programs annually review these data and not only make application decisions on the basis of what they find but also judge programs' academic rigor and the quality of their annual student cohorts using their "selectivity in admissions" as a compelling indicator.

In certain respects, graduate creative writing programs are more popular than any of these professional degree programs—over the last twenty years the field of graduate creative writing programs has expanded more rapidly than that of any other type of graduate degree—and yet acceptance rates to these programs have historically not been available. There are many reasons for this, including that the number of graduate creative writing programs was still relatively small as late as the mid-1980s, and admissions decisions are made almost exclusively on the basis of an unquantifiable measure: the literary quality of an applicant's creative writing portfolio. A more esoteric explanation is that graduate creative writing programs have not historically kept records with the same rigor that professional postgraduate programs do, and students and faculty in the field are particularly disinclined to introduce comparative measures—and therefore, in one view, overt competitiveness—into a discipline squarely within the arts.

The problem is that creative writing MFA and PhD programs are expensive, time-consuming, and, historically, poorly marketed. This makes it extremely difficult for applicants to find clues as to which program will be the best fit for them. We've already discussed the problems with choosing a program by its faculty, and since many other program measures, like pedagogy and program duration, are relatively consistent across the range of US graduate creative writing programs, applicants can easily feel undernourished by the lack of hard data. Useful points of distinction among programs, like credit requirements, program size, and the availability of cross-genre study, are only intermittently found in programs' printed promotional materials or on their websites.

With all this in mind, we come to the key questions asked by this chapter: how valuable is it to know that your application to a given graduate creative writing program will be subjected to a "selective" admissions process? How meaningful is the distinction between a "very selective" admissions process and a "moderately selective" one? Do acceptance rates tell us anything about the quality of a program's curriculum, faculty, or students? How should applicants make use of this information, particularly when they know only some programs provide it publicly—and very few of these systematically?

I want to be transparent here and tell you that the official position of the Association of Writers & Writing Programs, the trade organization for creative writing institutions in the United States—and the position of nearly all of their member institutions, with only a handful of exceptions—is that you as an applicant are not entitled to ask, or receive, information about any individual program's acceptance rate. AWP does not publish this data at the program level as a matter of longstanding policy, and the overwhelming majority of programs do not release it (they say) as a matter of principle. Yet all agree that one of the hallmarks of a strong creative writing program is that it has a selective admissions process rather than merely admitting everyone who applies, regardless of their skill-set. Still, few programs are willing to act on this consensus.

Of the 250 full-residency graduate creative writing programs in the United States, about ten routinely publish their annual acceptance rate. Another thirty or forty do so every other year or so. These latter programs' periodic informal reporting of their acceptance rates is what makes it possible for a book like this one to publish an ordered list of graduate creative writing programs from most to least selective. While not every program has sufficient data to allow it to be entered into this sort of chart, many do.

Is a list of the most selective writing programs useful to you as an applicant? Yes. Acceptance rates are a function of two numbers of significant relevance to you: the number of applicants a program receives and the number of students in the program's annual incoming cohort.

Since the mid-2000s, graduate creative writing program applicants have congregated in large numbers online to discuss which programs are worth applying to and which are not, so the grad-school application decisions of many aspiring poets and writers are not being made in a vacuum. In a field in which most programs poorly market themselves and provide little critical program data to potential applicants, the opportunity for applicants to share and compile research online is invaluable. In a succession of high-traffic online applicant communities since 2004, applicants have congregated to discuss not just the hard data of individual programs (e.g., program size, program duration, cost of living, and acceptance rates) but also more inchoate concerns like the quality of a program's faculty, the satisfaction of current and former students, and the utility of curricular prerequisites and requirements. Were creative writing a field like law, medicine, engineering, or business, perhaps applicant communities of such size and scope would never have been formed; as it is, creative writing is a field in which applicants must often take their lead from research done by their predecessors.

For this reason, the number of annual applicants to a given graduate creative writing program *does* matter. Polling shows that the overwhelming majority (more than 97 percent) of such applicants are not limited by geographic concerns, and in the online communities I'm speaking of the names, locations, and website addresses of all extant creative writing MFA programs are readily available—so when we discover in these communities certain application trends, these data are meaningful. Programs with a high number of applicants are, on balance, more likely to have been spoken of positively within the applicant community on the basis of their "hard" and "soft" features alike.

The other number we use to develop acceptance rates for individual programs is the number of students who matriculate at each program annually. You'll note here that we do *not* use information on the number of students each program *accepts* annually, as that information has been made available by only two of the 250 graduate creative writing programs in the United States—and even then only intermittently. For this reason, we cannot determine the "yield" of any program, this being the percentage of admitted students who choose to matriculate at a program once they've been accepted. For instance, if a program offers admission to ten students and five accept, the "yield" for that program, for that year, is 50 percent. Most programs manage their yield with sufficient care that their annual cohort size remains consistent across many application cycles.

So when we order programs by "acceptance rates" in the field of creative writing, what we are doing is dividing a program's annual cohort size by the total number of applicants it received in a given year. We call this a "yield-exclusive" acceptance rate because it does not take into account applicants who were accepted to a program but declined to attend. Make no mistake: it would be *wonderful* to have yield data, as it would give us an indication of how students feel about a program once they've been accepted to it and therefore have had a chance to take a closer look at it. And this, frankly, is why such data isn't available: on this particular point, graduate creative writing programs would prefer you have less information rather than more.

So why should you care about "cohort size," the second number we use to determine a program's degree of selectivity? Because cohort size gives you some indication of how much attention you can expect to receive from faculty if you decide to matriculate at a program. While by no means is a smaller program always a better one, it's true that the larger a program's annual cohort is, the easier it is for an individual poet or writer to get lost in the mix. (See Chapter 8 for more on student-faculty ratios.)

Let's say you agree that it's a good sign when many applicants want to attend a program; let's say you agree, too, that there's some value in attending a program with a relatively small annual cohort. Does this mean that a program with a 5 percent yield-exclusive acceptance rate is "better" than a program with a 25 percent yield-exclusive acceptance rate?

The answer is yes and no. And *both* answers are somewhat controversial.

The answer is yes because the data suggests there is a meaningful, persistent connection between a program's yield-exclusive acceptance rate and how it performs in terms of less ambiguous measures like postgraduate fellowships and job placements. In other words, programs with a more selective admissions process either graduate stronger job and fellowship candidates, do a better job of advancing their students' postgraduate candidacies through their curriculum selection and career services resources, or both.

Another reason the answer is yes is that in the realm of graduate study, perception often becomes reality—fairly or otherwise. A program with a low acceptance rate enjoys the benefit of a "virtuous circle": it is perceived as top-notch, so more and stronger applicants apply, and so its reputation for being top-notch gradually moves from theory to rumor and from rumor to reality. Note that this happens in every academic discipline. In every discipline there are schools with perhaps outsized reputations that were earned in part through the inertia of just such a virtuous circle as I've described. We could complain that this is unfair, or we could note—quite fairly—that as every program is aware of how and why this virtuous circle operates, every program has a natural incentive to be as attractive as possible to applicants and to keep its cohort size at a manageable level. Over time, this institutional concern for students' preprogram and in-program experiences dramatically benefits applicants, students, and alumni.

But the answer to the question of whether acceptance rates matter is also, and perhaps equally, a resounding no. When we laud, say, Harvard Law School for having a low acceptance rate, all we are saying is that the students it admits have very high LSAT scores and very high GPAs—as for all intents and purposes, these are the only two measures used in deciding which students will be admitted to a given law school. If you agree that high LSAT scores and a high GPA tells you who's going to be a good attorney when they're ten years on from law school, then yes, Harvard Law School's acceptance rate is an extremely telling piece of data. If, however, you believe good lawyering is born of a personal commitment to the job, a strong work ethic, the ability to listen and learn and empathize and all the other things that go into being a superlative professional, you may think LSAT scores and GPAs are only a very distant indicator of future success. Sure, it takes some admirable qualities for a pre–law school student to do well on the LSAT and maintain a high GPA, but those are only some of the qualities an attorney needs, and they may not translate as well into legal practice as we expect. When I was an attorney, I saw no correlation between a peer's abilities and their alma mater's acceptance rate.

In this sense, if perhaps in few others, law schools are analogous to writing programs. Because admission to graduate creative writing programs isn't based on standardized testing or GPAs but rather on a small number of persons' subjective responses to your creative writing portfolio, it's hard to say what any one admissions decision tells us about the student it accepted or declined. Conventional wisdom tells us that if one student is accepted and another rejected at a certain program, it likely means no more than that the former is currently more "polished" than the latter. By this we mean that the former currently exhibits better "craft" in their chosen genre. Does this make it more likely the former will have a successful publishing career? No one can say. There are so many intervening factors that will decide that question—time, learning curve, work ethic, mentorship, the natural and unpredictable development of any artist's imaginative faculties—that program admissions decisions are never more than a guess.

What we know for sure is that certain types of applicants are disadvantaged by the graduate creative writing program admissions process, and for this reason we must be very careful about calling the hard data of that process meaningful. What about the writer whose poetry or prose is so formally challenging that faculty members fear they wouldn't be good instructors for a student with such advanced ambitions? What about the writer who routinely creates dynamic multimedia and transmedia art? What about the writer whose choice of topic is unappealing to members of the program's faculty for reasons having everything to do with them and nothing at all to do with the applicant? These are not rare scenarios; they arise at every program during every application cycle. And what that means is that if you write something other than lyric-narrative poetry or literary fiction; if you write about potentially off-putting topics or use multimedia in your art; if your formal innovations are inscrutable to most application readers, whether due to your shortcomings or theirs; the selectivity data tables in this book won't give you a good indication of the odds you're facing at a given graduate creative writing program. What you'll have to do, instead, is research programs that cater to your specific vision, perhaps by thinking of authors you admire and seeing whether they teach in a program.

For the overwhelming majority of readers of this book, however, selectivity data will give you an "all-things-being-equal" sense of which programs on your application list are long-shots, and which are this discipline's version of a "safety school." You'll notice that I've put "safety school" in quotes; that's because there really are no safety schools in this field. While an especially new or regionally oriented program may be essentially nonselective, at least half the nation's graduate creative writing programs are difficult to get into by any measure. And since a clear majority of applications go to just fifty or so programs, applicants' assumption should be that at none of the programs they're considering are they a shoo-in. Thinking otherwise courts disappointment come spring.

FREQUENTLY ASKED QUESTIONS: SELECTIVITY

Q1: What do we mean when we say that one program is more popular than another?

A1: The difference between two programs' annual applicant pools can be *dramatic*. There are programs near the top of the heap in terms of applicant popularity that receive more than 1,000 program applications each year. Meanwhile, recently founded programs in their first few application cycles can get as few as ten applications. And that's not a typo. So to the extent the "applicant popularity" listings in this book give you a sense of how popular a program is among the best-researched applicants—the ones who congregate online to benefit from the research and advice of others in the MFA community—you should pay close attention to them. And because most MFA programs are relatively modest in size, matriculating between twenty and thirty poets and writers each year, it's often the case that a program with a low acceptance rate got that way because the other figure in the acceptance-rate equation (applicant pool size) is very high. These are things to keep in mind as you're constructing an application list.

Q2: Does the number of applicants to a program fluctuate significantly year to year?

A2: It fluctuates, yes. "Significantly" might be a stretch. But just as there are more teaching jobs available in a given genre in some years versus others, for various reasons—often having to do with the national

(Continued)

economy—in certain years applications will be down and getting admitted to a program with funding will be *marginally* easier.

Q3: How do applications break down by genre at most programs?
A3: All MFA programs offer poetry and fiction tracks, and well over half offer creative nonfiction as well. The general rule is that for every six applicants in fiction nationally, there are three poetry applicants and two nonfiction applicants. For this reason, many programs have a lower acceptance rate for their fiction track than their poetry track, and a slightly higher acceptance rate in nonfiction than either of the other two genres.

Q4: If my application is denied, will I be told how many applications the program got?
A4: Rarely. Most programs closely guard this information—for good and bad reasons.

Q5: What if all the programs I'm interested in have very low acceptance rates?
A5: It's okay to apply only to highly selective programs, provided you're willing to be denied admission across the board. I don't say that unkindly. One of the great things about being a graduate creative writing program applicant rather than a law or business school applicant is that your admission isn't time-sensitive. You can wait to get into the program of your choice, applying in consecutive years as necessary, because an MFA or PhD in creative writing doesn't substantially alter your earning potential. When the time is right, you'll get into your program of choice, get into a comparable program, or learn from successive years of applying that graduate school in creative writing might not be for you (remember, this discovery might be a function of aesthetics and not skill).

Q6: Is it sometimes the case that a program's fiction or poetry program is *especially* competitive, whatever the overall acceptance rate of the program may be?
A6: Absolutely. That happens a lot, actually, as there are a number of programs that are considered particularly strong in one genre and therefore attract a particularly large number of applicants for that track. It's one reason we offer one-genre popularity rankings in this book as well as two- and three-genre rankings. Genre-specific popularity rankings give you a sense of whether a program's fiction, poetry, or nonfiction program is especially attractive. If it is, and if you're planning to apply in that genre, adjust the program's "overall" acceptance rate downward when calculating your own odds of admission.

Q7: Can you talk more about "yield"? It seems like a pretty important measure.

A7: It is. Think of it this way: a program with 100 percent yield—a program at which every accepted student accepts their offer of admission—has an acceptance rate that's simply its cohort size divided by its applicant pool size. Meanwhile, a program with a 50 percent yield—one that only gets half its initial admittees—has an effective acceptance rate that's *twice* as high as its cohort size divided by its applicant pool size. That can mean the difference between a 6 percent acceptance rate and a 12 percent one, 13 percent and 26 percent, and so on.

The bad news here is that, particularly at larger and less popular programs, yields fluctuate wildly from year to year and are not reported. So in a given year a program may see half its initial accepted students say yes, and then the next year only a third. That's why yield-exclusive acceptance rates are much better at giving you a sense of how competitive the admissions process is in *general* than distinguishing between two clearly competitive programs. On the other hand, it can definitely help you see the difference between a competitive program and an essentially nonselective program.

Q8: If I'm accepted to a program, will I know whether I was in their first round of selections? Should I ask the program if they don't volunteer that information?

A8: No and no.

Q9: I know that, at the most competitive programs, a lot of people get waitlisted each year. How long are waitlists, and how do I manage being on one?

A9: The length of a waitlist varies from program to program, as the programs determine the length of their waitlists on the basis of their yield in the preceding year(s). Nearly every program—even one that routinely gets a 90-percent or better yield from its first round of acceptances—will have a waitlist long enough to accommodate a yield as low as 50 percent. Meanwhile, programs that generally see less than a 50-percent yield may prepare themselves for yields as low as 10 percent or 15 percent. Depending upon the size of the program, this could mean a waitlist of four people or a waitlist of forty. As for how to act when you're on a waitlist, the answer is professionally. Program administrators get extremely busy when the time for sending out acceptance letters comes, so if you're calling them for any reason other than an emergency

(Continued)

you might be risking their ire and thereby casting a shadow over your application. Even so, it's always appropriate to contact an administrator if you're on his or her waitlist and then get accepted to another program. That situation entitles you to inform the program you're waitlisted at that you've been accepted elsewhere, and to politely ask if they have a general sense of where you are on their waitlist and when they think you might hear a final answer from them. Most administrators will be candid with you under these circumstances; while they won't reveal their program's yield, they may say that it looks like they're not going to go very far into their waitlist and you should therefore seriously consider taking your existing offer. Or they may tell you that you're very high on the waitlist and beg for you to be patient and hold off as long as you can in giving an answer to the program you've already been accepted by.

As a general rule of thumb, the only other acceptable time to call a program and ask about the status of your application is if (a) everyone else who applied to that program received, two or more weeks earlier, an acceptance, rejection, or waitlist notification and you've not heard anything at all, or (b) it's within a few days of the April 15 deadline for students who've received funding offers to let those programs know whether they'll be attending. Of course, this deadline will only matter to you if you have a funded offer of admission elsewhere, which as I note in Chapter 2 is already a situation in which it's generally acceptable to contact a program's administrator.

As for following up a second time with an administrator when you're on their waitlist and have been accepted elsewhere, do this only when you're in the final two or three days before you have to accept or decline another offer. As you can see, your aim is to call programs to ask about the status of an application as infrequently as possible.

Q10: How common is it to have to apply in multiple application seasons?

A10: Very common. There's no shame in this whatsoever. Just keep plugging away at your creative portfolio and reapply whenever you think you're ready. Though I know it might feel otherwise, there really *is* no rush. Every year a substantial percentage of applicants either receive no acceptances or turn down the acceptances they receive due to a lack of funding. (Keep in mind that, though there's no shame in reapplying in successive years, there's no need to draw attention to this in a statement of purpose.)

Q11: After how many successive cycles of applying and not getting in should I give up?

A11: You should *never* give up on your writing. That said, if you've applied three years in a row and not received even a waitlisting, I'd take a break for a few years and do a lot of reading, writing, and local workshopping. Attend readings and lectures and try to meet more writers so that you can benefit from being in a community of literary artists.

CHAPTER SIX

Cost of Living

In the same way that Chapter 8 discusses student-faculty ratios as a stand-in of sorts for the question of faculty mentorship, calculating the cost of living at each school you're applying to not only helps you determine the real value of a program's funding offer but also directs your attention to the critical issue of program location. According to large-scale polls of MFA applicants, the location of a program is about as important as its funding package—and these two program features are considered more influential in application and matriculation decisions than any others. There's a good reason for this: because writing program workshops usually meet only once or twice a week, and because your other credit requirements will likely be rather flexible, you're going to spend well over 90 percent of your time just living and writing in your program's host location. Sure, you'll spend some time each week reading peers' work, perhaps writing papers for any academic courses you're required to take, and meeting up with professors and fellow students, but for the most part a writing program is a town or city you move to for two or three years. What sort of locale would you most like to live in—and is that locale actually conducive to you spending two or three years writing productively? How does your ability to afford basic necessities affect your well-being and creative focus?

From a certain view, cost of living isn't deserving of an entire chapter—after all, it's an easily locatable and quantifiable measure. All you have to do is go onto "Sperling's Best Places" online (or any similar site) and you'll immediately be able to compare the cost of living at your current location and any future one you might land in, or even compare the cost of living at two programs you're trying to decide between. But what does that number really tell you? Does the fact that New York City is much more expensive than a rural town in the South mean that the latter will be a better fit for you than the former? Conversely, does the expensiveness of New York City automatically confirm that it offers more of value, and more access to desirable commodities, than you might find in that small Southern town? I don't take any position on that, but I do want to direct you to obscure but quantifiable ways cost of living can matter very much.

First, and most importantly, a cost-of-living assessment helps you determine the actual value of a program's funding package. That's why this book uses cost-of-living adjustments to compare funding packages, and why I urge you not to simply accept the value of a funding package as listed on a program's website. The dollar figure a program attaches to your teaching assistantship stipend could go up or down by *many thousands* depending upon the cost of living in a program's host location. Because we do have a sense of what constitutes an even theoretically livable stipend (about $10,000 for a nine-month academic year) we can use cost-of-living adjustments to determine whether programs that claim to be fully funded really are. Don't allow the "five-figure trick"—a program pushing its stipend just over $10,000 to make it appear to be a livable wage— to fool you into penury and unwanted loans for the duration of your writing program.

Of course, many aspiring poets and writers would prefer to live on something more than $10,000 over nine months, so a second utility in knowing the cost of living at the programs you're applying to is allowing you to figure out how much student loan debt you will accrue while in-program. There's nothing wrong with borrowing a *very* small amount of money—no more than $10,000—to supplement your stipend for two or three years, but any more than that and you've run afoul of this book's "don't go into substantial debt for a nonprofessional degree" admonition. When you run a cost of living calculation for your first-choice program, you may well find that not only is their stipend not a livable wage, the total cost-of-living in the program's host location will cost you tens of thousands of dollars you don't have during the course of the program. While it's all right, simply because you only live once, to break the $10,000 debt-limit in order to attend a "dream" program, you owe it to yourself to have a sense of your future debt before you matriculate. Think a bit about how much you want your financial security, credit rating, or ability to buy a home to be affected by choosing MFA X over MFA Y.

A third reason cost of living matters is that it points you toward "objective" assessments of individual program locations. I strongly urge you to use online reference guides and articles—essays with titles like "The Best College Towns in America"—to get a sense of which locales are most admired by those tasked with assessing locations' livability. I can say with confidence, having done much research on this topic myself, that the same towns and cities appear and reappear on these lists over and over. And fortunately for you, many of the most livable towns and cities in America play host to at least one graduate creative writing program. So how does cost of living fit in? Well, while it's an imperfect science, it's true that there's a relationship between cost of living and livability; often, though not always, more expensive locations do indeed offer more amenities and are more prized by people looking for new places to live. Needless to say this isn't a maxim, and there are many "hidden gems" across the country that are both inexpensive to live in and offer surprisingly dynamic culture, cuisine, and entertainment. But if you aren't able to visit all the programs you've been admitted to, and if you're hearing conflicting reports about a given location, cost of living may give you a small indication of how many people are scrambling to live in the location you're researching.

If we're going to talk program location, however, we have to once again return to your own idiosyncrasies as an author and human. Are you someone who loves cities? Do you want to be close to the great outdoors? Will you feel bereft if there isn't a Whole Foods nearby, or a Trader Joe's, or, for that matter, a good barbeque joint or a professional sports team? Is the location of the program you're interested in right in the middle of a city or on its outskirts, and which would be preferable to you? Does a program advertise itself as being "just outside" a very desirable location, but when you use Google Maps to figure out the driving distance you find out that it's over an hour away? How often will you drive an hour to find culture, cuisine, and entertainment you can't find in your program's host location? All these questions and more are ones you must ask about each program you apply to, just as you would if you were considering moving tomorrow to a new location for several years. Because that's just what you'll be doing.

FREQUENTLY ASKED QUESTIONS: COST OF LIVING

Q1: Can you recommend websites or articles that assess program locations' livability?

A1: I hesitate to offer any such recommendations, as each website or article that addresses this topic has its own methodologies—which you should read carefully. One assessment may consider crime rate, another may not; one assessment may weigh heavily considerations you know are meaningless to you, while another eschews them altogether. Look for towns and cities that appear on all or most of the lists in their category (as towns and cities of different sizes are usually assessed on different lists).

Q2: Putting aside tuition, is attending an MFA expensive?

A2: It can be, but it certainly doesn't have to be. Many of the MFA students I've met and spoken to over the years didn't have a car, shared an apartment with a roommate, cooked rather than eating out, wore clothes purchased from secondhand stores, and spent all their available money on pens, notebooks, poetry collections and novels, and of course the occasional concert. (Also alcohol, to be honest.) This somewhat archetypal writing program lifestyle might not be for you, but it's worth noting that when you're in an MFA or PhD program in creative writing you have a lot of free time, and it's easy for some of that time to be spent spending money. Unfortunately, unless you're already wealthy, you can't count on a teaching assistantship stipend to do much more than help you pay rent, buy food, and get the occasional beer (or whatever your pleasure) on the rare occasions to go out to be with friends rather than hanging around in someone's apartment or a park somewhere. You'll be tempted—I know I was—to get supplemental loans to live on, perhaps to make certain you can have your car with you or take a plane to see family or a significant other on occasion. Just make sure you don't overdo it. I've said that $10,000 is a pretty good benchmark for how much additional student loan debt one should be willing to go into to do a writing program, and I'd stick with that if at all possible. If you take out the maximum in federal loans each year you're in-program, you could be paying $50,000 for what was *supposed* to be a "fully funded" degree.

Q3: I'm worried that I'll hate my program's location. Any words of encouragement?

A3: Most of the MFA students I speak to tell me that they enjoyed or disliked their MFA experience almost entirely due to one of two things: (a) the people they met there, whether peers or faculty or (hopefully) interesting people from other academic programs; and (b) the quality of the work they think they produced while in-program. There's no question that longtime city-dwellers sometimes complain about having ended up in a college town, but that sort of homesickness or disappointment with your immediate environment can be significantly placated when you have friends and/or feel like you're writing the best work of your life. And besides, faculty and students at most programs have long since discovered the best local spots, so unless you're somewhere really out of the way, asking around will help you find restaurants, museums, galleries, parks, or other spots you might enjoy even if you don't love the town or city you're in as a whole.

On occasion I've known poets or writers to leave a program altogether because of dissatisfaction with their program's location. But usually these poets and writers are also struggling to produce work they're happy with—a circumstance that makes every kind of disappointment one is feeling even worse. As an educator, though, my advice to you would be this: consider that, in certain rare instances, standing in a slightly adverse position relative to your geography and culture might aid rather than hinder you writing your most dynamic work. Find the source of your angst and do something generative and interesting with it if you can. Writing programs aren't quite as long as they seem—21 months for a "two-year" program and 33 months for a "three-year" program—and with the right network of people around you, you can get through just about anything.

Q4: Do MFA programs assist students they've admitted in finding housing off-campus?

A4: Yes, they often do. Your program coordinator may be able to point you in the right direction, or put you in contact with a graduating student who is vacating an apartment.

CHAPTER SEVEN

Funding

You shouldn't go into substantial debt for a graduate creative writing program. You'll hear that many times between the time you decide to apply to programs and the day you decide whether and where you'll attend. There's a reason for that: it's true.

The reason not to go into debt for a graduate creative writing program, as I've mentioned elsewhere in this book, is that the MFA is a nonprofessional fine arts degree and having one will do very little to help you earn your tuition money back. An MFA alone, with the academic job market as it is now, is unlikely to get anyone much more than—at best—an adjunct teaching position with no healthcare benefits or job security. And outside the field of creative writing you'll encounter a lot of prospective employers who have no idea what to do with the fact that you have a fine arts degree in creative writing. Nor will your professors be much use on the employment front; most programs have no dedicated career services professionals on their program staff, and as much as some would like to think that networking with professors can land you not only a book deal but also a teaching gig, I'm here to tell you that that's not so. So you don't go to an MFA program for financial reasons. In other words, don't go into substantial debt for an MFA.

In consequence of the "no-debt" mantra that first became conventional wisdom among graduate creative writing applicants when Tom Kealey wrote about it in *The Creative Writing MFA Handbook*, funding has become the number-one consideration for applicants in choosing a graduate-level creative writing program. And it's not just applicants who value a strong funding package: the only large-scale survey of MFA *faculty* suggests that they too think funding is the most important consideration. I've heard many stories of faculty members telling students they've accepted—mind you, students they've *accepted*—not to come to the program unless and until they're told they have full funding. I've also heard many stories of faculty members saying to an applicant something like, "Only come here unfunded if you have no funded offers elsewhere." Why do they say this? Because it's true. Don't go into substantial debt for an MFA.

The problem with funding being such an important consideration in the graduate-school application process is that the overwhelming majority of creative writing programs do not fully fund all their incoming students. Only fifty-one graduate creative writing programs are fully funded for all matriculants, which leaves around 200 that are not. Of those 200, perhaps a quarter fund an appreciable percentage of their incoming students, usually somewhere between 33 percent and 75 percent of each cohort. That still leaves a lot of students at those programs out in the cold, and of course a hundred or more programs that offer less than a third of students full funding. While increased discussion among applicants of the need for full funding is slowly driving more and more programs to become fully funded, that's a long-term process and we're still only at its beginning.

Some of you reading this may be asking, why should these programs be fully funded? Don't most people have to pay for their master's degrees? While it's true that many disciplines don't fully fund their master's degrees, the reason is because those degrees are nonterminal; it's a convention in the United States for terminal degrees to be fully funded. Since the MFA has been the official terminal degree in the discipline of creative writing since the 1970s, it by all rights should be a fully funded degree. Those who treat the MFA as a run-of-the-mill master's degree that should no more be fully funded than a master's degree in a hard or social science are not only diminishing the status of the MFA but are directly contradicting the governing body in creative writing— the Association of Writers & Writing Programs—which has been very clear about the terminality of the MFA. While AWP takes no position on whether a program must be fully funded to fully honor that terminality, it says, in its "Hallmarks of a Successful MFA Program in Creative Writing," that "an effective MFA offers financial aid." Indeed it does.

A second issue with the focus on student funding that we've seen over the last decade is that many programs—some intentionally, some not—make it very difficult to find out what their funding package is. That makes it hard on you, the applicant, and hard on me, the researcher, as we both try to determine which programs are adhering to the spirit of AWP's "Hallmarks" and funding as many incoming students as they can. I can't emphasize to you enough how much difficulty you will have, when looking at certain programs, determining whether or not any funding is available at all, let alone what each available funding package looks like. While program administrators will sometimes be more forthcoming if you speak to them on the telephone, many won't—and all are wary of giving out financial aid information that, they increasingly believe, will shortly find its way onto the internet and into the sizable applicant community that congregates there. So I'll tell you now that even if you've decided not to go into debt for a program, you may be playing a cat-and-mouse game trying to figure out how to do it.

When you learn, as you will in this chapter, about how complicated MFA funding packages are, you'll be all the more disinclined to spend much time on programs that give you little or no financial aid information in their promotional materials. Because the fact of the matter is that it's not only the amount of the stipend associated with an assistantship that must matter to you, but also scores of attendant details that can make that topline number either meaningful or meaningless. For instance, the first question you should ask of any funding package is how is this funding being delivered to me? Am I being asked to teach? Must I edit a literary magazine? Will I be assisting a professor with research? Will I be doing administrative busywork in the program office? Or will I be given the money with no responsibilities attached to its receipt, which on some level is lovely but won't help me at all if I really want to gain teaching experience?

The second question to ask is how much work does this assistantship require (if it is an assistantship), and how enjoyable or educational will that work be, and how much or little will it affect my writing schedule? For instance, as I discuss more in

Chapter 9, teaching assistants can be given a light teaching load or a heavy one, and can be offered the chance to teach creative writing in their genre or tasked with teaching a subject many poets and writers are less enthusiastic about creating a syllabus for, like freshman composition. By the same token, there's interesting administrative work and soul-crushing administrative work, magazines that function well and are fun to work on and those that will be a good deal more work than you expect to keep up and running.

Now that you've figured out where the funding will come from, and about how much work will be asked of you, you have to determine if your funding offer is *renewable*. A renewable funding offer is one that follows you as you move through the program without substantial downward changes (and perhaps even a slight increase). A nonrenewable aid offer is one you can only count on for your first year in the program; it may or may not return, which could leave you holding a rather big bag tuition-wise.

And tuition—specifically, tuition remission—is going to be the next thing you'll want to focus your attention on. Not every teaching assistantship comes with full tuition remission, and the ones that don't can leave you on the hook for a sizable percentage of what's likely to be a hefty annual tuition bill. Make sure you calculate the tuition owed before you look at the stipend associated with any teaching assistantship. That stipend doesn't mean very much if most of it is going to go toward tuition payments.

Another adjustment you must make to your stipend is a cost-of-living adjustment (COLA). Ten thousand dollars at your program's host location may be worth much more—or less—than that same amount in the town or city you currently live in, so only looking at the COLA will allow you to answer a key question: "Can I live for nine months off this stipend?" It's okay if the answer is "no," but not if that means you're going to have to take out much more than $10,000 in loans over the course of your writing program.

But the stipend amount you see on a program's website requires yet another alteration, and that's to account for the cost of health insurance. It is absolutely vital, and I can't emphasize this enough, that your assistantship includes healthcare. If it doesn't, and you must purchase insurance separately through the college or university, that could be as much as $1,500 knocked off what already is likely a modest stipend.

Unfortunately, there's one more deduction you need to know about, and that's a tricky category called "student fees." Student fees are fees charged to all students at a college or university. Usually they go toward the budgets for student activities or maintaining a student center or other student services. While they undoubtedly go toward a good cause, student fees can reduce the amount of your stipend by $500 to $1,500, and most graduate writing programs won't tell you about them in advance.

And while it shouldn't influence whether you accept an assistantship or not, be aware that many schools don't make their first payment to teaching assistants until the end of September or early October. So you may be responsible for your moving costs, your first and last month's rent, and a security deposit before you've seen even a single paycheck.

One question you may be asking, having read now about all the ways your stipend can actually be much lower than initially advertised, is this: "What actually qualifies as 'full funding,' then?" This is a tricky question to answer, as of course your stipend is paid out over nine months, so we can't treat it as an "annual" salary. For instance, if your stipend is $9,000 over the nine months of the academic calendar, it's the "equivalent" of a $12,000 annual salary. And indeed many students try to find some employment over the summer to supplement their stipend. That's going to be critical, because even a $12,000 annual salary is very low; the federal poverty line in 2017 was an annual salary of $13,860. So according to the government, a single person making $13,859 per year (or $10,395 over a nine-month academic year) is living in poverty.

No program whose teaching assistantship stipend—when adjusted for cost of living, health insurance costs, and tuition owed—is less than $10,395 can be considered fully funded. So when the term "fully funded" is used in this book, that's what it means. Programs that offer smaller stipends may be giving students as much money as they're able to give, and certainly can be construed as more "generous" than programs that don't fund their students at all, but the term "fully funded" must remain a jealously guarded one. Only programs that keep students off food-stamp eligibility qualify.

FREQUENTLY ASKED QUESTIONS: FUNDING

Q1: Should I fill out the Free Application for Federal Student Aid (FAFSA), even if I'm looking to attend a fully funded program?
A1: Yes. Some schools offer need-based grants based on FAFSA data, and you never know if you'll want to take out a small federal loan to ensure your stipend is livable.

Q2: Can I negotiate for more funding, once I get a funding offer?
A2: Generally speaking, no. Most programs have lines of funding that are relatively static. A few programs have wiggle room, but it's a small minority of all programs and it's considered gauche to try to haggle. That said, you can certainly inform a program of any competing offers you have—be tactful—and if they want to increase their "bid" for you by augmenting your stipend with what are called "topping up" funds, they will. "Topping up" funds are intended to bring students who normally would be less than fully funded up to full funding, but I've seen programs use them to land top picks, too.

Q3: Are there any circumstances under which I should attend a program unfunded?
A3: No. Even if you're a millionaire, the mere fact that a program has admitted you without funding means that you would be better served by continuing to work on your creative portfolio for a year or two more and then reapply to fully funded programs. Getting full funding to do an MFA is not merely nice from a financial standpoint, it's also a clear signal that those with the expertise and experience to know have adjudicated your work as being promising enough to warrant graduate study. I suppose that, if you were a millionaire, and you simply wanted to get an MFA for fun, without any ambition beyond that, it would be fine to go into significant debt for an MFA. But keep in mind that when we discuss an aspiring poet or writer going to an MFA program with no funding, we are talking about someone who is about to go into debt by as much as $100,000 for a nonprofessional degree. That's poor financial planning—for anyone.

Q4: Is in-state residency and in-state tuition possible for my first year at a state school?
A4: Sometimes. In some states, nonresidents need only establish residency a month or more before seeking in-state tuition rates. So if

you're from outside the state and can move to your program's location by July 1, depending on state law you might be in the clear. Research this issue carefully, however, as there's often a big difference between in-state and out-of-state tuition rates. Contact the program coordinator to see if it's possible to establish residency before matriculating. But don't be surprised if the answer is "no"; some states require many months of residency before you officially become an 'in-state' student.

Q5: Can international students get funding?
A5: At some programs yes, at some programs no. You'll have to contact any programs you're interested in to find out their policies, as most programs are silent on the issue.

Q6: An MFA rejected me, and then offered an unfunded spot in its MA program. Should I go?
A6: No. When a program runs both an MA and an MFA, invariably the students in the former are given short shrift. You should never go into *any* debt for a nonterminal MA.

Q7: How do I calculate funding at MFAs where you compete for second-year funding?
A7: You should always assume that if a line of funding is not yet promised to you, it will not be offered. Mind you, that's not me being cynical or proposing you issue a negative judgment on your own teaching or writing— it's just good financial sense. Don't count on money that has been dangled in front of you but not yet promised to you. The only exception would be if over 90 percent of each cohort gets the competitively awarded grant, fellowship, or assistantship. Those are reasonable enough odds that you can think of the money in question as part of your funding package. But even then, have a backup plan.

Q8: I've heard that at programs at which students receive different levels of funding, there's a lot of competition and resentment between members of the cohort. True?
A8: Yes and no. Yes, to the extent that whenever you put a large group of poets and writers together, there will always be resentments. This poet will resent that one for their talent; this fiction-writer will resent that one for being a given professor's favorite student; this memoirist will resent that one because that one throws better parties and everyone knows it. You get my point—writing programs are intimate communities in which many petty jealousies can thrive, and being bothered that someone else

(Continued)

was given $1,000 more than you (which comes out to about $100 a month over an academic year) would fall into that category. So when I say that "no," such competition and resentment doesn't occur, I mean that it very often doesn't occur and when it does, it shouldn't and should be ignored. Don't decline a program's funding offer solely because not all students at that program are funded; if you matriculate at that program, you can be certain that you'll meet and befriend poets and writers who don't give a fig about your funding package.

Q9: I keep hearing of a "Council of Graduate Students Resolution" (CGSR). What is it?

A9: A long list of colleges and universities are signatory to an agreement that says, in sum, that all *funded* offers of admission to a graduate school *must* be held open until April 15 of each year. This means no program whose college or university is a signatory to the agreement can force you to give them a response to a funded offer of admission prior to April 15. Here's the problem: many such programs *will* pressure you in this way, and there's not much you can do beyond asking to have until April 15. If they persist, you can hold firm, but (a) you may be burning a bridge with the very program you're considering attending, and (b) they may retract your offer in violation of the CGSR and then implicitly dare you to do something about it. It's an ugly situation all around.

Why do some programs violate the CGSR? First, because they can; the only people who ever call them on it are applicants, who as you know by now are in a disadvantageous position, power- and authority-wise, with respect to the graduate creative writing programs to which they apply. Second, and perhaps more commonly, they do it because if they only find out you're not coming to their program on April 15, they may in the meantime have lost out on several waitlisted candidates who they would have been perfectly happy to take in your stead. So they see you holding out until April 15 as you—and I've heard faculty say this directly— "screwing them over." That's unfair and untrue, but it's how some faculty see it and it's therefore how they call it.

The rule of thumb when you receive a funded offer is to give the program that's offered it a response as soon as you reasonably can. You needn't in any sense create a logistical problem for yourself by hurrying to give an answer—for instance, by foregoing hearing from another program that you'd rather attend if they accept you and give you funding—but don't hold onto a funded offer for no reason, either. That's not fair to the program and, more to the point, it's not fair to applicants who may be on the waitlist.

As you might imagine, programs are much less likely to hurry you to accept or reject an *unfunded* offer, though on the other hand such acceptances are not covered by the CGSR and therefore can be assigned an expiration date other than the CGSR's April 15 deadline. As for programs that assign early expiration dates for funded offers—which, again, they're not supposed to do—it's really your call. If you love the program and are willing to accept their offer before hearing from other schools, say yes; if you're not willing, say no and see what happens. If they're classy about it, that's a good sign. If they're not, ask yourself, do you really want to go to that sort of program anyway? Sometimes the way a program treats its applicants is emblematic of how it treats its students. Keep that in mind not just with respect to the CGSR but generally.

Q10: What is a "funding waitlist"?

A10: Not only do programs have admission waitlists, programs that cannot fully fund all students have another waitlist for fully funded spots. Often a student will be admitted without funding and then, based upon decisions made by other applicants, will move up the funding waitlist into a funded position. It can't be counted upon, but it does happen.

Q11: Will programs pay for me to make a campus visit, if I'm admitted?

A11: Generally speaking, they won't—though you're free to ask. A small number of programs have admitted student weekends for which the program partially or fully foots the bill. Often you're paired with a current student and stay with them while you're in town. An even smaller number of programs don't have special weekends for admitted students but do pay for campus visits for their top picks. Making an unfunded visit is almost always an option. If you do make an unfunded visit, make sure you tell the program *in advance*. They'll treat you well, show you around, and maybe buy you a meal.

Q12: I'm trying to decide between a fully funded two-year program and a fully funded three-year program. Just how important is having that third year of study?

A12: Unless you're in a particular hurry, that third year is crucial. Consider that most students spend their first semester adjusting to their program and their second-to-last semester applying to jobs, fellowships, or PhD programs—so a two-year program is really two semesters of worry-free study, and a three-year program is twice that. In a certain respect, then,

(Continued)

a three-year program feels twice as long as a two-year program. Many graduate students take a while to hit their stride in-program; a two-year program increases the chance you won't get to where you want to be while getting paid to write.

Q13: What about postgraduate program funding? Is that a thing?
A13: For the overwhelming majority of programs, the answer is no. For a very small number of programs (see Chapter 18 for a partial list) a number of postgraduate fellowships are available for select students. As a general rule, unless a program guarantees all alumni a postgraduate lectureship, fellowship, or grant—and explicitly says so in its program materials—you should not assume that one will be forthcoming.

CHAPTER EIGHT

Student-Faculty Ratio

It may seem odd to devote an entire chapter to student-faculty ratios, but these data are used in this book as a proxy for a question whose importance is unchallenged: the amount of access any individual student has to any individual faculty member while studying in a full-residency graduate creative writing program. Because many applicants choose which programs to apply to in part on the basis of their faculties, knowing that you'll actually have regular access to these people who have been so important to your application and matriculation decision is no small matter. And what we find when we look at student-faculty ratios is that some programs hire so many full-time faculty members that ready access to these members is virtually assured to every student in the program; other programs are staffed largely by part-time faculty surrounding a small core of full-time faculty, and in these programs it may be more difficult to access full-time faculty and for professors to pay meaningful, long-term attention to any individual student.

Student-faculty ratios are not conclusory, however. We can say that they're instructive without presuming they tell a complete story. There are poets and writers who teach in writing programs and can simultaneously pay attention to a large number of students no matter how many peers they have or how many students they teach. But because, as an applicant, you're charged with working in an "all-things-being-equal" environment—as you won't have the time or resources to find out every detail about every program you wish to apply to—using student-faculty ratios as an imperfect stand-in for a question that you definitely *should* be considering is not a bad idea at all.

The question of how and whether a program uses part-time faculty rather than full-time faculty is presently consuming higher education. Part-time faculty generally cost less—in part because they often don't receive healthcare benefits—and are much easier to fire if they're found to be underwhelming in the classroom. On the other hand, in the context of a creative writing program one benefit to having many part-time faculty members is that it increases the size and diversity of the faculty, giving students many more options as to who to study with or (in some cases) be well mentored by. Perhaps the most well-known graduate creative writing program, the Iowa Writers' Workshop, has for years had a visiting-faculty program that students are enthusiastic about even though it technically reduces the size of the "permanent" faculty. And of course just because a faculty member is full-time rather than part-time doesn't mean they won't take regular sabbaticals, take a job elsewhere and leave a temporary hole in the faculty, or simply be, for whatever reason, less accessible than part-time peers.

But as an applicant you must approach these questions with that "all-things-being-equal" mantra in mind. All things being equal, a full-time faculty member is likely to be on campus more often, be more involved in a program's social and creative culture, and be more engaged in the construction and execution of program curricula than a part-time faculty member. Simply put, a full-time faculty member has obligations that a part-time faculty member does not. While this doesn't by any means translate into full-time faculty members necessarily being better educators than their part-time peers—and I don't know of any study that answers that question one way or another—it does mean you're a bit more likely to have access to full-time rather than part-time faculty.

For this reason, this book calculates student-faculty ratios as a function of the number of students a program matriculates annually and the number of full-time, tenure-track creative writing faculty members it has. Adjuncts, lecturers, and visiting faculty are not included in this calculation, not because they're not important or a critical presence in the programs in which they teach but because, as noted, their mentorship and program service obligations are not the same as those of their tenure-track peers. By the same token, our assessment does not include full-time faculty members who are not creative writers. Many programs include, in their promotional materials, "affiliated faculty" who are not literary artists themselves but may teach individual courses within the program from time to time. As with adjuncts, lecturers, and visiting professors, these tenure-track faculty members are likely a significant boon to the students they teach. They are not, however, primarily responsible for students in the program; indeed, they are more properly "counted" toward their home departments.

The reason I explain the methodology behind this book's student-faculty data in such detail is that what you are finally attending a writing program to do is to learn. I am one who believes you learn the most from your peers, rather than faculty members, but as we can't know in advance who your peers will be or what relationships you will form with them, we can only look at the information we *can* rely upon—in this case, that portion of a faculty roster unlikely to change much over time—in determining what kind of instruction you might expect to receive. Student-faculty ratios won't tell you who's great in the classroom, who tries to get students to write exactly like they do, or who acts creepily around certain students or in certain social situations; all of those things may come to mean a great deal to you, but we simply can't capture them here. Instead, you'll have to do your own legwork and speak to current and former students at the programs you're interested in to get the skinny on their current or former professors. But what hundreds and hundreds of interviews *do* tell us is that students in programs with low student-faculty ratios report, on average, having better access to faculty than their peers attending high-ratio programs. By the same token, we more often hear of professors "picking favorites" in programs with high student-faculty ratios, perhaps because professors are overwhelmed by the size of each incoming cohort and choose (rightly or wrongly) to focus the bulk of their attentions on just a few poets and writers.

Student-faculty ratios should be just one factor in your application and matriculation decisions. After all, many applicants wary of programs with high student-faculty ratios nevertheless want to attend a large program, and as you'll see from the data tables at the end of this book, the larger a program is, the more likely it is to have a large student-faculty ratio. So balance your desire to have ready access to faculty, and your confidence you'll receive consistent attention during the course of your writing program, with any concerns you may have about attending a program that is very small. Smaller student cohorts can become close-knit or, due to interpersonal strife, quickly come unglued; in my time at several universities, I've seen both things happen. So treat student-faculty ratios as part of a larger data matrix with other constitutive elements such as program size, any anecdotal information you turn up about individual professors at each program, and the extent to which you hope to learn from living among peers rather than an ongoing mentorship relationship. And in considering all this remember, too, that even when program faculty are readily available, you may or may not find their personalities, teaching styles, tastes, or readings of your work to be conducive to an ongoing mentor-mentee interaction.

FREQUENTLY ASKED QUESTIONS: STUDENT-FACULTY RATIO

Q1: Is there an "ideal" student-faculty ratio?

A1: Not really, though I'll say that while a student-faculty ratio can never really get "too low"—even a 1:1 ratio would be considered favorable to student learning—it can definitely get "too high." As a point of reference, imagine a program with a 25:1 ratio. This means each full-time faculty member has final, long-term supervisory authority over *at least* twenty-five students (as they may still be in touch with and mentoring former students) in addition to trying to write their own poetry or fiction, performing service for their program and their university, and traveling around the country promoting their writing through readings, lectures, interviews, conferences, and so on. All things being equal, how much individual attention would one of those twenty-five students expect from that professor? How much could they expect if, unbeknownst to them, the professor had only lukewarm feelings toward their writing? You see my point.

Q2: Which is more important: a program's size or its student-faculty ratio?

A2: That's got to be up to you. But it's a good question for you to ask.

Q3: Does the student-faculty ratio matter if a program caps workshop enrollments at 12?

A3: It does matter, and not only because, in smaller programs, you may well enjoy the benefit of workshops with fewer than twelve people in them (the difference between an eight-person workshop and a twelve-person workshop can be profound). It also matters because you will often want to gain access to professors you aren't currently studying with, and your ability to do that is in part a function of the program's *overall* student-faculty ratio. Remember that however large any given workshop is, the workshop leader is not only teaching that class, but perhaps other classes, and not only teaching other classes but also supervising the thesis work of students in their last year of the program.

Q4: Are you saying in-class attention doesn't matter?
A4: Actually, it matters quite a bit, and should you discover that any of the programs you're applying to regularly enrolls fewer than ten students in their workshops, you'll want to take that into account—as it'll mean much more instructional time for you than would otherwise be the case. That said, a workshop is not a one-on-one meeting in the guise of a classroom session. While in a workshop you should be thinking about the emotional well-being and intellectual heft of the conversations you're having with your peers, not just waiting for feedback from your professor and ignoring everyone else. In a classroom with vibrant discussions among peers, input from the professor is usually de-emphasized rather than the opposite; by the same token, writing classrooms in which students hang on their professor's every word and have little regard for one another's opinions are not productive for anyone. So be sure to distinguish between the student-faculty ratio—which may tell you something about how often you'll have one-on-one office meetings with professors, and how long and generative these will become—and the way individual workshops are conducted. Getting data on the latter is hard, and will probably require you tracking down current or former students from the programs you're applying to.

Q5: Are there benefits to a larger program, despite its higher student-faculty ratios?
A5: Absolutely. The larger a program is, the more diverse—all things being equal—it will be both in terms of student work and student demographics. You may find it easier to make friends with people whose company you really enjoy and whose feedback you really benefit from, as you'll simply be exposed to many more people during the course of your program. If you're a loner who's mostly going to a writing program so you have time and space to write in solitude, larger programs allow you to lose yourself in the crowd a bit, if that's what you're after. Larger programs may also be more likely to have regular student-run literary
(Continued)

events and social programming. They may have more staff available for university-run literary magazines, and therefore the operation of those magazines may be more likely to have a national rather than merely local scope. If you can find a way to network with your peers without being off-putting about it, a larger program will offer you many more opportunities to do so. So is a larger program right for you? It depends on who you are as a writer and person and what you're looking for.

Q6: What sort of value do adjuncts, lecturers, and visiting professors bring to their programs, given that you aren't counting them toward student-faculty ratios?
A6: They bring an enormous amount of value, particularly in small programs where such participants in the program's community may offer a welcome change of pace—or change of face—from the program's usual conglomeration of personalities. These educators are often hoping to be tenure-track faculty at some point, which gives them a significant impetus to work hard, accrue good student recommendations, and make an impression on the institutions at which they run their workshops. Programs may also use part-time or nontenure faculty as a way of bringing into the campus community for a delineated time poets and writers who don't *want* to teach full-time. Students then get to access ideas and styles they might not have been exposed to otherwise. While it's true that nontenure faculty don't have the same service, mentorship, or even (in some cases) teaching responsibilities tenure-track faculty do, and while their possible impermanence in the program community may mean you can't learn their names in advance of matriculating, many students report excellent interactions with nontenure-track faculty. In fact, according to both the AWP and this book, a vibrant graduate creative writing program will—whatever its use of adjuncts, lecturers, and visiting professors as semester-long workshop leaders—make sure to bring many visiting poets and writers to campus to lecture, give readings, and meet one-on-one with students. So please don't take student-faculty ratios as a judgment on the value of nontenure-track faculty. What we're doing is trying to focus on those aspects of a program that are *most predictable*. Rest assured there will be many more program features—or bugs—that will become significant to your experience and which you couldn't have known about in advance.

CHAPTER NINE

Assistantships

If you've been offered a funding package at a program that qualifies as "fully funded" or nearly so, chances are it will be attached to a teaching assistantship. Teaching assistants are graduate students who teach undergraduate courses as though they were adjunct faculty, though they're not considered faculty or given an "adjunct" designation. Basically, teaching assistantships are a way for programs to give you teaching experience, pay you a modest stipend, and get the university to waive some or all of your tuition. Teaching assistantships are grand and, all things being equal, they're what you're shooting for when you're applying to graduate creative writing programs.

There are other types of assistantships, but they're vanishingly rare. On occasion (less than 10 percent of the time) the awarding of an assistantship will be for a "research assistantship," editorship, or "project assistantship"—or you will receive a nonteaching fellowship instead. So if you receive funding at a program, you likely *won't* be assisting a professor with their next book (research assistantship), working as a paid editor for the program's literary magazine (editorship), assisting the program coordinator (an example of a project assistantship), or earning enough to live on without any instructional duties whatsoever (a nonteaching fellowship). Rather, you'll likely be assigned to teach one of four subjects to undergraduates: rhetoric, composition, literature, or creative writing.

Of these four types of teaching assistantships, a teaching assistantship in creative writing is the hardest to find, and therefore is especially prized. The reason these assistantships are so popular is, I suppose, obvious: a teaching assistantship in creative writing allows you to instruct undergraduates in the very subject you yourself are studying. The second-most popular teaching assistantships are probably the ones in literature, as they often allow you to teach contemporary literature, sometimes works you yourself have chosen in your genre of choice. Rhetoric and composition are actually a lot more fun to teach than you'd think—there are countless imaginative ways to teach freshmen how to speak and write well—but as many creative writers waived out of taking such classes themselves, they feel some understandable trepidation about them.

Whatever sort of teaching assistantship you receive, don't be surprised if there's substantial oversight of your syllabus coupled with relatively little assistance in how best to run a classroom. Many incoming MFA students have never taught before and are terrified to do so, yet many writing programs do not run semester-long pedagogy courses that instruct new instructors on how to instruct. The result is that a number of creative writers who may not be well suited to the classroom—either because of a lack of interest, the wrong temperament for teaching, or shyness—are put in classrooms with little preparation for the experience. In this context, a program putting limits on what you can and can't teach, or even giving you a stock syllabus to teach from, may actually be a blessing. Some new instructors appreciate limitations being put on their course content, as it can take a lot of the guesswork out of weekly lesson planning.

One important thing all teaching assistants should remember, and at some programs you'll be told this explicitly, is that unless you're a creative writing graduate student absolutely *certain* you want to be a professor one day, you're not attending a writing program to learn how to teach. And that means that teaching should always be a secondary priority for the typical creative writing MFA student. This doesn't mean you shouldn't do the best job of teaching you possibly can; it just means that the moment doing the best job you can begins to directly interfere with your writing, even if that interference relates only to your emotional well-being, you need to pull back a bit. Because half of MFA students don't intend to ever teach undergraduates, and less than 1 percent will ever do so full-time, MFAs allowing largely training-free teaching-assistant programs to dramatically affect anyone's educational experience would be deeply unfair. That's why programs only ask you to do the best you can under the circumstances; they're not expecting classroom brilliance—though of course they won't object to it.

The purpose of this introduction to teaching assistantships isn't to educate you on proper classroom etiquette and the latest creative writing pedagogies. More important is simply that you understand that to be fully funded in writing programs you'll likely have to teach, that teaching is difficult work, and that programs will, on average, woefully underprepare you for educating undergraduates. That said, as a longtime educator I can tell you that you have a number of advantages on your side: students don't really know how scared you are, so you enter the classroom with a great deal of authority; there are countless ways, even while working with a syllabus that someone else has selected for you, to bend your classroom time toward topics and exercises you're already comfortable with; a significant part of being an effective educator is creating a welcoming classroom environment, which you can easily do whether or not you have teaching experience; and as long as you're giving students the guidance and occasional free rein to think critically and creatively, communicate in writing and orally, and work collaboratively, you're helping them learn the five basic skills the best creative writing courses emphasize. Hardened "knowledge bases"—for instance, rote memorizations of texts, facts, definitions, or rules—are as likely to hamper a creative writer as to help her, so don't overexercise yourself about your students becoming "experts" on any given topic. The important thing is that your classroom should be a place students can flex their critical and creative faculties.

What I do hope you'll take from this introduction to teaching assistantships is a series of questions you should be asking yourself when applying to programs or deciding where to attend once you've applied. For instance, will I have to teach to be funded? What subject(s) will I teach, or can I teach? Will I be given any instruction in pedagogy before I enter the classroom? How much control will I have over my curriculum? How important is my performance in the classroom to my success in the program? Will I get regular performance reviews? How do I know when I'm pushing myself too hard as a new and only lightly trained educator? These are all important questions.

FREQUENTLY ASKED QUESTIONS: ASSISTANTSHIPS

Q1: How often will I have to teach?
A1: It depends on your program, of course, but in general you'll teach either one or two classes per semester. Avoid, at all costs, any program that requires you to teach three classes in any semester. In fact, many students find that even teaching two classes per semester hampers their writing and their enjoyment of their program, so think carefully before you commit to a program that requires you to take on that kind of teaching load.

When looking at schools, you may see designations for student "teaching loads" that look like this: 0/1, 1/0, 1/1, 1/2, 2/1, 2/2. In each case, the first number is the number of courses you'll teach each fall semester, and the second number is the number of courses you'll teach each spring semester. A few programs are on the trimester system—with three ten-week terms between August and June rather than two fifteen-week terms—so for these programs you'll see notations like 1/0/1, 1/1/1, and so on.

As for how often each class you teach will meet every week, that depends on your program. It's rare, though not unheard of, for undergraduate classes to meet once a week or, at the other end of the spectrum, four times a week. Much more common are classes that meet two or three times per week for roughly an hour each class session. In my experience, one only gets the opportunity to teach a once-a-week undergraduate course if it's an advanced creative writing course, and one only gets stuck teaching four times a week if it's an introductory composition course for first- or second-semester freshmen. As a general rule, you'd always prefer to teach fewer times per week rather than more—even if sessions are generally longer for classes that meet less frequently—as this minimizes any interference with your regular writing practice.

Keep in mind that college instructors spend about as much time reading student work and grading papers as they do in class, so you should expect that a course with three hours of instructional time per week will take six hours out of your weekly schedule, and that two such courses would set you back twelve hours per week. If your program requires you to teach non-creative writing courses that have more than the usual number of students for a workshop—twelve—your reading and grading time will increase significantly. Be certain you understand what a position entails before taking it.

Q2: Will the quality of my teaching affect my progress in the program?
A2: Almost certainly not. While some programs will schedule classroom visits, check-ins with faculty mentors, or an expansive review of end-of-term student evaluations, the most that usually results from any of these is a stern talking to about how to improve your in-class performance. Only a significant classroom malfeasance—for instance, threatening or harassing a student; sleeping with a student; encouraging your students to engage in illegal behavior; or behavior directly contrary to university regulations—is likely to lead to you losing your assistantship. That said, untrained educators are more likely to do all of the proscribed things I just mentioned, so do realize that being a classroom instructor is a responsibility you must take seriously. While you struggling to be an effective teacher can and will be forgiven by your program, violent or otherwise inappropriate comments or behavior absolutely will not be. And remember that losing one's assistantship can mean losing one's full tuition remission, too. So the cost of acting irresponsibly in the classroom—or toward students outside of it—can be grave.

For this reason, I recommend three simple rules of thumb for teaching undergraduates: first, no matter how close in age they are to you, do not hang out with them outside the classroom. Second, do your best to focus on the curriculum, rather than bringing your personal opinions—whether on the state of the world or the personality of individual students—into classroom conversations. And finally, seek advice from faculty mentors or other teaching assistants the moment something happens in class you're unequipped to face. Unexpected things do happen in classrooms, of course, and the key is simply learning over time how best to deal with them. You can't know everything in advance, so you will, certainly, make mistakes. That's okay; be forgiving of yourself. And assuming that the mistakes aren't catastrophic ones, your program will be every bit as forgiving.

Q3: What am I supposed to be teaching these students?
A3: Those of you who end up tasked with teaching an introductory literature course will likely be familiar with these from high school and have some sense of what they look like. Rhetoric and composition courses are the ones most likely to come with preset syllabi, but even when they don't,

(*Continued*)

you'll likely have the assistance of an established university freshman composition program to help you in planning your curriculum. Chances are, if you've gotten into a program via a fully funded teaching position, you know how to write; rhetoric and composition courses generally use themed writing assignments and exercises to teach skills you probably already possess to others.

The bigger question is what you should be teaching students if you're assigned to teach a creative writing workshop. Here's a simple answer: do not spend your classroom time trying to get your students to write as you do, or to write toward some imagined ideal that you've derived from reading literary magazines and full-length collections of poetry or prose. That's not the purpose of a creative writing classroom. The purpose of the creative writing workshop, broadly speaking, is to help individual students master basic techniques as they develop an idiosyncratic relationship with language, culture, genre, and self-identity—a relationship that empowers them to author unique works of literary art that no one else would have thought to create. In other words, encourage your students in a lifelong exploration of language, not a semester-long deduction of the various rules, practices, and compositional gestures that make for "great writing." While it's true that, in fiction and nonfiction at least, a certain amount of superficial polish is necessary for publication, with undergraduates the development of this polish is less important than the encouragement of the daring that makes creative writing so worthwhile.

With that in mind, you should certainly work with your creative writing students on matters of "craft," but also give them time and space to dispute craft conventions and explore innovative ways to subvert them. Some of your students will likely be straining at the bit to create such freedom for themselves anyway, so emphasizing that you encourage rather than oppose it will be a win-win situation for both you and your class. And as writing workshops are graded mostly on class participation and the effort shown by students across the various drafts of their individual works, you won't need to test students on narrow bands of knowledge that will, in fact, kill their imaginative spirit.

Q4: What do I get out of teaching?
A4: Hopefully, teaching undergraduates will be satisfying on a number of levels: working with students on their critical or creative writing may illuminate issues you'd never considered in your own work; developing a facility for "giving back" to the writing community through the instruction and support of other writers will be useful to you when, post-program, you seek to create new writing communities wherever you live; and within a

few years the writers you teach will be part of the national community of publishing authors alongside you, so developing these connections and associations is—odd as it sounds—all part of figuring out what it means to be a lifelong working author.

You'll notice that I didn't mention "teaching experience." While of course teaching undergraduates is useful experience for those who wish to one day teach undergraduates full-time, so few MFA alumni (less than 1 percent) will end up teaching undergraduates full-time that it'd be foolish to say that the primary benefit of a teaching assistantship is teaching experience. That said, it takes a lot of work and a real sense of responsibility to be a college-level educator, so even if you don't end up trying to get a full-time teaching position at a college or university, having an assistantship on your resume underscores to potential future employers that you've held serious employment in the past. For younger students without a long work history, this is invaluable.

Finally, there's a benefit to running undergraduate creative writing workshops—if you get the chance to do that—that's hard to detect but as important as any other: running a workshop gives you a much better understanding of what it means to be a positive contributor to a workshop. Workshop leaders are generally better able to see than are workshop participants which types of classroom contributions are helpful and which are disruptive. They develop a keen sense for a healthy classroom environment, and therefore are better able to help construct that sort of environment in their own graduate workshops. What you'll probably find, and pretty quickly, is that aesthetic rigidity, impoliteness, and dogma of any kind is destructive to a workshop; meanwhile, a flexible and inquiring mind, an appreciation for the diversity of reasons writers come to writing, and an even temperament are critical to *any* creative writing workshop.

Q5: What about editorships? Is there any value to these, or should I avoid them?

A5: If you have a chance to get involved with your program's literary magazine, whether in a paid or unpaid position, try to do so. Here's why: the long-term benefits of working at a literary magazine while attending an MFA or PhD program in creative writing outweigh the transient hassle of taking a little time away from your own writing.

Only a small number of programs will offer incoming students editorships or project assistantships to work on a university publication.

(Continued)

Many programs, however, encourage students to join these publications as staff. While as a general matter most university literary publications are only lightly read outside their host university and, moreover, are more prone than independent publications to aesthetic conservatism, as a staff member a student learns a lot about what it means to be a successful author.

First, working for a literary magazine gives you an opportunity to see what sort of work others in your field are writing. You'll very quickly come to recognize common—often somewhat uninteresting—compositional gestures in your genre that you will then redouble your effort to eradicate in your own work. You may be inspired to conduct new literary experiments and flex creative muscles you didn't even know you had by a particularly superlative work that you find in the "slush" pile (the pile of unsolicited submissions). You may discover new authors to read, and perhaps even have an opportunity to initiate contact with those authors and develop further relationships with them and their work. You'll develop a keener editorial eye for your own writing and be better able to judge which of your works is readily publishable, which unpublishable, and which publishable only with a publisher of suitable daring. Second, working for your program's literary magazine is always a good professional decision, as it gives you significant work experience in publishing—a field that many graduate creative writing students become interested in as a full-time career postgraduation.

Q6: What if I want teaching experience, but I'm not given a teaching assistantship?
A6: You may be able to apply again for a teaching assistantship in your second (and/or third) year, and many programs sponsor or are at least aware of nonprofit teaching opportunities in their local area—for instance, teaching creative writing to prison inmates or at a local high school. While you'll definitely want to do all you can to get a university teaching assistantship if your ambition is to be a creative writing professor, there are other avenues to at least begin the process of building a teaching-oriented CV.

CHAPTER TEN

Curriculum

When we talk about writing program curricula, what we're really talking about is the creative writing workshop. Nearly all creative writing programs are today built upon the workshop model, in which students pass forward poetry or prose at an allotted time and their peers take a week to write comments on that poetry or prose. After a week, those peers present their findings as part of a classroom discussion the author herself is not permitted to participate in—not even to ask questions, offer clarifications, or add thoughts that are only indirectly related to the piece under review. This, in a nutshell, is the creative writing workshop. While sometimes your workshop experience will be gussied up with additional accoutrements like directed in-class writing prompts, take-home writing exercises, brief reading assignments, oral presentations, field trips, written or dialogic analyses of already published work, reflection papers, and so on, at the core of your program experience will always be the writing workshop. So if you really dislike workshopping, the creative writing MFA is not for you; you can expect that the better part of each class session will be taken up by workshopping the work of your peers.

Of course workshops aren't the only classes you'll take during the course of your writing program. It's just that the others are graduate-level or even undergraduate courses in subjects you're already familiar with like, for instance, literature. It's not my place to explain what such classrooms are like, as you've already experienced them to some degree or another during your undergraduate years. Suffice to say that if you're required to take graduate courses you will find yourself in a simultaneously more and less intense academic environment—one in which your classmates may well be doctoral students in another subject, and therefore naturally enthusiastic about much of the course material. If you dislike academic courses—which, in my experience, a large percentage of poets and writers do—you may not love taking graduate English courses, as the atmosphere will be more relaxed than undergraduate courses even as the material is more difficult, the classroom discussions more byzantine, and the students almost cloyingly more self-motivated. Still, an MFA or PhD program in creative writing can't be all workshops, and frankly you wouldn't want it to be. So make sure you know what percentage of your credits will come from workshops versus academic courses.

Fortunately, many programs will allow you to take out-of-genre workshops, independent studies, or courses well outside the English department in fulfillment of at least a few of your credit requirements. You'll be able to tell rather early on in your visit to a program's website just how flexible their curriculum is. You'll find, I think, that a flexible curriculum is always better than an inflexible one; you never know how you'll feel once you're on campus, what sort of interests you may develop, and what sort of stomach you'll have for one type of course or another. Best to know in advance that you'll be given an opportunity to chart your own course.

One item here in particular is worth additional discussion: cross-genre study. As I discuss more elsewhere in this book, not every program allows you to take workshops outside the genre in which you were admitted to the program, and even some of those programs that allow cross-genre study limit your access to it considerably. For instance, a program might declare that you can only take one out-of-genre workshop for credit, or only one out-of-genre workshop, period. If you've no desire to write in any genre other than your preferred one *and* have no ambition of ever teaching creative writing at the university level, restrictions on your ability to study across genres shouldn't matter much to you. If, however, you want to develop your skills in multiple genres, or want to be free to hand in cross-genre work in any workshop you take, or want to learn the craft of a second genre so you'll be a more attractive job candidate later on, your program's openness to cross-genre writing and study will mean a great deal to you. Increasingly, academic job candidates with classroom, teaching, and publishing experience in many genres have a *substantial* leg up on other job applicants. I can't stress this enough for anyone reading this who wants to teach: learn how to write well in a second (or third) genre if you can. You'll thank me later.

Whatever courses you take or are allowed to take, whether you enjoy your MFA experience will usually come down to whether you enjoy your workshops. And that's surprising, in a sense, as very few graduate creative writing programs do much to prepare their students in advance to ensure they are happy and productive and congenial in workshops. There seems to be an assumption that everyone comes to a writing program already knowing the rules of the workshop because they've workshopped before, usually in college. The problem, of course, is that many young workshoppers develop bad workshopping habits in their undergraduate years, and if the graduate faculty do nothing to help students work through these issues, they typically continue. And if you or a peer is struggling to stay focused or positive in a workshop, the domino effect on your classmates will be keenly felt. Workshops just aren't large enough to mask the unhappiness or, worse, the unruliness of even a single participant.

If you're reading this, you probably know the basics of workshopping: don't offer purely "affective" (emotion-based) feedback; don't try to convince others to write as you do; see others' work through their eyes, and in the context of their own ambitions, rather than yours; don't talk over your classmates, and don't pick fights with them by pretending there are always clear right and wrong answers in what is essentially an art class. Other admonitions: don't take criticism personally; learn to recognize which comments will be helpful to you and which won't be, taking the former to heart and letting the latter go; don't, under any circumstances, speak while being workshopped, or get defensive about your work when (or if) you're allowed to speak once your peers are done talking; don't assume that it's only your intent, and not the subjective experience of your audience, that matters. All this is easy to remember and to practice in workshop.

What's much more complicated is having the will to approach a workshop *differently* than those of your peers who think a graduate creative writing workshop is essentially identical to its undergraduate iteration. The fact is, the two are—or should be—as different as night and day. In a graduate workshop, for instance, you should feel confident enough in your abilities that you're willing to do what all workshoppers are technically called upon to do: workshop *unpolished* work. All too often, students will bring in their most finished poetry and prose with the aim of garnering praise from their peers and their professor. And it often works; the praise often comes. The problem, of course, is that you haven't really learned anything new, and likely didn't stretch your legs much with the work you handed in—as any risk you took in the writing of the work would've increased exponentially the chances of garnering someone's disapproval. And you know what? You're right. Workshopping poetry and prose that takes substantial risks and puts you outside your comfort zone *is* more likely to receive a harsh critique from your peers and your workshop leader. But this is graduate school, and you're in class not because you have to be but because you *chose* to be—and can prove that by realizing that you often learn more about the author you do and don't want to be from a "bad" workshop session than a praise-filled one.

But there are other infirmities within the workshop model that have nothing to do with you at all. For instance, many outside the discipline of creative writing would find it odd that the workshop tasks eleven people with (at worst) copyediting or (at best) providing extemporaneous critique of a single person's work—and not work that they've spent a great deal of time with, at that. Wouldn't it make more sense for a "workshop" to be structured so that each session benefits the *eleven* far more than the one? Could we not see "being workshopped" as sacrificing one's ego for the sake of the class by providing, in the form of an unpolished draft, an opportunity for classmates to engage in an open-ended discussion of "big" in- and out-of-genre ideas? Why must workshopping be deductive in its logic, rather than gleefully inductive? Why shouldn't discussion of a work go wherever the class wants to take it, rather than a narrow focus on "perfecting" a work that was supposed to be unfinished and risk-filled to begin with?

Right about now you might be wondering why a book on applying to graduate creative writing programs is taking the time to critique a century-old writing pedagogy. And I'll admit that one reason for this is that this particular author studied the history of the creative writing workshop as part of his doctoral program in English. But a far more important reason is this one: in the hundreds of interviews and discussions I've had with former creative writing students over the past decade, one constant has been a sense of despair in discussing the endless workshopping of the MFA-program pedagogy. Basically everyone, almost without exception, is tired of workshopping by the time they get to their last semester—and often much earlier than that. Students feel that they've already heard everything their peers have to say or will ever say, and feel, too, that they know well enough what their strengths and weaknesses are that they no longer have to be told. They feel, in short, like their education as a writer is finished and completing their program is just playing out the string of a ballgame whose outcome is predetermined.

Of course, the opposite is true: MFA and even PhD students in creative writing are at the very beginning, rather than at the very end, of their education as writers. They should leave their programs with more questions and doubts—provided they're generative rather than debilitating ones—than they had when they arrived. Whether or not you leave your writing program feeling as though you have evolved as a poet or writer, you should certainly leave feeling *ready* to evolve. You should be able to look behind you and see scores of misperceptions about writing in your wake. In many respects, being a dynamic and successful literary artist is all about upending your most deep-seeded authorial prejudices. If your workshops aren't helping you to do that, and encouraging you to risk more than enough each time you write to be in danger of falling flat on your face, there's a problem. I say this even though I realize that many reading this now are aspiring novelists who love literary fiction and believe, as many professors do, that there's a sort of formula to writing such fiction that is reliable and responsible.

They may be right—though the fact remains that most of the great works of American literature are idiosyncratic in some way, or many ways, that would have made it difficult to workshop them. Or they are difficult in ways that would have earned them substantial criticism in a workshop. So even if you're a committed lyric-narrative poet or literary fiction novelist, as you learn intermediate or advanced craft in a writing program don't forget to also develop your "poetics," too. "Poetics" is the term we writers use to denote the idiosyncratic relationship each poet or fiction-writer develops with their own language, genre, self-identity, and culture—and the ways in which that idiosyncratic relationship finds genuinely unreplicable and irreplaceable expression in the literary forms they've chosen for themselves. As you know, the world's bookstores and libraries are glutted with books no one is reading; the best way to avoid that fate is to offer the literary world something they've never quite seen before. And the best way to produce such work is to determine what it is about your temperament, experience, knowledge, skills, traumas, and ambitions that makes your relationship with writing idiosyncratic.

What I'm saying, as delicately as I can say it in a reference guide, is that if you find your workshops unsatisfactory that's likely the fault of the pedagogy. But the situation might well be exacerbated by an approach to workshopping that you developed in your undergraduate years and which, for whatever reason, your writing program does little to dissuade you from. Hopefully something I've said here will be useful as you develop your "ethos" as a workshop participant and a writing program community member.

So what does all this have to do with adjudicating the curriculum of an MFA or PhD program in creative writing? It underscores that you'll want to think about the role of the workshop in each program's curriculum before you apply. Some programs are what we call "studio-oriented," which means over half your credit requirements can be fulfilled via in-genre workshops, out-of-genre workshops, independent studies, internships, or studio courses in the nonliterary arts—for instance, the performing or material arts. By comparison, an "academics-oriented" program requires that you spend at least half of your credits completing conventional academic coursework.

Many reading this may assume that a studio-oriented MFA program is preferable to an academics-oriented MFA program, and, depending upon your proclivities and temperament, you may be right. But remember what I said about the chief complaint I hear from MFA alumni: "I got sick of workshopping." Very rarely do we hear complaints about the art history class someone chose to take as an elective because they'd always been interested in the subject. While it's true that academic courses might subject you to conventional grading schemes rather than pass/fail rubrics— and I know a few of you may not be very fond of conventional grading schemes—remember that you won't likely be showing your transcript to many people unless you apply for a PhD or decide to go into academia. And the truth is, most graduate-school faculty will cut you slack when they realize you're a writing student rather than a PhD candidate in English.

The good news in all this is that programs are more transparent about their credit requirements than almost anything else. For some reason, this is the one piece of information that's quickly discernible on almost any MFA or PhD program website. So make sure you study it carefully and think about what all those credit requirements will feel like in real time. And just because workshop hours are a given doesn't mean that learning how to workshop well isn't a skill you'll have to work very hard at to master.

FREQUENTLY ASKED QUESTIONS: CURRICULUM

Q1: Are some programs known to be more open to experimental poetry and fiction?
A1: Yes, though they're relatively few in number (see Chapter 18 for a partial listing).

Q2: Are there programs in literary genres other than fiction, poetry, and nonfiction?
A2: Absolutely. While there are far fewer of each of these than there are conventional two- or three-genre programs, at various schools around the country you'll find MFA or even PhD programs in playwriting, screenwriting, writing for television, writing for children, comics and graphic narratives, translation, editing, publishing, young-adult fiction, genre fiction, experimental and documentary arts, and several others. Note, though, that in most of these categories only a handful of programs are available.

Q3: Can I change my genre of study after I'm admitted?
A3: Almost never.

Q4: How much access will I have to professors in the other genres at my program?
A4: Honestly, not much. They'll likely meet with you if you ask, but as they have their own roster of students to supervise and to mentor, any time they spend with you is in a certain sense "off the clock." Keep that in mind when seeking to meet with them.

(Continued)

Q5: I have a teaching assistantship. Will I take a pedagogy course to help me prepare?

A5: Many programs will informally—and a number of programs will formally—help you prepare for your teaching duties with either an ad-hoc discussion section or a full-blown pedagogy course. If you're looking to teach long-term, you'll find either of these invaluable; if you're not, it will at least reduce somewhat any anxiety you feel about having to teach. My best advice to those who have been given teaching duties and are feeling some stage fright is this: never forget that you enter the classroom with an enormous amount of gravitas, much of which is earned because you really do know more about your subject—and perhaps much else—than many or all of your students. Whatever you may think they're thinking, your students usually don't know how prepared or unprepared you are, or how nervous or not nervous, just by looking at you. It takes a lot to lose their faith and trust, and provided you take your teaching duties seriously and are respectful to your students, they'll roll with the punches even as and when your inexperience becomes obvious. Remember that they *want* the class to be an engaging experience; they're rooting for you whether they're fully conscious of it or not. Pedagogy workshops or courses can help you prepare syllabi or homework assignments, but finding real joy in lecturing, or running a workshop, or discovering what the students think about writing and being aspiring writers is more or less entirely up to you.

Q6: Should I workshop a novel or short stories in my fiction-writing program?

A6: Short stories are much easier to workshop; the workshop format is conducive to analyzing discrete texts and less apt for projects whose endpoint is uncertain. If you're able to do so, workshop your short stories and spend time on your novel outside of class. Ask your professors if they ever run "novel workshops"—workshops specifically geared toward the special instructional needs of those writing novels. Certain professors may disallow workshopping novels, so don't be surprised if this happens. Most will allow it, though they may encourage students to workshop short stories whenever possible.

Q7: How much does a "curriculum" really matter if I'm going to be doing most of the real work myself, alone, writing within my genre as best I can and as often as I can?

A7: That's a great question. It's true that you'll spend far more time outside classrooms during your MFA years than inside of them. And I'll say from experience that I've written some of my strongest work during workshops that I didn't particularly enjoy, and some of my weakest work during semesters where the workshop experience felt especially pleasant. There isn't necessarily—odd as it is to say—a direct correlation between the writing you produce and the courses you take. Sometimes the influence will be direct and obvious, sometimes indirect or only implicit, but there will also be many things you write that are primarily the product of you having sufficient time and space and energy to write them. So while you shouldn't ignore the importance of a program's formal curriculum, you should also give thought to other program factors (like location or funding) that will govern how comfortable you feel every time you sit down to write.

Q8: Are there postgraduation implications to choosing one type of program over another—for instance, a studio-oriented program over an academics-oriented one?

Q8: Absolutely. If you think you might want to teach at the university level some day, having the chance to study multiple genres is critical; if you think you might want to attend graduate school in English after your MFA, you'll want to land at a program with conventionally graded courses that are likely to have eligible transferable credits for a doctoral program. If you don't know what you plan to do after your MFA, you may want to find a program whose curriculum is flexible enough that you can take electives in areas of study that could, one day, become professional interests for you. And more than any of these possibilities is the very real likelihood that studying subjects other than creative writing—indeed, perhaps as distant from creative writing as physics—will help you to become a more dynamic and idiosyncratic author. Having taught creative writing now at three large universities, I can say that some of my strongest students have been those whose background is *not* in the humanities. So you should feel free to stretch yourself a bit and take courses in subjects that interest you even if they're not closely linked to the degree you're currently earning. Enter that political science course with the mindset of a poet or novelist and I promise you'll find ways to integrate what you learn into your writing. And your writing will be much better for it.

Q9: Are there "dual" MFA curricula? Like an MFA/JD program or MFA/PhD program?

A9: Yes—see Chapter 18 for a partial listing of such programs.

(Continued)

Q10: What can I do the summer before I begin a writing program to prepare myself?

A10: Read extensively in your genre. That's good advice whenever, but it's particularly important when you're about to enter a program that will have you writing regularly and perhaps reading slightly less than you'd expect. Don't try to write too many poems or stories "in advance"— an MFA has much less educational value if you produce all your work beforehand—but do begin thinking seriously about where you're at as a poet or writer. Which writers act as models for you, if any? What do you like about them? How can you not merely replicate what they're doing but build off it substantially in a way only you, with your background and temperament and personality, would think to do?

Some students will join a local workshop or apply for a residency over the summer, just to prepare themselves for regular writing and workshopping in the fall. This isn't a bad idea—unless you're the sort of person who burns out on workshopping easily or really needs to clear your head before you dive into an MFA for two or three years. I promise you that you'll get all the workshopping and peer-to-peer interactions you can handle in your program. If you have the opportunity, try to give a reading of your work somewhere so that you're better prepared for reading your work aloud in class. Likewise, you might consider submitting a few things for publication, so that when publishing conversations arise in your program, you won't feel quite so out of the loop.

Summer workshops and residencies that you can apply to include the Juniper Summer Writing Institute, the Tin House Writers' Workshop, the Bread Loaf Writers' Conference, the Summer Literary Seminars, the Gotham Writers' Workshop, Grub Street, the Iowa Summer Writing Festival, the Writers' Studio, and the Vermont Studio Center.

CHAPTER ELEVEN

Fellowships

Two or three years of graduate study in creative writing may sound like a long time, but many aspiring poets and writers find that it's not nearly long enough. Some students hope to go on to teach creative writing full-time—and while most fully funded graduate creative writing programs offer teaching assistantships (see Chapter 9), not every assistantship allows one to teach creative writing. By comparison, many post-MFA creative writing fellowships offer their fellows teaching opportunities, and nearly all of these involve teaching creative writing (and usually within a fellow's primary genre).

So what exactly is a postgraduate fellowship? Well, it's a funded position at a school or nonprofit organization that allows you significant additional time to write following your graduation from an MFA or PhD program in creative writing. Positions in this category range in duration from one week to two years, are located all around the country, and vary significantly in the duties they demand from fellows. Some fellowships require one to teach in exchange for a stipend, while others do not; some fellowships incorporate an educational component, requiring fellows to continue to attend writing workshops, while others do not. Most fellowships are attached to institutions of higher learning, but some are associated with secondary schools or nonprofit organizations.

When it comes to fellowships, one thing is true across the board: they're almost impossible to get. Acceptance rates at the most-coveted post-MFA fellowships are as low as they are at the most competitive MFA programs, which isn't surprising when you consider that the applicant pool for these post-MFA opportunities often comprises only the most committed MFA-holders—those who want to continue to dedicate themselves full-time to creative writing. Not to put too fine a point on it, but between 2001 and the present around 1 percent of MFA graduates have gone on to a post-MFA fellowship. While many graduates don't apply to these fellowships, meaning that more than 1 percent of those who apply are admitted, a good rule of thumb is this: a highly regarded postgraduate fellowship program is likely to accept well less than 2 percent of applicants, and no fellowship program, no matter its duration or its reputation, should be assumed to have a yield-excusive acceptance rate of over 20 percent.

The intense competition for fellowship positions means that one must never make a postgraduate fellowship the focus of one's postgraduation plans. While many students in the last year of a program will consider applying to a few fellowships, only the truly foolhardy do so *instead* of looking for other employment. The wisest course of action for any poet or writer interested in a postgraduation fellowship is to apply to a number of these alongside other opportunities: for instance, creative writing doctoral programs; graduate study in another field, such as library science (MLIS), comparative literature (PhD), rhetoric and composition (PhD), poetics (PhD), or English (PhD); or employment in the public or private sector in fields unrelated to creative writing.

So if postgraduation fellowships are only available for a small number of graduates, why are so many people so interested in them? In my interviews with MFA alumni I've found that there are many reasons for a poet or writer to seek a fellowship after graduation, some of which are strong justifications and others of which, well, less so. For instance, some MFA graduates have no desire to teach but only found their footing as poets or writers late in their program experience. Understandably, these graduates want a chance to continue the fine work they began doing during the final semester or two of their program. This scenario is a common one in MFA programs, and nothing to be ashamed of—as creative writing is a lifelong endeavor, it's no surprise that certain periods of instruction or writing will be more fecund for a literary artist than others. Even the poet or writer who sails through their graduate program assuredly writing the best work of their life will be (assuming they continue reading and writing regularly) an immeasurably better literary artist just a few years after graduation. That said, the simple fact is that the MFA is not for everyone, and many MFA students will take a long while transitioning to the life of a graduate student. Those who only become comfortable with that life, or the trajectory their creative writing is taking, at the end of their program may seek a fellowship to ensure any inertia they've built up isn't wasted.

Of course, many students who've had thoroughly enjoyable and instructive MFA or PhD experiences may nevertheless find that the many years they've had in-program are insufficient to complete a book-length project. While every MFA program requires a thesis, and all require that a student hand in that thesis before graduating, both faculty and students understand that any MFA thesis is, at best, an advanced draft of a work that's yet to be perfected. Putting aside for a moment the many poetry MFA alumni who decide not to publish their theses at all, some do find that they need two or three years postgraduation to swap out the weaker work in their manuscript; likewise, novelists may find that their MFA thesis is sufficient to draw interest from an agent but not yet ready (in their own view or, more commonly, their agent's) to submit to publishers. Still other poets and writers will graduate from their MFA program with an eminently publishable thesis, but want an extra year or two to place it with a publisher. These recent graduates may seek out fellowships as a way to stay funded, continue teaching, and maintain a flexible schedule as they look for a publisher. Often, these writers apply for a full-time teaching job as soon as their first book is under contract.

To be clear, fellowships are not intended to be, and cannot become, a way of life. In recent years some poets and writers have found themselves hopping from fellowship to fellowship for years on end, never landing in a full-time job and in some cases never publishing that ever-elusive first book. The temptation to do this is understandable; what we often find is that a poet or writer whose work is attractive to one fellowship will likewise find that that same work is attractive to other fellowship committees, which opens up the possibility of "fellowship-hopping" as a middle-term lifestyle choice. Unfortunately, given the small number of fellowships and their low acceptance rates, even a writer successful at securing a succession of fellowships will soon enough see their luck run out. For this reason, my advice is to apply to fellowship programs only when you consider it *necessary* to your future plans. If you just want more time to write, you're better served figuring out now, rather than later, how to organize a professional life around that ambition. Participating in a fellowship forestalls that eventuality, and therefore is useful primarily in the scenarios I've described in the previous paragraphs.

While there has never been, and should never be, a ranking of fellowships—they usually lack curricula and are deeply personal experiences, so there's no point in arguing one is categorically preferable to another—it's true that certain fellowships are more widely esteemed than others. The esteem in which a fellowship is held is usually a function of who has held it in the past; how frequently the holders of a given fellowship have found placement in full-time teaching positions at the university level; how long the fellowship has been around; how selective it is thought to be (acknowledging that we have precious little hard data on the subject); and, as much as anything, its duration and location. Generally, fellowship applicants choose longer fellowships over shorter ones and a fellowship in a location they wish to live in versus one in what they consider an undesirable location, assuming these two analyses don't conflict.

Having said all this, I can note that there are nine fellowship programs often mentioned by recent MFA graduates as the most desirable, for the aforementioned and other reasons: the Stegner Fellowships at Stanford University in Palo Alto, California; the Wisconsin Creative Writing Institute Fellowships at the University of Wisconsin in Madison; the Hodder Fellowships at Princeton University in New Jersey; the Fine Arts Work Center Fellowships in Provincetown, Massachusetts; Emory University's Creative Writing Fellowship in Atlanta; the Stadler Fellowship at Bucknell University in Lewisburg, Pennsylvania; the Gettysburg Emerging Writer Lectureship at Gettysburg College in Pennsylvania; the Ruth Lilly Poetry Fellowships granted by the Poetry Foundation in Chicago; and the Steinbeck Fellowship for Fiction Writers at the Center for Steinbeck Studies at San Jose State University in California. Among the very short-term— weeks-long—fellowships, the most prized, per interviews with current and former MFA students, appear to be the Sewanee

Writers' Conference Fellowships at the University of the South in Sewanee, Tennessee (including, at last analysis, Borchardt, Dakin, Elkin, Justice, McCorkle, Nemerov, Ralston, Sewanee, Taylor, Van Duyn, Wall, and Williams Scholars and Fellows), the Bread Loaf Writers' Conference Fellowships ("waiterships") at Middlebury College in Vermont, and fellowships offered by the Vermont Studio Center.

One important caveat about fellowships: what it means to be admitted to a given fellowship is no more or less than that the very small number of judges who were tasked with choosing new fellows liked your work. The taste level of these judges is often unknown or (when and where they are anonymous) unknowable, though the history of most fellowship placements, on the evidence gathered for this book, is that these postgraduate opportunities favor—at this moment in American literary history—conventional lyric-narrative verse and literary fiction.

I mention the aesthetic proclivities of fellowship programs because you'll find, in Chapter 17, tables regarding which MFA programs have met with the most success in placing graduates in fellowship programs. Keeping in mind that really it is the *graduates* who place *themselves*—as most programs do little to assist students in securing fellowships besides writing recommendation letters, reviewing students' poetry and prose in their regularly scheduled workshops, and perhaps giving them a short list of fellowships to apply to—we should also note that having many postgraduate fellowship placements doesn't mean a graduate creative writing program is superlative. Rather, what it means is that that program admitted a large number of students whose work was subsequently found acceptable by the readers at fellowship programs. While this does indicate that programs that perform well in the Fellowship Placement Table do a good job of matriculating relatively strong lyric-narrative poets and literary fiction-writers, if those camps aren't your bag, that table should only mean so much to you.

I think the best way to summarize this book's assessment of fellowship-program placement is this: programs that perform well in the Fellowship Placement Table at the end of this book are definitely competitive programs with strong student cohorts, but that doesn't mean programs that *don't* place well according to that one measure are *not* strong.

FREQUENTLY ASKED QUESTIONS: FELLOWSHIPS

Q1: How do I apply to a postgraduate fellowship?
A1: The process is almost identical to the MFA application process, though certain items you needed for your MFA application will be immaterial now. For instance, while you'll certainly submit a creative portfolio, and almost certainly both recommendations and a personal statement of some kind, the chances that your GPA will be considered are low, as there's no longer any graduate-school GPA requirements to be met. Indeed, if you're asked for a transcript it will mostly be to confirm you have a terminal degree in creative writing and that there are no warning signs in your academic record—for instance, a number of failed courses with no explanation given. In applying to postgraduate fellowships, remember the advice I offered previously: only apply when your portfolio is truly ready; ask for recommendations early; avoid oversharing in a personal statement; and make sure you have enough money for any transcripts you need. Fortunately, you won't have to worry about more standardized test-taking, so you'll save money there.

Q2: Can I apply for postgraduate fellowships if I just earned a creative writing PhD?
A2: Generally yes, but do carefully check the fellowship's application requirements.

Q3: Can I apply to postgrad fellowships if I haven't earned a creative writing MFA?
A3: Generally no—but again, check the fellowship's full application requirements.

Q4: What kind of "program culture" will I find in a fellowship program?
A4: With few exceptions, not much. That's only because most fellowship programs accept only one or two poets and/or writers a year. Notable exceptions include the Stegner fellowships and the fellowships at the Wisconsin Creative Writing Institute. That said, short-term fellowships such as Sewanee, Bread Loaf, and the Vermont Studio Center often offer excellent—if short-lived—camaraderie between accepted fellows.

Q5: Can I get hired into a full-time university teaching position without a fellowship?
A5: Yes! A fellowship strengthens a job application, but is by no means essential to it.

Q6: Do I teach in a fellowship? Take workshops? Give readings? Participate in events?
Q6: It varies from fellowship to fellowship. If you're accepted to the Stegner Fellowship you'll both teach and take workshops; on the other hand, if you're awarded a "writer-in-residence" position somewhere you may simply be required to offer a lecture or reading or two and hold occasional office hours for undergraduate students. Make sure you fully understand all the responsibilities that come with a fellowship before you apply to it.

Q7: How much can I expect a fellowship to pay me?
A7: Fellowship stipends are usually slightly above—or even well above—MFA stipends.

Q8: Are there any program-sponsored postgraduate fellowships?
A8: A few programs offer these to recent graduates (Chapter 18 offers a nonexhaustive list).

Q9: Will getting a fellowship help me get a job outside the field of creative writing?
A9: Probably not, though any university-level teaching experience you acquire during a fellowship is important professional work experience and may be useful to your CV.

Q10: How important is a fellowship's duration, when I'm deciding whether to apply?
A10: If your goal is to strengthen your job application for a university teaching position, a fellowship of any duration will help you to do that merely by appearing on your CV. If, however, you're looking to finish writing a book or get substantial teaching experience, a fellowship program that's less than a year in duration may not be a good fit. Even in a year-long fellowship you have to begin applying for next year's opportunities within weeks of your arrival; that sort of frantic application-writing coming so early in your fellowship isn't conducive to you getting a lot of writing done. In this respect, fellowship programs are like MFA programs—if they're too short, you spend your time in-program trying

(Continued)

to decide where you're headed next rather than enjoying the view from where you are.

Q11: Some say certain fellowships promote literary hierarchies. What do you think?

A11: Personally, I dislike any institution that seeks to establish subcultural hierarchies—I think it distracts from the hard work of writing compelling poetry and prose—but your mileage may vary. Whatever your view, the fact remains that short-term fellowships, perhaps because they don't require the same sort of time commitment as fellowships that bring assistantships with them, are often used by literary artists as markers of talent and success. There are even some fellowships with tiered admission systems that entrench the idea that some poets and writers are categorically more important people than their younger, less-published peers. I could tell you now that I find that kind of "sorting" distasteful, but I wouldn't want it to chill you from applying to whatever fellowships you think will assist you in advancing your writing. Just make sure you're attending these brief-term fellowships in the right frame of mind: yes, there's surely some networking to be done, and yes, certain attendees will be people whose work you admire, but few of us got into poetry or prose simply to reestablish the sort of insidious social hierarchies that pushed us toward the arts in the first place. So if fellowships are for you, by all means apply to them. Just don't confuse admission and attendance with a guarantee that your work will find an audience or even that it necessarily should. Keep working as hard as you can on your writing whether or not you secure a fellowship; making superlative literary art is a long haul best measured in decades rather than days.

CHAPTER TWELVE

Job Placement

Talk to applicants to graduate creative writing programs, and about 50 percent will tell you that they'd like to teach full-time at a college or university upon graduation. Talk to current creative writing MFA students and about 33 percent will tell you the same thing. But if you talk to MFA alumni, they'll give you the real story: fewer than 1 percent of MFA graduates will ever teach full-time at the college or university level, and even those who do secure jobs usually do so several years after graduating from an MFA program.

So why is it so hard to get a teaching job, especially when there are so many undergraduate and graduate creative writing programs out there? That's a really good question, and the long answer would be complicated. The short answer, in four parts, is this: (a) the earliest sizable generation of creative writing professors, those who were hired during the creative writing "boom" of the 1990s, have not yet reached retirement age; (b) some programs are trying to replace full-time faculty members with part-time faculty members; (c) increasingly, hiring committees are looking for applicants with a creative writing doctorate as well as an MFA, making the hiring process a tough slog for MFA-holders with no PhD; and (d) the publishing record expectations for new university hires in creative writing have skyrocketed, such that many MFA graduates who would've once been competitive applicants are no longer quite so competitive.

Let's start with that last issue first. How much do I need to have published in order to get a teaching job after I graduate from my MFA or PhD? Twenty-five years ago, the answer would have been that a large number of magazine publications is enough; ten years ago, the answer would have been that a single book, even one merely under contract but not yet published, even one published by a small indie publisher, would be enough; but these days, the most competitive applicants in poetry already have two books published (or one book that won a major national prize) and the most competitive fiction applicants have at least one book published with a major trade press (or under contract and due to be published, if the book won a major prepublication prize or was the subject of a bidding war between highly regarded publishers). If that sounds daunting, it should: the belief that the MFA is a professional degree that guarantees its holder a teaching position at the university level is one that needs to be excised from our disciplinary discourse immediately. Not only do few MFA graduates get these jobs, but as you can see from the publication expectations that attach to these positions, it's difficult for a recent MFA graduate to even be well-qualified to apply to them.

What many MFA grads who want to teach do, instead of immediately applying for "tenure-track" positions—these being full-time professorial placements that can lead, in five or six years, to tenure—is apply for adjunct (part-time) teaching positions, a creative writing PhD, or a postgrad fellowship. The theory is that hiring committees don't like "gaps" in applicant CVs, so they expect that you've spent your time preparing yourself for academia by seeking more teaching, studying, and writing experience.

Some of you may be a bit startled, given that this book focuses primarily on creative writing MFA programs, by my statement that hiring committees are now ardently looking for applicants with both an MFA *and* a PhD in creative writing. I wish I could give you better news; certainly, a decade ago the MFA and PhD in creative writing were truly co-equal terminal degrees, with neither having a particular advantage as far as university job applications were concerned. Indeed, the conventional wisdom as late as 2009 was that the creative writing PhD would, at most, be used as a "tie-breaker" in a close competition between a potential creative writing hire with an MFA and one with both an MFA and a doctorate. Unfortunately, that's no longer the case. Hiring committees have a clear preference for those with *both* of creative writing's two terminal degrees. While surely some of this is explained by creative writing PhD-holders having had more time to hone their work, publish books, accrue teaching experience, and meet potential recommenders—and while we'd expect PhD graduates to be strong job candidates, as they went through the ringer of the graduate creative writing program application process *twice*—this doesn't tell the full story.

The full story is that because hiring committees often have members whose non-creative writing disciplines *only* accept new faculty with a PhD, there has always been pressure on creative writing hiring committees to follow suit. In recent years, the number of applicants to, and therefore the number of strong poets and writers graduating from, creative writing doctoral programs has increased substantially enough that hiring committees can *always* find a well-qualified PhD to bring on board. And as doing so meets their needs *and* the demands of their colleagues, why shouldn't they?

Chapter 14 discusses the value of creative writing doctoral programs at more length, and I discussed postgraduate fellowships in Chapter 11, but what about adjunct teaching positions? Are these a smart way to prepare for a university teaching career?

The answer is yes and no. Adjunct positions give you valuable teaching experience, which you'll sorely need if and when you apply for a teaching position at a college or university. They teach you about how to create a syllabus, how to teach a course while being observed—which may well happen if you make it to the second or third round of the hiring process at a given school—and ensure that you have no gaps in your CV suggesting a waning interest in teaching as a career. Many poets and writers find teaching inspiring and say that it helps them to be better writers; others simply enjoy remaining in a literary community upon the completion of their MFA programs.

On the other hand, most adjunct positions are extremely poorly compensated, offer no healthcare benefits, overwork you terribly and leave you little time to focus on your own writing. Worse still, they may never lead to full-time employment at the institution you're working at, and their value as an entry on your CV is relatively modest. Being a workhorse for a university with too few full-time professors is not the same thing as finding the long-term teaching career you always wanted. Yet if the option is leaving academia altogether or being an adjunct; and if you really want to teach full-time some day; and if neither a fellowship nor a fully funded doctoral program is an option, I would say an adjunct position is the way to go.

I mentioned that the creative writing job market might improve in the coming years, as the generation of creative writing professors hired during the creative writing "boom" of the 1990s will one day begin retiring en masse. I'll add to this that MFA alumni are much shrewder now than they were years ago about whether a university teaching career is really right for them, so we're seeing more young professors leave academia altogether and more current MFA students realizing the academic job market is too competitive to be a safe bet. Ironically, this might ease its competitiveness a bit.

Just how competitive is the market? Well, at the risk of scaring you, I'll offer up some hard facts: most years there are well under 100 full-time college or university jobs, across *all* genres of creative writing, in the whole of the United States—and a pool of tens of thousands who are qualified to occupy them. Don't believe me? Consider that, according to data from the Association of Writers & Writing Programs, the average MFA program has 20 students. There are roughly 250 such programs in the United States, which means 5,000 newly minted MFA alumni in poetry, fiction, and nonfiction each year. Over the course of a fifteen-year "generation" of writers, that's 75,000 MFA-holders. Needless to say, only a small percentage of these will apply for a full-time teaching position, but polling tells us that about a third were interested when they graduated from their programs, so it's reasonable to expect that the annual number of applicants for full-time creative writing professor positions numbers in the thousands.

An additional complication is that the number of jobs available in each major genre of creative writing annually rises and falls. In one recent year, there were eleven full-time poetry teaching jobs in the United States—that's right, eleven. MFA graduates who happened to go onto the job market in that year had a far lower than normal chance of being hired, and I know that fact was an unhappy discovery for a great many of them. Even those applying for a job in an "up" year for job openings in their genre sometimes encounter other unexpected roadblocks, like the need to buy your own ticket and hotel room for initial job interviews at either the MLA or AWP conferences. All in all, applying for full-time employment as a creative writing professor is something you should only do if you're deeply committed to teaching and academia and not only creative writing. Being a good—and happy—creative writing professor is about much more than liking writing and reading, so consider carefully whether this relatively narrow career choice is for you. Most importantly, don't be fooled by programs' promotional materials or anecdotal evidence of a given poet or writer quickly getting hired by a university to teach. The overall hard data on MFA graduates getting teaching positions is what it is, and in the interest of helping you to make whatever decision is right for you, I urge you to consider large data-sets rather than advertising or anecdotes.

Though the creative writing MFA degree has been around since the 1930s, there has to date been not one longitudinal study of how successful graduate creative writing programs are at placing students in jobs—academic or otherwise—postgraduation. One reason for this is that such programs do little if anything to assist recent graduates in finding jobs, so calculating their success at that endeavor would be a little misleading. Another reason is that many MFA graduates don't enter the full-time job market postgraduation, but instead seek out fellowships, part-time teaching positions, further graduate study in creative writing or another subject in the humanities, or matriculation in a professional course of study (most commonly, law or library science). So even if we had data on the jobs poets and writers get after completing their MFA degrees, it would be difficult to say whether it was the degree that got them the job or the other activities they engaged in postgraduation but pre-hire. In this book, we look at how different MFA programs perform at placing graduates in full-time, tenure-track teaching positions not to imply that top-performing programs have robust career services departments (they do not) but to see measures we might use to determine what we broadly term "cohort quality."

If a given graduate creative writing program is placing a relatively large number of recent graduates in full-time, tenure-track university teaching positions, it tends to suggest that its students are publishing regularly and producing highly competent work. It also suggests a certain level of commitment, among some subsection of that program's student body, to rigorously thinking about creative writing and staying within the field long-term. As I mentioned in discussing fellowship programs (see Chapter 11), this *doesn't* mean that the poets and writers at such programs are categorically "better" than the poets and writers elsewhere, as that's a wholly subjective determination. But it might—probatively, if not scientifically— suggest that there is a strong aptitude for lyric-narrative poetry and literary fiction at any program that performs well in job placement.

We might surmise this because these two aesthetic spheres comprise much of contemporary literature and nearly all of what is taught in graduate creative writing programs. So aptitude in these styles is desirable in the view of many hiring committees.

> ## FREQUENTLY ASKED QUESTIONS: JOB PLACEMENT

Q1: Can I get a job with an MFA but no PhD and no book?

A1: Yes, but more in the same way that people say "anything can happen" than in the sense of it being likely. Keep in mind that when you go on the academic job market you are competing with literally thousands of MFA graduates—and likely several hundred for any individual job—many of whom have books and doctorates. Those who hold doctorates are likely to have much more teaching experience than you (particularly if you didn't hold an assistantship during your MFA program) and will have had many more years to hone their work and seek publication. So when I say an MFA holder with no other degrees and only magazine publications may secure an adjunct teaching spot and only if lightning strikes a full-time position, I say it not to wound but to be candid.

Q2: Is it possible to be *too* qualified for a teaching position?

A2: Oddly, there are many indicators suggesting that you *can* be "too qualified" for a teaching position. Those who've hopped from fellowship to fellowship for many years, and/or adjunct position to adjunct position, may inadvertently be communicating to prospective employers either that they're unwilling to commit to full-time teaching duties or else have tried repeatedly to secure these without any success thus far. Meanwhile, those who have many books but little or no teaching experience may have a great pedigree and publishing record but no evidence of a commitment to teaching. Even those with a strong pedigree, lots of teaching experience, and a handful of books may inadvertently scare off hiring committees who fear that, upon their hire as a first-year assistant professor, such an eminently qualified poet or writer will immediately go looking for an even better position elsewhere. (And when this happens, as it sometimes does, it only confirms that fear.) This leads academic job applicants to want to hit the "sweet spot" in applying for jobs: a strong pedigree; teaching experience in multiple genres (or other areas besides creative writing); and two books with a reputable publisher for poets, or one with a nationally recognized trade press for fiction-writers.

Q3: You just mentioned "pedigree" several times. That's a topic that hasn't really been discussed yet. How much does the name of the school I graduate from matter?
A3: If you're a poet and you don't plan on seeking a full-time university teaching position, the name of the school you attend matters virtually not at all. It's a myth that poetry editors care about submitters' alma maters; they don't, and I say that having been an editor at many different publications. I've seen no evidence that other poets care, either. That said, if you're poet and you want to teach, any hiring committee looking at you is going to be thinking, to some degree, about their institution's marketing and enrollment goals—meaning, they'll want to hire someone who "on paper" as well as in reality appears to be a particular asset to their community. So in rare instances, the name of one's graduate poetry-writing program might matter a bit.

For fiction-writers, things are a bit more complicated, and there's a one-word reason for that: agents. Agents are swayed not just by good writing but also by strong pedigrees, in part because they believe publishers respond to these. Your degree from one of the older and more established fiction-writing programs makes their job trying to sell your novel or short story collection that much easier. Having said that, agents' knowledge of creative writing programs is remarkably shallow; they're familiar with what they consider the top ten or so programs, which generally are whatever programs were ranked in the top ten by *U.S. News & World Report* over two decades ago, but know little about any of the other 200+ graduate creative writing programs in America.

So what does this mean for you? It means you might have a slightly easier time finding an agent if you attend one of the programs that was highly regarded more than two decades ago, and that you will not have that advantage—but won't necessarily be at any specific disadvantage—if you do not. For all other purposes, fiction-writers' pedigree matters about as much as it does for poets: your peers largely won't care, as they'll judge you primarily on your writing, and since no one outside the field of creative writing has heard of any writing program other than (at most) the Iowa Writers' Workshop, no one else will really care, either. So

(*Continued*)

when I discuss pedigree in this book I hope to acknowledge that while it *can* matter in a small number of situations, it is far more commonly beside the point. The best program for you is the best program for you, whatever *U.S. News & World Report* may have said about it (if it existed) over twenty years ago, or this book may say about it now. Remember that MFA programs are nonprofessional programs, so you don't choose them in the way you might choose a law, business, or medical school.

Q4: What are some things I can do to make it marginally more likely that I'll find placement in a teaching job after graduation, besides publish my work in a book?

A4: The first and most obvious response is that you must—absolutely must—get some college-level teaching experience. This means that if you want to teach, a program that gives you no teaching experience, for whatever reason it does so, is not a very good fit for you. Fortunately, the programs that offer teaching assistantships to a large number of incoming students are also the ones that use those assistantships to fully fund most or all of their first-year poets and writers. So that's a win-win situation for you.

A second response, equally important, is one you're not likely to come across in many places besides a book like this one: you must do everything you can to develop proficiency in a second (and if possible a third) genre of creative writing. That includes taking workshops in a second genre, teaching workshops in a second genre if possible, and seeking to publish in a second genre. Why is this so important? It's important because colleges and universities have become increasingly spoiled by the glut of humanities-oriented job candidates on the academic market, and one result of this is that they are looking for "unicorns." In this context, a "unicorn" is a job candidate who miraculously can fill so many different roles for their prospective employer that that employer is saved from having to hire for two separate "lines" ("line" meaning a line of funding dedicated to a particular faculty position within a department). For instance, if a hiring committee can hire someone to teach both poetry and fiction rather than hiring one poet and one novelist, they will be very strongly inclined to do so.

As you might imagine, this admonition to pick up a second or third genre while in-program means that only programs that allow this sort of study will work well for applicants who want to teach postgraduation. Programs that instead blockade you into a single "silo" (a term used in academia to discuss a narrow area of study) will be deeply harmful to you if you're hoping to get one of the nation's few full-time university teaching positions upon graduation. And because getting two MFA degrees—one in each of two primary genres—is time-consuming, expensive, and frankly just difficult to pull off from an admissions standpoint, you're really going to want the one program you attend to be the one program you need to prepare yourself for the academic job market.

Finally, while some programs mandate pedagogy courses or practicums, if your program offers these and *doesn't* mandate them you should take them anyway. They're excellent professional development opportunities for those who want to teach later on.

Q5: Are all creative writing jobs equally difficult to get? Is there a way to up my odds?
A5: Almost every aspiring professor's "dream" creative writing job postgraduation is a "1/1" tenure-track professorship in an MFA program. (A "1/1" means that you only teach one class in the fall and one in the spring.) Poets and writers report being more interested in teaching graduate students than undergraduates, and believing that teaching in an MFA program is more prestigious than teaching in an undergraduate program—perhaps in part because MFA professors are only obligated to teach courses within their preferred genre. Whether or not graduate teaching positions are more prestigious than undergraduate teaching positions, and whether or not that matters, the fact remains that very few MFA positions open up annually and almost none of them are 1/1 teaching positions. These are generally reserved for more experienced professors or nationally renowned authors getting a teaching job for the first time. On the other end of the spectrum is the most difficult sort of appointment, broadly speaking, that one could possibly have: a 5/5 teaching load working as an adjunct at a community college, particularly a teaching load that requires you to teach subjects other than creative writing in addition to a workshop or two. This can be a tough spot to be in not only because a 5/5 is a staggeringly heavy teaching load, but also because adjuncts generally don't get healthcare benefits and community colleges may lack the resources to pay well and attract strong undergraduate creative writers. I'm putting aside here the obvious and entirely fair objection that if you love teaching you should want to teach those who most need you to teach them well—and perhaps least expect that you can or will.

Not surprisingly, the "typical" job you might hope to find postgraduation is in the middle: a 3/3 teaching load tenure-track position at a four-year undergraduate institution, during which you'll be asked to teach other

(*Continued*)

subjects besides creative writing (usually composition and literature). A 3/3 load is about the maximum teaching load most poets and writers can handle before their writing time and emotional energy is compromised. One's ability to handle that load, or anything heavier, is related to how many of the courses you teach are writing workshops and how large your classes are. Community colleges are likely to have larger courses due to having less money for faculty; public universities, particularly land-grant universities with large research budgets, are more likely to be able to cap workshop enrollments at a reasonable level.

So if you're thinking about teaching, ask yourself: What sort of teaching job would excite me, and what sort of job would be more than I can handle? If you'd only accept the first sort of job I've described—the one at an MFA program—you'll want to focus your post-MFA job search on professions other than academia, applying to work at an MFA program only on the rare occasions that sort of position opens up. It won't be often, I can tell you. On the other end of things, if a 5/5 adjunct position at a community college doesn't sound like something you could handle—and I'll say here that those who can and do handle it with aplomb are heroes of mine—realize you've narrowed your employment options considerably. And the field of options was narrow to begin with.

Q6: Do the data tables in this book distinguish between *types* of job placements?
A6: They do not, for a number of reasons. First and foremost is logistics: the size and scope of a data table cross-indexing both how often a given graduate creative writing program places graduates in a full-time teaching position and exactly what the teaching load and curriculum assigned to each such teaching position is would be prohibitive. But secondly, those who hope to teach postgraduation are first and foremost just looking for full-time employment as a university lecturer or professor. We all know that your first job may not be your last job, and that waiting for the perfect job to come around means, in this job market, waiting forever. There are no perfect jobs—or, there are few enough of them that we need not waste time discussing them here.

This doesn't mean that distinguishing between types of placements is pointless, as some of you *would* find certain types of placements unacceptable. Rather, I make this point about job placements so that you'll take job-placement data with a grain of salt. As I've argued, these data can be useful in assessing cohort quality—however indirectly—but should not be taken as a guarantee of postgraduation employment.

Q7: Are there any programs that offer an extensive career services suite to students?

A7: Not really. While many programs run one-off workshops for current students detailing the fellowship and job-application process, no more than a handful give students ready in-program access to too much more than this. And only a fraction of *those* programs advertise these offerings. Programs may well encourage you to access their host university's general career services operation—the one open to all students, undergraduate and graduate—but the field of creative writing is idiosyncratic enough that you'd likely get more benefit out of reading this book than almost anything you'll hear from a career services employee with no expertise in creative writing jobs. That's no insult to hardworking career services professionals; rather, it's intended to confirm that creative writing is in many ways a universe unto itself. So you should assume that, as to finding a university teaching position, you'll largely be on your own postgraduation.

Q8: I don't want to teach. How do I make the most of a writing program in terms of preparing myself for future employment? What can I expect to do after I graduate?

A8: There are no longitudinal studies of what happens to MFA students after they graduate, though there should be. This book addresses the three readily observable outcomes for MFA alumni: placement in a fellowship, placement in a teaching position, and acceptance to a doctoral program in creative writing. But at best this accounts for only 10 percent or so of MFA graduates. What happens to the other 90 percent? Nobody knows; it appears, indeed, that virtually no one has asked. In my experience, some go on to law school, some to obtain Master of Library Science (MLS) or Master of Library and Information Science (MLIS) degrees, some make an effort to become "creatives" in new technologies such as immersive realities (XR), and some, unfortunately a vanishingly small number, get book deals with large advances and live off that for awhile. All told, this may account for another 10 percent of MFA alumni. But what about the remaining 80 percent? I imagine that some of these would like to go into publishing if possible, which is why I always recommend that MFA students work with their program's literary magazine if at all possible (or start a new one, if one doesn't exist already or you don't care for the one your program already has) or look into local and program-sponsored internships with book publishers. Many programs also have

(*Continued*)

courses available in literary publishing, and you should definitely look into these. You can also dedicate yourself to taking as many courses as possible outside the discipline of creative writing—perhaps even outside the humanities—with an eye toward discovering new fields you might want to work or pursue further study in. I don't necessarily recommend a part-time job, as it might detract significantly from your in-program writing practice, but certainly colleges and universities have a lot of interesting research going on, so you might find that there's something you can do that will pay you a bit and expose you to a possible future career.

One's MFA years go by quickly, and if one doesn't approach the experience mindfully from the start, it's easy to graduate with debt and few marketable skills. Most MFA alumni can write well, but while there are many jobs available as a "technical writer" this isn't the sort of writing skill most graduates have acquired by the end of their MFA. So do consider, while still in-program, seeking out instruction in forms of writing—for instance new media journalism, professional writing, technical writing, and so on—that are more conspicuously marketable than the ability to write a competent poem or short story. The one thing you must *not* do is be corralled into a postgraduate position that's not right for you just because you don't know what else to do. That means you should only apply to a doctoral program, fellowship, or law school if that's really what you want to do. Don't let the discipline of creative writing's inattention to student outcomes keep you from doing the legwork needed to plan your future now.

CHAPTER THIRTEEN

Low-Residency Programs

Not every MFA applicant is looking for a full-residency graduate-school experience. Some are happy in their current jobs, or happy with the place they live, and have no wish to upend their lives to spend several years pursuing a nonprofessional degree far from home. Others feel, rightly or wrongly, that they're too old to go back to school. Perhaps they don't like school very much—preferring to avoid classrooms and awkward peer interactions—and hope to earn a degree without subjecting themselves to the accoutrements of higher education. These are just a few reasons an aspiring poet or writer might choose to apply to what's called a "low-residency" MFA program.

As a general rule, low-residency MFA programs require that students be on campus for less than three weeks a year, usually in two ten-day increments. The rest of the year students engage in online workshopping and, more notably, one-on-one electronic correspondence with a faculty mentor. Because students aren't on campus very often, they're saved the cost of room and board for a full academic year; on the other hand, because students aren't on campus very often they also can't be offered teaching assistantships (unless they happen to be local) and therefore are unlikely to be "fully funded." The idea with low-residency programs is that low-residency students don't mind as much not getting substantial student funding because their MFA program allows them to stay in their jobs. Low-residency programs also tend to be more flexible than full-residency MFAs in terms of how long you can take to finish the degree.

As you might expect, low-residency students are, on average, slightly older than full-residency students. The median age for full-residency students, according to polling, is around 27, and around 37 for low-residency students. Other differences between full-residency and low-residency programs include the following distinctions: low-residency programs usually offer more genres of study than full-residency programs, as well as more opportunities for cross-genre study; they tend to be housed at smaller, regional, and less well-known colleges and universities, as they have lower overhead than full-residency programs and therefore don't require substantial institutional resources to operate; they're usually "money-makers" for their host schools, as they bring in tuition while paying out little financial aid; they tend to have faculties full of literary luminaries, as low-residency faculty can live wherever they want, and therefore may take on such a position as a side job; and finally, and most controversially, they have a scattershot record in terms of fellowship placement, job placement, and, significantly, selectivity.

The simple fact is that many (but by no means all) low-residency programs are relatively nonselective, meaning they will seek to matriculate most applicants who come to them—regardless of skill level or native talent. Due to this, the quality of the "pedigree" attached to a low-residency degree is not the same as a full-residency MFA.

That said, low-residency programs are increasing in number right now at a much higher rate than full-residency programs, and comprise half of all new MFA programs in the United States since 2000. Because the increasingly crowded low-residency field harbors within it a small number of programs that predate the low-residency "boom," there are a few schools offering the low-residency MFA that have benefited from being among the first in the field—and have even developed a certain amount of cachet. Three programs in particular answer to this description: Vermont College of Fine Arts, Warren Wilson College, and Bennington College. A handful of other programs approach this top group in terms of their popularity among applicants and the esteem in which they are held, but these three have thus far separated themselves quite capably from the pack. That said, in the last two years a few well-respected "national brands" have entered the low-residency creative writing MFA market—the most notable being New York University—which may, in short order, throw the whole pedigree question into a new stage of flux.

There's a real question, however, as to whether pedigree can or should matter in a low-residency program. After all, didn't we establish in Chapter 12 that pedigree is mostly useful when seeking a full-time teaching position in higher education? And don't low-residency students already, by definition, have jobs and possibly long-term careers? All this is true. However, fiction-writers who attend low-residency programs—especially any but the three mentioned above—may have a slightly more difficult time accessing agents than do their peers at highly regarded full-residency MFA programs. (Of course, the same can be said of those who attend a less well-known full-residency MFA, so this point should by no means prevent you from considering a low-residency program.)

In any case, interviews with low-residency MFA students suggest that their chief concerns are not pedigree or job placement but pedagogy and job retention. In other words, low-residency poets and writers prefer long-distance education and one-on-one mentorship to the conventional creative writing workshop, and/or value staying in their current job—or in any case, their current living situation—more than placing themselves in academic employment somewhere down the line. Hopefully it goes without saying that there's no right or wrong approach here. Whether a low-residency or full-residency program is right for you depends entirely on your circumstances and your priorities.

This book focuses somewhat less on low-residency programs for three reasons: first, there are far fewer low-residency programs (81) than full-residency programs (176) and an even greater disparity in the number of applicants to the two types of degrees; second, low-residency programs are a much newer phenomenon, and therefore much that can be said about them is not yet known or knowable; and third, because of their age and sophistication, their narrower range of program options, and their more idiosyncratic program-selection methods, low-residency applicants are less likely to find a book like this one useful.

In writing about low-residency programs, I therefore want to be cautious about applying "full-residency logic" to low-residency scenarios. Many of the critiques I've made in this book of, for instance, the workshop method don't apply to the more customized, idiosyncratic, technology-oriented low-residency pedagogies. Just so, assessments of programs' funding packages—so important to full-residency applicants—are more or less moot in the low-residency context. Realistically, few students admitted to a low-residency program get funding, and those who do are given well below the cost of attendance.

The question of pedigree is a more difficult one to tackle, as low-residency students are in theory paying full freight not just for the ease of staying at home and the opportunity to get extensive one-on-one mentoring, but also for the "brand" attached to their degree. Is it worth it to go into substantial debt, or to substantially degrade one's financial position, for a degree from a largely unknown college or university, even if one can learn a great deal by attending that program? That's really up to each applicant to decide, so it's not something I can speak to. Suffice to say that, as with full-residency programs, there are alumni who swear by the low-residency format and those who critique it. And you'll find every imaginable reaction in between these two poles.

One thing we can definitively say about low-residency programs is that it is their online pedagogies that distinguish them more than anything else. Putting aside a handful of programs, most low-residency programs admit a majority of applicants and therefore cannot be distinguished by their selectivity. Likewise, since almost no low-residency programs offer substantial funding packages and (apropos of Chapter 2) it's unwise to select a creative writing program by its faculty, these measures aren't very helpful to us either. But the teaching methods a low-residency program uses to dispense its curriculum to students? These we can discuss comparatively, if not quantitatively.

At least we *would* be able to do that, if low-residency programs were rigorous about describing their pedagogies to prospective students, which they are not. For that matter, neither are full-residency programs, though this is less of an issue because most such programs use the conventional creative writing workshop exclusively for their writing instruction. Low-residency programs have an opportunity to be more creative and tech-savvy about how they deliver course content, but to access that sort of information you may have to not only scour a program's website but also quiz current and former students, faculty, and administrators. In any case, this much is clear: if you're applying to a low-residency program it will not be duration, location, funding, student-faculty ratio, fellowship placement, job placement, or perhaps even pedigree that will or should matter to you. Rather, your focus is likely to be on pedagogy, program cost, and the degree to which the program allows you to work in any and all genres of your choice.

For those wondering about the roughly three weeks per year you'll spend on-campus, these two "residencies" are like high-intensity full-residency MFA programs: lots of workshops, lectures, readings, and social events held over a very short span of time. The hope is that you'll get to know your cohort members so that you can put faces to names when you later encounter them online, and perhaps even develop personal and professional relationships with your peers despite not seeing them in the flesh very often. There's not much more to say about these residencies because they vary only slightly in duration from program to program; while arguably the location of these residencies may matter a great deal to individual applicants, for instance if one program meets in Paris while another meets in a relatively sleepy rural town, it's debatable whether one should select a low-residency program on the basis of its residency's location. After all, the point of the residencies is first and foremost to read, write, study, and discuss texts within your genre, and secondarily to socialize with your peers, so exploring a lovely new vacation spot should probably be a much lower priority.

As the number of low-residency programs increases, and particularly as well-known brands in higher education begin to enter the low-residency market, it's inevitable that the latter programs will become even more established and highly regarded in the field of creative writing. At the moment low-residency programs are having a "boom" in program creation, even as they have not necessarily become dramatically more popular among applicants. The fact that colleges and universities can create these types of graduate creative writing programs at little cost and with great financial returns ensures that we will continue to see many new low-residency programs pop up in the years ahead. If these programs take advantage of their flexible, interdisciplinary curricula to offer students access to genre tracks, pedagogies, and technologies they wouldn't otherwise encounter, they'll be a valuable addition to creative writing as a discipline. While it might take a bit longer for agents and hiring committees to view any but the oldest low-residency programs as competitive in their admissions and therefore august in their pedigrees, undoubtedly that day will come.

FREQUENTLY ASKED QUESTIONS: LOW-RESIDENCY PROGRAMS

Q1: Are these vanity degrees?
A1: I answer this question first because it's a question some have about low-residency MFA programs. The answer is a resounding no. While these programs are indeed money-makers for their host institutions, and while they're popular among older poets and writers looking more for enlightenment or validation than pedigree or a networking tool, the low-residency faculty members I've spoken with are serious about what they do. They want their students to have the best MFA experience possible, and recognize that many low-residency attendees take that route because other obligations make it impossible for them to attend a full-residency program. Having said that, it is never wise to attend a truly nonselective graduate program, whether low-residency or otherwise, as doing so fails to confirm—through a rigorous application and admissions process—that you're ready for graduate study in the field of creative writing in the first instance. So while the more selective low-residency programs have strong faculties, strong cohorts, and even a bit of cachet, in the literary community, unless they feature special indicia of quality, the very smallest and very newest ones should be given some time to grow before you commit yourself to them for two to four years.

Q2: Why has there been such exponential growth in the number of low-residency MFA programs, if demand for them has not increased commensurately?
A2: The answer is that low-residency programs have low overhead, as often their faculty are paid per student rather than per class. This means that faculty members can fully participate as faculty members while supervising just a handful of students and earning a relatively modest salary. Having said that, it's possible that there are more low-residency programs currently operating than the academic market can support, which is why I caution readers about those programs within the field that are truly nonselective. These programs are useful for those who live near them and cannot travel a great distance even for two residencies a year; otherwise, they have not yet proven themselves to be more than fundraising apparatuses for their host institutions. While I've no doubt their faculties work diligently with all their students, if those students have been selected as the result of merely filling out an application it

limits what even a long period of one-on-one mentorship can realistically accomplish.

Q3: Are there other reasons to attend a low-residency program, besides convenience?

A3: Yes! In fact, besides their tendency to encourage and facilitate interdisciplinary and cross-genre writing, one easily overlooked reason is that it is only low-residency programs that will admit students who are interested in, and already committed to, genre or young-adult fiction. At full-residency programs your portfolio must be composed of literary fiction or (at most) magical realism; however, there are several low-residency programs offering genre fiction or young-adult fiction as a track. So if you're interested in one of these subgenres of fiction, a low-residency program may be your only option.

What's odd about the presence of genre fiction and young-adult fiction at low-residency programs but not full-residency programs is that these subgenres are, as of 2018, far more popular among creative writers than literary fiction ever has been—and, I'll add, more lucrative by a fair margin—so it continues to surprise me that so few full-residency programs have moved into the genre fiction and young-adult fiction markets. This means, too, that agents looking for work within these two subgenres are less likely to be skeptical of a low-residency degree, as low-residency programs are where the most committed genre and young-adult writers who go to graduate school are studying.

Q4: Are there any funded low-residency programs?

A4: Fully funded? No. But as with every general rule, there's an exception or two, so when I say that low-residency programs don't offer substantial funding, you'll find the occasional exception. One or two programs may even offer as much as a 50 percent tuition break for the most qualified applicants. Keep in mind, however, that a tuition break isn't a stipend with full tuition remission, so even the most generous low-residency funding packages fall well short of "full funding."

CHAPTER FOURTEEN

Creative Writing Doctoral Programs

Creative writing is the only academic discipline I'm aware of with *two* terminal degrees—which tells you something about how chaotic and even underdeveloped the discipline still is. But it's true what you've heard: both the creative writing MFA and the creative writing PhD are considered terminal degrees in the field of creative writing. Why? Because creative writing doctoral programs have largely arisen at universities that disapprove of a master's degree being considered a terminal degree, so they've created the PhD in creative writing as an alternative to, rather than expansion upon, the MFA.

If you understand how academia works, this struggle over "terminality" isn't as surprising as it sounds. In nearly every field of study, the PhD is the terminal degree, so there's a great deal of pressure applied to creative writers working within higher education to conform to that convention. At some universities, the "price" creative writers must pay for being allowed to develop a terminal degree in their discipline is that they must hew to convention and call it a PhD rather than an MFA. You may recall that early on in this book I observed that the "Iowa model" (the MFA) was rejected for decades before a few colleges and universities picked it up in the 1960s. This is a further development in that vein, as certain schools that rejected the Workshop's model held out on adopting the MFA until much later—the 1980s and beyond—and when they did finally develop a graduate creative writing program, they opted for the PhD, instead.

All that is confusing enough, but what makes it more confusing is that MFA students quite understandably think of the creative writing PhD not as an alternative to the MFA but as the next step one takes in the discipline post-MFA. And they're not wrong. The universities that developed creative writing doctorates realized in the 1980s, 1990s, and 2000s that they could attract the most talented MFA graduates in the United States if they turned their degrees into coterminal post-MFA educational experiences. It kept them from having to directly compete with MFA programs for students, while ensuring they'd get strong cohorts—students likely to publish and teach—every year.

Today, the mission of creative writing PhD programs has changed so much that they almost never accept students without an MFA. You should assume, therefore, that the only appropriate time to apply to a creative writing PhD is in the last year of your MFA. That's one reason I don't address the topic of creative writing doctoral degrees very often in this book; by the time one applies for such a degree, one has already been through the MFA application process, and the PhD application process is remarkably similar. What changes are the GRE requirements, the foreign language requirements, and the necessity, at some institutions, of submitting a critical writing sample as well as a creative portfolio. Other than that, by the time you get to applying for creative writing PhD programs you'll be familiar with the drill from this book and your own experience.

I mentioned that creative writing doctorates are confusing, and they are—for more reasons than I've noted. Contrary to the expectation some had in the 1990s and 2000s that the creative writing PhD would eventually supplant the creative writing MFA, that now seems unlikely to happen. Hardly any new creative writing doctoral programs have been created in the last decade, even as new low- and full-residency MFA programs have appeared at an almost alarming rate.

If you've followed the history of the creative writing PhD as laid out in this chapter, you won't be too surprised by the lack of growth in the area. After all, the degree was intended as an alternative, not a follow-up, to the MFA, so colleges and universities that already had the MFA were loath to build out a PhD, and schools with neither an MFA nor a PhD in creative writing feared that any

PhD they created would simply compete with the more popular MFA. The result is that deeply committed poets and writers use the creative writing PhD as a four- or five-year extension of their MFA experience rather than an entirely new sort of degree program. Attending such a program gives them more time to publish and more teaching experience, and therefore strengthens their hand if they want to go on the academic job market down the line. Increasingly, it's not a bad strategy: as we've noted, university hiring committees looking for new creative writing faculty have shown a marked preference, in recent years, for candidates with a doctorate. It's nearly to the point at which anyone who wants to teach creative writing at the university level *has* to get a creative writing doctorate first.

The increasing ubiquity of the creative writing PhD on the academic job market is in a sense unfortunate, because the degree really isn't for everyone. Keep in mind that for the first three years of study, a creative writing PhD is almost indistinguishable from a PhD program in English, English literature, or literary studies—you have to take a lot of academic courses and then, at the end of three years, you must pass your "comprehensive exams" ("comps") in order to move on to the dissertation stage. While poets and writers getting doctorates in creative writing are allowed to take workshops for credit, whereas their academic-degree peers almost universally are not, that's small comfort for those literary artists who detest academic coursework and difficult exams.

Most of those who pursue a creative writing PhD anticipate getting most of their writing done during the three-year "dissert-ation" phase of their programs. While a dissertator you'll have no coursework obligations, only teaching obligations—assuming you have a teaching assistantship—and periodic check-ins with your dissertation committee chairperson. When your dissertation (a full-length book) is complete, you "defend" it by going before a committee and discussing your process, your influences, and your ambitions. Most programs also require you to write a critical introduction to your project, so you may be asked about any theory or literature that influences you as a writer. While comprehensive exams can be difficult, the overwhelming majority of poets and writers are able to pass their dissertation defense with relative ease, making one's dissertator period more like a paid fellowship than an academic course of study.

Because the PhD in creative writing is coterminal with the MFA, you should have the same expectations of funding for the former as the latter. In the United States, any terminal degree worth its salt is fully funded for its duration. That means my advice to you regarding the creative writing PhD is exactly the same as for the creative writing MFA: *do not go into substantial debt for a creative writing doctorate.* While some creative writing PhD programs do not fund first-year students, on the grounds that during the first year of the program you're technically earning your nonterminal MA degree, many MFA graduates have enough transferable credits to skip this year of the program. Certainly everything after that point should be fully funded through a fellowship, teaching assistantship, research assistantship, or some form of grant. PhD programs that offer students unfunded admission to five or six years of nonprofessional doctoral study should have their entreaties ignored, and I'm telling you now that the faculty and administrators at these programs would privately agree with me. Such a small percentage of MFA or PhD graduates get tenure-track professorships in creative writing that asking aspiring poets or writers to pay for their terminal degrees is wrong.

All that said, this book provides you with a listing of the most popular creative writing PhD programs in the event that this course of study is right for you. And certainly, if you receive a fully funded offer, don't mind some academic coursework and testing, and believe you need an extra four or five years to work on your writing and gain teaching experience, a creative writing PhD may well suit your needs perfectly.

FREQUENTLY ASKED QUESTIONS: CREATIVE WRITING DOCTORAL PROGRAMS

Q1: Can I get a full-time, tenure-track teaching job without a PhD in creative writing?
A1: As of 2018, it's still possible—but it's difficult. I just don't know if it will be possible by 2025. The fact is, so many of the strongest poets and writers graduating from MFA programs are going on to do creative writing doctorates that the job market is glutted with writers who have

almost ten years of teaching experience and about that much time under their belt writing and submitting their work for publication. That can make it very difficult for someone who's only taken two or three years of graduate study in creative writing. Please know that I hate to say that; the idea that one should have to study creative writing for nearly a decade to get a full-time, tenure-track professorship teaching creative writing would have been horrifying to most poets and writers a decade ago, and it still horrifies me now. But my job here is to tell you the truth, and the truth is that a creative writing PhD is a sizable advantage on the academic job market.

Q2: Should someone who *doesn't* want to teach do a creative writing PhD?

A2: No. The creative writing PhD offers a professional pedigree only for those who want to be professors; it does not appreciably improve your CV should you go looking for other kinds of employment. While one can learn a lot from doctoral coursework, and while it's nice to have a few extra years to write, the fact is that eventually you will have to learn how to integrate a regular writing practice into your daily life—so you might as well start doing so immediately after your MFA. The crutch a doctoral program offers to writers, that being a dissertator period with few responsibilities and ample time to write, is an unrealistic turn away from the realities of being a poet or writer that will follow you for a lifetime. You will almost certainly find yourself, years from now, trying to write creatively while working on some other career, and that ability to multitask is a critical skill that one can't learn from the relative safety of a doctoral program. Besides, due to low stipends many doctoral students will have to take out small loans each year to live, and by the time you've done that for four or five years you've racked up quite a bit of debt. So: you may be tempted to apply to a creative writing PhD postgraduation simply because you don't know what else to do, but my recommendation is that you avoid the temptation and think about other ways to build off your MFA experience. The creative writing PhD really is there for those who want to teach at the university level.

Q3: Can I apply to a creative writing PhD with just an undergraduate degree?

A3: At many PhD programs, you technically can—though your chances of admission are very slight, given that you're competing for a spot with some of the top MFA graduates in the United States. My advice is to

(Continued)

apply to MFA programs instead, and to move on to the PhD only if you decide, in the last year of your MFA, that being a university professor is for you. You might well think that's your future from the vantage point of having just completed an undergraduate degree, but as I've discussed elsewhere in this book the percentage of poets and writers who want to teach full-time drops markedly pre-MFA to post-MFA. You don't want to commit yourself to a career path before you've given it a test run via the MFA. If you do decide to apply to a creative writing PhD straight after college, make sure you've confirmed with any program you apply to that they're willing to take applicants with no MFA. Many will say yes; some may not.

Q4: Can you say more about these "comprehensive exams"?
A4: Comprehensive exams, or "comps," are usually taken at the end of a doctoral student's third year of study, and represent the gateway you must pass through to get from the academic coursework phase of the program to the dissertation phase. Usually this exam involves you selecting, with the assistance of an advisor, a very large reading list and then, a few months later, taking an essay test in which you discuss all of the books you've read. You may also be asked to describe what you've learned to a committee, a process that's colloquially called "orals." Usually a program's website will tell you whether you're obligated to take *both* comps and orals or exclusively comps.

The overwhelming majority of students pass their comps and orals, though technically it is possible not to pass and to have to take them again (most programs will give you at least two shots at it). Having gone through the experience myself, I can say that it's a bit nerve-wracking but ultimately nothing near as bad as taking a bar exam or the medical boards. If you really hate academics, you'll hate this—in fact you'll hate the first few years of a creative writing doctoral program, most likely—so take that into account when deciding whether a creative writing PhD program is a good fit for you.

Q5: For those not interested in teaching, but very interested in publishing poetry or fiction, how does the creative writing PhD compare to the MFA in terms of pedigree?
A5: First, and most importantly, if you're a poet forget about pedigree. No one cares. If you're a fiction-writer, the simple truth is that the top creative writing MFA programs generally enjoy *more* prestige than the top creative writing PhD programs, in no small part because of the history of the two degrees that we've been discussing. In many respects

the creative writing PhD is a competitor to, rather than a continuation of, the creative writing MFA, and the last few decades has shown the MFA to be the winner in that tilt. The only exception, as already noted, is on the academic job market. But as for agents, they're not going to care one way or another if you have a PhD in creative writing as well as an MFA in creative writing. As long as you attend an MFA program they're familiar with you will have gotten all the mileage out of your "pedigree" you can.

Q6: What type of teaching experience will I gain in a creative writing PhD program?
A6: One of the perks of the creative writing PhD is that you almost always are given a teaching assistantship, and that teaching assistantship almost always involves teaching creative writing—and, moreover, teaching within your preferred genre. That's a perk because MFA assistantships only sometimes allow you to teach creative writing, and only rarely a course that's restricted to your preferred genre.

CHAPTER FIFTEEN

Applicant and Faculty Surveys

I mentioned earlier that graduate creative writing applicants are forced to stand on the shoulders of the applicants who came before them. Because MFA and PhD programs release little hard data themselves, the collective research of applicants, and the archive into which this research is put, becomes invaluable to their successors. One type of research that applicants are unlikely to conduct, however, has to do with their own interests and values. These are of course being expressed daily in the discussions they have with one another, but this is a very different matter than surveying applicants en masse to determine who they are and what they want.

Unfortunately, very few such qualitative surveys have ever been done. On the other hand, all of the ones that have been done are in this chapter. We also, to boot, have the one survey ever taken of MFA faculty on the subject of which program features *they* think are the most important.

Between 2008 and 2013, thousands of applicants were asked to reveal their thinking on a range of topics, all of which relate to applying to graduate creative writing programs. Their responses follow. Each survey is introduced with a brief recitation of its query, date of collection, and methodology.

The abbreviation "n" at the end of each survey indicates the number of applicants surveyed.

SURVEY 1

Survey year: 2009

Query: "Which of these is most important to your decision about where to apply?"

Options: location, funding, faculty, reputation, selectivity, curriculum, none.

Additional instructions: respondents were permitted to select multiple answers.

Survey location: *The Creative Writing MFA Blog*

Survey web address: http://creative-writing-mfa-handbook. blogspot.com/

Interface application: sponsored by Google

Results (top four responses only):

1. Funding (56%)
2. Reputation (45%)
3. Location (32%)
4. Faculty (18%)

[n = 502.]

SURVEY 2

Survey year: 2010

Query: "If you are a current creative writing MFA applicant, which of the following program features are among your top five reasons for choosing to apply to a particular program?"

Options: alumni, cost of living, curriculum, duration, faculty, funding, internship opportunities location, postgraduate placement, reputation, selectivity, student-to-faculty ratio, size, teaching opportunities, and other.

Additional instructions: respondents were permitted to select multiple answers.

Survey location: *The Creative Writing MFA Blog*

Survey web address: http://creative-writing-mfa-handbook.
blogspot.com/
Interface application: sponsored by Google

Results (all):

1. Funding (68%)
2. Reputation (61%)
3. Location (59%)
4. Faculty (50%)
5. Teaching opportunities (41%)
6. Curriculum (28%)
7. Cost of living (23%)
8. Alumni (21%)
9. Duration (19%)
10. Size (13%)
11. Selectivity (13%)
12. Postgraduate placement (11%)
13. Student-to-faculty ratio (10%)
14. Internship opportunities (6%)
15. Other (5%)

[n = 909.]

SURVEY 3

Survey year: 2011
Query: "As part of your research into MFA programs, how many
current or former MFA students or faculty have you spoken
to?"
Options: 0, 1–2, 3–5, 6–10, 11 or more.
Additional instructions: respondents were limited to one answer.
Survey location: *The Creative Writing MFA Blog*
Survey web address: http://creative-writing-mfa-handbook.
blogspot.com/

Results (all):

   1.   1–2 (34%)
   2.   3–5 (27%)
   3.   0 (25%)
   4.   6–10 (7%)
   5.   11 or more (4%)

   [n = 686.]

SURVEY 4

Survey year: 2011
Query: "Have you received advice from an undergraduate creative
   writing faculty member in applying to MFA programs?"
Options: yes, no, and not yet but I plan to.
Additional instructions: Respondents were limited to one answer.
Survey location: *The Creative Writing MFA Blog*
Survey web address: http://creative-writing-mfa-handbook.
   blogspot.com/

Results (all):

   1.   Yes (59%)
   2.   No (30%)
   3.   Not yet, but I plan to (10%)

   [n = 860.]

SURVEY 5

Survey year: 2011
Query: "On a scale of '1' to '10', how important are (or were)
   print-published national creative writing MFA rankings to your
   decision regarding where to apply for your MFA? ('1' is 'entirely
   irrelevant', '10' is 'singularly essential')."
Additional instructions: respondents were limited to one answer.

Survey location: *The Creative Writing MFA Blog*
Survey web address: http://creative-writing-mfa-handbook.
blogspot.com/
Interface application: sponsored by Google

Results (all):

1. 8 (17%)
2. 7 (15%)
3. 1 (12%)
4. 5 (10%)
5. 6 (9%)
6. 9 (9%)
7. 3 (8%)
8. 4 (6%)
9. 10 (6%)
10. 2 (3%)

[n = 519.]

Results (grouped by positive [6–10], neutral [5] and negative [1–4] scores):

1. Positive (58.9%)
2. Negative (31.1%)
3. Neutral (10%)

[n = 519.]

SURVEY 6

Survey year: 2011
Query: "What are the top ten things that turn you off to, and/ or lead you not to apply to, a particular creative writing MFA program?"
Options: a heavy teaching load, high application fee, high GRE minimums, impolite admissions staff, language requirements,

low national ranking, no cross-genre work, no health insurance, no opportunity to teach creative writing, not CGSR-compliant, not selective enough, poor funding, poor placement record, program too large, program too small, too long duration, too much academics, too short duration, undesirable faculty, undesirable location, and other.

Additional instructions: respondents were asked to select up to ten answers.

Survey location: *The Creative Writing MFA Blog*

Survey web address: http://creative-writing-mfa-handbook. blogspot.com/

Interface application: sponsored by Google

Results (all):

1. Poor funding (79%)
2. Undesirable location (65%)
3. Low national ranking (42%)
4. High GRE minimums (38%)
5. High application fee (33%)
6. Heavy teaching load (32%)
7. Undesirable faculty (30%)
8. Impolite admissions staff (29%)
9. No chance to teach creative writing (28%)
10. Language requirements (26%)
11. Too much academics (25%)
12. No cross-genre work (25%)
13. No health insurance (25%)
14. Program too large (25%)
15. Poor placement record (23%)
16. Too short duration (18%)
17. Not selective enough (18%)
18. Too long duration (16%)
19. Not CGSR-compliant (13%)

20. Program too small (8%)

21. Other (8%)

[n = 395.]

SURVEY 7

Survey year: 2011

Query: "What do you consider the most important factors in deciding which MFA programs to apply to?"

Options: advice from family, advice from friends, advice from other applicants, aesthetic diversity of students, alumni: publishing success, alumni: quality/aesthetics of work, alumni self-reporting, application requirements: app fee, application requirements: GRE test, career services/advising, cohort quality: selectivity, cohort quality: talent, community service opportunities, cost of living, cross-genre opportunities, curricular emphasis, curricular flexibility, curricular intensity, demographic diversity of students, editing opportunities, faculty: accessibility, faculty: quality/aesthetics of work, faculty self-reporting, faculty teaching aptitude, faculty: visiting writers, funding, graduation requirements: foreign language, internship opportunities, location, networking opportunities, other [non-listed], presence of reading series, program duration, program fellowship placement, program job placement, program size, program visit, program website, student body: program atmosphere, rankings: applicant's genre, rankings: overall, recommendations: undergraduate professors, student-to-faculty ratio, student self-reporting, teaching load, teaching opportunities, and workshop format.

Additional instructions: respondents were permitted to select multiple answers.

Survey location: *The Creative Writing MFA Blog*

Survey web address: http://creative-writing-mfa-handbook. blogspot.com/

Interface application: sponsored by Google

Results (all):

1. Funding (65%)
2. Location (53%)
3. Faculty: quality/aesthetics of work (41%)
4. Student body: program atmosphere (40%)
5. Cost of living (40%)
6. Teaching opportunities (37%)
7. Rankings: applicant's genre (34%)
8. Faculty: accessibility (34%)
9. Recommendations: undergraduate professors (33%)
10. Rankings: overall (32%)
11. Alumni: publishing success (31%)
12. Faculty: visiting writers (31%)
13. Program size (30%)
14. Networking opportunities (29%)
15. Cohort quality: talent (29%)
16. Curricular flexibility (29%)
17. Alumni: quality/aesthetics of work (28%)
18. Cross-genre opportunities (27%)
19. Editing opportunities (25%)
20. Workshop format (24%)
21. Faculty teaching aptitude (24%)
22. Program duration (24%)
23. Program job placement (24%)
24. Internship opportunities (23%)
25. Student-to-faculty ratio (23%)
26. Application requirements: GRE test (22%)
27. Cohort quality: selectivity (21%)
28. Advice from other applicants (21%)
29. Teaching load (21%)
30. Student self-reporting (20%)*

31. Program fellowship placement (19%)
32. Curricular emphasis (19%)
33. Curricular intensity (17%)
34. Alumni self-reporting (17%)*
35. Application requirements: app fee (17%)
36. Career services/advising (16%)
37. Program website (15%)
38. Presence of reading series (13%)
39. Demographic diversity of students (12%)
40. Aesthetic diversity of students (12%)
41. Faculty self-reporting (10%)*
42. Graduation requirements: foreign language (9%)
43. Advice from friends (9%)
44. Advice from family (6%)
45. Program visit (5%)
46. Community service opportunities (4%)
47. Other [non-listed] (3%)

[n = 603.]

*"Self-reporting" refers to accounts of the program provided by members of the listed group (variously, current students, program alumni, and current program faculty).

SURVEY 8

Survey year: 2011
Query: "If you are a current creative writing MFA applicant, how old will you be when you begin your program, assuming you're admitted this year?"
Options: 21–22, 23–24, 25–26, 27–28, 29–30, 31–32, 33–34, 35–36, 37–38, 39–40, older than 40.
Additional instructions: respondents were limited to one answer.

Survey location: *The Suburban Ecstasies*
Survey web address: http://www.sethabramson.blogspot.com/
Interface application: sponsored by Google

Results (all):

1. 23–24 (18%)
2. 25–26 (16%)
3. 21–22 (13%)
4. 27–28 (11%)
5. Older than 40 (10%)
6. 29–30 (8%)
7. 31–32 (6%)
8. 33–34 (5%)
9. 35–36 (4%)
10. 37–38 (3%)
11. 39–40 (2%)

[n = 1,937.]

SURVEY 9

Survey year: 2011
Query: "How old are you?"
Options: Under 21, 21–22, 23–24, 25–26, 27–28, 29–30, 31–32, 33–34, 35–36, 37–38, 39–40, older than 40.
Additional instructions: respondents were limited to one answer.
Survey location: *The Creative Writing MFA Blog*
Survey web address: http://creative-writing-mfa-handbook. blogspot.com/
Interface application: sponsored by Google

Results (Survey A: "X" or time-of-survey):

1. 23–24 (24%)
2. 25–26 (19%)
3. 21–22 (17%)
4. 27–28 (13%)
5. 29–30 (8%)
6t. 31–32 (5%)
6t. Older than 40 (5%)
8t. 33–34 (3%)
8t. 39–40 (3%)
10t. Under 21 (1%)
10t. 35–36 (1%)
12. 37–38 (0%)

[n = 75.]

Results (Survey A: "X + 1" or time-of-matriculation):

1. 25–26 (21%)
2. 23–24 (19%)
3. 27–28 (16%)
4t. 21–22 (9%)
4t. 29–30 (9%)
6t. 31–32 (8%)
6t. Older than 40 (8%)
8. 33–34 (7%)
9. 35–36 (3%)
10t. 37–38 (0%)
10t. 39–40 (0%)

[n = 75.]

Results (Surveys B and C):
[In 2006, Stanford University lecturer and novelist Tom
Kealey surveyed two dozen current creative writing MFA

students to determine their present age. He reported their average age to be 28, suggesting an average matriculant age of between 26 and 27. In 2008, an informal poll of nearly eighty commenters at *The Creative Writing MFA Blog* revealed an average age of between 25 and 26 for full-residency applicants and 35 and 36 for low-residency applicants. These figures translate, respectively, to "26–27" and "36–37" for matriculants.]

SURVEY 10

Survey year: 2012
Query: "What is your primary genre?"
Options: fiction, poetry.
Survey location: Facebook (MFA Draft 2012 Group)
Survey web address: http://www.facebook.com/
Interface application: sponsored by Facebook

Results (all):

1. Fiction (70%)
2. Poetry (30%)

[n = 234.]

SURVEY 11

Survey year: 2011
Query: "What is your primary genre?"
Options: fiction, poetry.
Survey location: *The Creative Writing MFA Blog*
Survey web address: http://creative-writing-mfa-handbook.
   blogspot.com/
Interface application: sponsored by Google

Results (All):

1. Fiction (63%)
2. Poetry (37%)

[n = 640.]

SURVEY 12

Survey year: 2011
Query: "What is your primary genre?"
Options: fiction, nonfiction, poetry, other.
Survey location: *The Creative Writing MFA Blog*
Survey web address: http://creative-writing-mfa-handbook.
   blogspot.com/
Interface application: sponsored by Google

Results (all):

1. Fiction (53%)
2. Poetry (28%)
3. Nonfiction (15%)
4. Other (2%)

[n = 701.]

Survey year: 2011
Query: "What is your primary genre?"
Options: fiction, poetry.
Survey location: *The Creative Writing MFA Blog*
Survey web address: http://creative-writing-mfa-handbook.
   blogspot.com/
Interface application: sponsored by Google

Results (Survey 12: poetry and fiction respondents only):

1. Fiction (65%)
2. Poetry (35%)

[n = 578.]

SURVEY 13

Survey year: 2008 to 2011
Query: "What is your primary genre?"
Options: fiction, poetry.
Survey location: *The Creative Writing MFA Blog**
Survey web address: http://creative-writing-mfa-handbook.
   blogspot.com/
Interface application: sponsored by Google

   Results (all):

   1. Fiction (70%)

   2. Poetry (30%)

   [n = 12,368.]

*Survey 13 compiles all available program-supplied hard data archived on
The Creative Writing MFA Handbook website between 2008 and 2011
(fiction and poetry applicants).

SURVEY 14

Survey year: 2010
Query: "Why do you want to get a creative writing graduate
   degree?"
Options: avoid work, community, credential, employability, mentor-
   ing, networking, time to write, validation, none of the above.
Additional instructions: respondents were permitted to select
   multiple answers.
Survey location: *The Creative Writing MFA Blog*
Survey web address: http://creative-writing-mfa-handbook.
   blogspot.com/
Interface application: sponsored by Google

   Results (Top 3 Responses Only):

   1. Time to write (55%)

   2. Employability (43%)

   3. Mentoring (36%)

   [n = 253.]

SURVEY 15

Survey year: 2011

Query: From *Poets & Writers*: "We asked directors, coordinators, and professors of full- and low-residency MFA programs to offer some advice for prospective students trying to decide which programs are right for them. Here's what they said."

Survey location: *Poets & Writers* (September/October 2011, pp. 85–107).

Description: In 2011, faculty at over a quarter of the world's (then) 162 full-residency MFA programs and 51 low-residency programs were interviewed by *Poets & Writers* to determine which program features faculty members felt should be most important in applicants' assessments of graduate creative writing programs. The results of this survey, outlined at the end of this description, suggest a synchronicity between many of the priorities reported by applicants in a similar survey. For instance, funding is the top priority among both survey groups, and location, the quality of faculty members' published work, the availability of teaching opportunities, program atmospherics, faculty accessibility, and curricular flexibility also are among the first fifteen priorities for both applicants and faculty. More broadly, there is a 60 percent correlation between applicants' and faculty members' top twenty priorities.

Notably, neither applicants (#21) nor faculty (#11) rate "teaching aptitude" high on their list of priorities in assessing creative writing MFA programs. While the reason for this comparatively low valuation is unknown, one possible reason is that few graduate creative writing programs release contact information for current students to prospective applicants, so applicants often do not have access to current-student self-reporting regarding their faculty members' teaching aptitude.

The differences between the responses offered by the two groups—MFA applicants and MFA faculty—are also substantial, however. For instance, the faculty cohort surveyed by *Poets & Writers* included "faculty self-reporting" among their first fifteen priorities in assessing a graduate creative writing program, while only 10 percent of applicants claim to use this sort of data. This may in part be explained by the fact that few MFA programs are known to offer prospective students contact information for full-time faculty prior to admission. Another area of divergence between applicant and faculty values is that faculty members indicate a strong preference that admitted students visit programs before matriculating; meanwhile, applicants generally place "program visit" much lower on their own list of priorities. Nationally, only a handful of MFA programs provide admitted students with the funds to make a program visit—a possible explanation for this statistical disparity in the two surveys. Finally, while only 12 percent of current MFA faculty members explicitly advise applicants against relying on published "rankings" of programs, applicants are even more circumspect than this, with 40 percent expressing a neutral or negative attitude toward such assessments. Oddly, while only 2 percent of MFA faculty members explicitly urge applicants to get advice from undergraduate creative writing faculty members, 69 percent of applicants nevertheless avail themselves of this opportunity.

The survey, structured as a qualitative study seeking narratives from current MFA faculty members as to how MFA applicants should select a program, has been reduced here to its quantitative form by itemizing how frequently the MFA faculty members surveyed cited individual program elements as important. While there was substantial overlap between the program features mentioned by both MFA faculty members and MFA applicants in their respective surveys, three considerations mentioned by MFA applicants were mentioned by *none* of the 42 MFA faculty members surveyed by *Poets & Writers*: the cost of a program's application (*Poets & Writers* studies published between 2009 and 2013 reveal that the cost of applying to a single program can range from a low of "free" to a high of $150); the ranking of a program within an applicant's genre; and recommendations provided to an applicant by other current applicants.

Results (all):

1. Funding (71%)
2. Faculty: quality/aesthetics of work (69%)
3. Student self-reporting (60%)*

4. Student body: program atmosphere (50%)
5. Faculty: accessibility (41%)
6. Teaching opportunities (38%)
7. Location (36%)
8. Editing opportunities (31%)
9. Workshop format (29%)**
10. Program visit (26%)
11. Faculty: teaching aptitude (24%)
    Curricular flexibility (24%)
13. Alumni: publishing success (19%)
    Faculty self-reporting (19%)*
15. Reading series (19%)
16. Curricular intensity (17%)***
    Program size (17%)
18. Alumni self-reporting (12%)*
19. Cost of living (10%)
    Internship opportunities (10%)
    Program duration (10%)
22. Curricular emphasis (7%)
    Faculty: visiting writers (7%)
    Program website (7%)
    Cohort quality (7%)
    Cohort quality (7%)
    Student-to-faculty ratio (7%)
27. Career services (5%)
    Cross-genre opportunities (5%)
    Student body: aesthetic diversity (5%)
    Student body: demographic diversity (5%)
    Teaching load (5%)
32. Alumni: quality/aesthetics of work (2%)
    Applicant self-reporting (2%)*****
    Community service opportunities (2%)

Networking opportunities (2%)

Program emphasis (2%)****

Recommendations: college faculty (2%)

Thesis protection (2%)^

[n = 42.]

*"Self-reporting" refers to accounts of the program provided by members of the listed group (variously, current students, alumni of the program, and current members of the program faculty).

**Includes workshop size, tone, feedback type, and philosophy (e.g., a focus on publishability versus innovation or vice versa).

***Number, type, and academic challenge of required courses.

****Sample themes advertised by individual programs include international writing, writing on the environment, and writing for children.

*****Refers to an applicant's self-assessment as to whether she has the necessary motivation to complete an MFA, whether she is at the right age and in the right circumstances to benefit from an MFA, and whether she is willing to attend and interested in applying to a large and diverse enough roster of MFA programs to make admission and a productive in-program experience likely.

^Whether a program embargoes theses or makes them freely available online.

CHAPTER SIXTEEN

Popularity Rankings

A Brief Note on the Rankings

Education rankings can be extraordinarily helpful, but they're also easily misused and therefore, in their way, dangerous. The most common misuse of an education ranking is to believe that it measures something it does not. So I hope it's clear that while the rankings that follow are exactly what they claim to be, they are not more than that. They are not an attempt to rank graduate creative writing programs by "overall program quality," as that phrase doesn't finally mean anything and couldn't be measured quantitatively if it did. You, as a prospective graduate student in creative writing, and me, as a former one, both know that every aspiring poet and writer is looking for something different out of a graduate degree in their genre of choice. So anyone who tells you they know for certain which program is the right one for you, or that one program is certifiably better for you than another, is trying to sell you something you shouldn't seek to buy. Even if you told me your hundred most important priorities in applying to a full- or low-residency MFA or PhD program in creative writing, the most I could do is say that a particular slate of programs is slightly more *likely* to meet your needs. But until you show up on campus and start meeting people, strolling about town, and taking classes, neither you nor I would know if I'd been right.

What the rankings that follow do establish, rather well if still unscientifically, is how popular individual programs are among *applicants*, compared to one another, at a given moment in time.

I've tried to enhance the utility of the rankings by restricting the survey site to the nation's largest online creative writing applicant community—a place known for near-obsessive data-gathering, data-sharing, and daily data analysis. The applicants in the annual applicant communities in which these surveys were taken are, beyond any doubt, the best-researched creative writing applicants in America. Their institutional knowledge of the nation's slate of creative writing program options outstrips what we could get from any one creative writing professor or, for that matter, an MFA alumnus who never joined such a community before applying to programs.

So right now you might be asking yourself, "Why should I care which full- and low-residency fiction, poetry, and nonfiction graduate programs are most popular with the nation's hardest-researching applicants?" The first reason is perhaps the most obvious one: because it gives you a general sense of how competitive the admissions process at a given program is likely to be. Given that acceptance rates change from year to year, are not available for every program, and are "yield-exclusive" even when we find them, long-term studies of individual programs' popularity among applicants are absolutely critical. For instance, the hard data compiled for the first chart in this chapter tells us that, over a ten-year period, more than 51 percent of the full-residency poetry and fiction MFA applicants in each admissions cycle applied to the Iowa Writers' Workshop. During the same period, less than 1 percent of each cycle's applicants applied to the graduate creative writing program at Northwestern University. Does that suggest some problem with the program at Northwestern? Not at all—it simply means that the program at the University of Iowa is on everyone's radar, while the program at Northwestern (which just went to "full funding") is not. So if you look into the latter program and it's perfect for you, the chart below turns out to be extraordinarily useful. While you ought not use the chart to make fine distinctions—the difference in popularity between a program ranked #63 in a popularity survey and one ranked #72 is quite small—because a good application list balances admission odds against much else, the bigger distinctions these charts allow you to make are invaluable.

A second reason to care about these charts is that while we can't really develop objective measures to determine how "good" a program is, we *can* triangulate among the available data to get a general sense of how certain people would answer that question. That's not the same thing as saying we have an objective measure of quality—we don't—but rather that applicants' particularly strong willingness to attend certain programs does tell us a few things worth knowing.

To contextualize all of this properly, we have to go back to the mid-1990s, when *U.S. News & World Report* (USNWR) ranked graduate creative writing programs for the first and only time (an unedited republication of its mid-1990s survey notwithstanding). What USNWR did was ask the nation's creative writing professors to rank every program on a scale of 1 to 5; it then totaled up these scores, averaged them, and used *that* as its only measure of a program's quality. It collected no admissions data, student-faculty ratios, or information on postgraduate outcomes; it didn't even glance at funding packages, program locations, or key program features like program size, duration, curriculum, and application prerequisites. Its theory, instead, was a simple one: if we can ask recruiters for law firms to rank the "pedigree" of individual law schools, why can't we ask a poet at University of San Francisco's MFA program to gauge the quality of fiction workshops at the creative writing MA program at Kansas State? Perhaps you see the problem: while USNWR was wise to seek out unbiased survey respondents for its law school surveys—we can all agree you'd not expect unbiased responses from the students at a given law school if they knew negative responses could diminish the value of their degree—there really is no analogy between corporate recruiters and working artists. It's not any creative writing professor's job to *care* how strong the workshops are at another institution, only to make sure their own are the best they can be. So asking a memoirist at University of Utah to rank "on a scale of 1 to 5" the young-adult novel workshops at Hollins University in Virginia is really a rather silly thing to do.

The only unbiased class of persons in the field of creative writing whose task it is to intelligently compare what different programs have to offer is the applicants to those programs. Just as a corporate recruiter asked to judge various law schools may have more knowledge about one program than another, and have intimate knowledge only of the program they themselves attended—which of course they're not allowed to rank, anyway—you as an applicant will naturally know more about some programs than others, and would never be asked to assess a program you'd actually attended. What you have access to, however, much like a corporate recruiter, is a community of other persons with similar interests who are themselves trying to adjudicate between programs. Spend enough time in the MFA applicant community, in other words, and you learn an enormous amount about a very large number of programs in a very short period of time. And then, from the outside looking in, you assess which programs appear most appealing to you. You're not making a final determination of the "quality" of each program—as how could you—but merely sizing up everything that can be known about a number of programs by an interested and unbiased observer.

Consider an analogy: you're trying to decide which of several hundred restaurants to eat at for dinner. You're not going to ask the advice of the chefs at those establishments, as they know that their honest answer (if negative) could cause the business they're so invested in to tank. And let's say that former diners at these establishments likewise can't be asked because they too may be negatively affected by giving a negative response—in much the same way MFA alumni won't denigrate their programs if they know a bad report of their alma mater will cause it to sink in a published ranking, thereby diminishing the value of their degree. What do you do in that situation? Well, you investigate a large number of restaurants and find as many indicators of quality as you possibly can short of stealing food from the kitchen. Is there only one waiter for every forty diners? That'd be bad. Are there indications that "post-dining outcomes" are somehow unfavorable? Is one restaurant so expensive only a very rich person could afford it? Are the pricing, menu, setting, and order-to-table time at one restaurant indicative of an appealing experience for, and caring attitude toward, each evening's diners that seems to be lacking at other restaurants? Is the restaurant going to be crowded, and are you going to be able to eat the sort of cuisine you already know you like? And so on. With enough research, you can make an incredibly informed decision about which restaurant you're most likely to enjoy. And if you participate in the right sort of online community, too, you might, on top of everything else, have in-person access to former diners (their potential biases notwithstanding) and to other restaurant investigators who themselves have talked to former diners you'll never meet.

USNWR realized that their ranking would never take into account even a fraction of the factors a book like this one discusses and catalogues, so it closed up its creative writing rankings shop within months of opening it. Another, more bizarre effort by *The Atlantic* in the mid-2000s—a single journalist visiting about 10 percent of the nation's programs and then issuing nonexhaustive, subjective lists of some of the better ones nationally—met a similar fate. Yet what the USNWR and *The Atlantic* rankings had in common was this: the programs themselves had little problem with them. The reason? The USNWR ranking asked the programs for their opinions, thereby appealing to their vanity, while *The Atlantic* was so careful about making its lists nonexhaustive that it offended precisely no one. Indeed, it was hardly making any judgments at all, certain programs' misleading use of the resulting 2007 article in *The Atlantic* notwithstanding.

By comparison, the majority of graduate creative writing programs categorically object to either hard-data collection about their program features or any surveying of their potential students. In fact, the programs so object to this sort of data being collected that it's part of the founding charter of their trade union (the Association of Writers & Writing Programs) that AWP will never collect data from programs in a way that can be traced to any individual program. Instead, we have an annual AWP "report" that tells you a bit about the *field* of creative writing but nothing about any individual program. The only program-specific reporting the programs permit, these days, is an annual compilation of each program's promotional materials in *Poets & Writers*. That's right— the only materials the programs are okay with you seeing are the ones they've compiled in the manner of a hard sell. The problem, as you might anticipate, is that a lot of the data the programs end up providing isn't vetted for accuracy, currency, or comprehensiveness. This guide attempts to solve those problems and give you hard-won data that the programs do not willingly release in any systematized way. By giving applicants a voice in that data, we help ensure that *applicants'* most important considerations—as embodied in their decisions about where to apply—are part of the assessment regime.

Indeed, that's what each of the popularity surveys in this chapter finally is: a summation of the values, interests, and calculations of individual poets and writers making one of the most important decisions of their lives. We're proud to feature *your* values—not the opinions or promotional materials of institutional actors—at the heart of our data here.

Full-Residency Fiction and Poetry MFA Programs

The data compiled for this guide suggest that for every eleven graduate-school applicants in the three "major" genres of creative writing, nine are applying in either fiction or poetry. For that reason, our first charts look at medium-term and long-term application trends in first the two genres together, and then each separately. While you may be tempted to focus exclusively on the ranking in your preferred genre, remember that the overall impression of a school held by thousands of well-researched applicants in Year X becomes, in time, the impression an entire generation of working poets and novelists has about a program in Year X+10. So these first charts, while they contain no break-outs by genre, tell us a great deal about how competitive individual programs are in their overall admissions and, as importantly, how a very large number of people who will soon be your professional peers think about each program. For many of you, this latter assessment cannot, should not, and will not matter, as your focus is first and foremost on nothing more than your own creative efforts. That's probably for the best. But for those of you looking to turn your degree into a job-application credential somewhere down the line, or who believe that more selective programs may have curricular and peer-study benefits that can't be easily quantified, these charts can help.

Full-residency Fiction and Poetry MFA Programs: Two-Genre Ten-Year Survey (2008 to 2017 Inclusive)*

(ranked by number of appearances on applicants' application lists)

Top 40

1. University of Iowa [Iowa Writers' Workshop]
2. University of Michigan

3. University of Wisconsin at Madison
4t. Brown University
4t. University of Texas at Austin [Michener Center]
6. Syracuse University
7. University of Virginia
8. Cornell University
9. Vanderbilt University
10. Washington University at St. Louis
11. University of Minnesota
12. New York University
13. University of Massachusetts at Amherst
14. University of Oregon
15. Indiana University
16. University of California at Irvine
17. University of Florida
18. University of Alabama at Tuscaloosa
19. Johns Hopkins University
20. Louisiana State University
21. University of Montana
22. Brooklyn College [City University of New York, or CUNY]
23. University of Houston
24. Arizona State University
25. Ohio State University
26. Virginia Tech
27t. Hunter College [CUNY]
27t. University of Mississippi
29. University of Illinois at Urbana–Champaign
30. Purdue University
31. University of Arizona
32. University of Notre Dame
33. Columbia University
34. University of North Carolina at Greensboro
35. University of Wyoming
36. McNeese State University
37. Oregon State University
38t. Southern Illinois University at Carbondale
38t. University of Colorado at Boulder
40. Boston University

Second Tier

41t. Colorado State University
41t. The New School
43. University of Texas at Austin [New Writers Project]
44. University of Arkansas at Fayetteville
45. University of North Carolina at Wilmington
46. University of Nevada at Las Vegas^
47. Hollins University
48. Bowling Green State University
49. University of Washington at Seattle
50. Virginia Commonwealth University
51. Sarah Lawrence College
52. Boise State University
53. University of California at San Diego^
54t. Florida State University
54t. University of South Carolina
56. George Mason University
57. Texas State University
58. University of California at Riverside
59. Rutgers University at Newark^
60. North Carolina State University
61. University of Miami (FL)
62. University of Maryland^
63. University of New Hampshire
64. West Virginia University^
65t. Portland State University
65t. San Francisco State University
67. Columbia College Chicago
68. Georgia College
69. Emerson College
70. San Diego State University
71. University of San Francisco
72. American University
73. Western Michigan University
74. University of Idaho
75t. University of Kansas^
75t. University of New Orleans^
75t. University of Pittsburgh^
78. University of Memphis

79. Iowa State University
80. University of New Mexico^

Third Tier

81. Eastern Washington University
82. Old Dominion University
83. University of Massachusetts at Boston^
84t. New Mexico State University
84t. Wichita State University
86. Minnesota State University at Mankato
87. Mills College
88. California Institute of the Arts [CalArts]
89. Rutgers University at Camden^
90. School of the Art Institute of Chicago
91t. Northern Michigan University^
91t. University of Alaska at Fairbanks
91t. University of Central Florida^
94. University of British Columbia at Vancouver (CAN)
95. California College of the Arts [CCA]
96. Saint Mary's College (CA)
97. City College of New York [CCNY]
98t. Queens College [CUNY]
98t. Temple University
100. Chatham University
101. Florida Atlantic University
102. Florida International University
103. Northeast Ohio Master of Fine Arts [NEOMFA]
104t. Georgia State University
104t. Northwestern University
104t. San Jose State University
107t. California State University at Long Beach [Long Beach State]
107t. Stony Brook Southampton [State University of New York, or SUNY]
107t. University of South Florida^
110. Oklahoma State University
111. Otis College of Art and Design
112t. University of Guelph (CAN)
112t. University of Missouri at St. Louis

112t. University of Utah
115. University of Missouri at Kansas City
116. Roosevelt University
117. Naropa University
118t. California State University at Fresno [Fresno State]
118t. University of Baltimore
118t. University of Victoria (CAN)

Fourth Tier

121t. Adelphi University
121t. Chapman University
121t. Pratt Institute
121t. Southern Connecticut State University
125t. Hamline University
125t. Kingston University (UK)
125t. Miami University (OH)^
125t. University of Central Arkansas
125t. Western Washington University^
130t. Butler University
130t. University of Tennessee at Knoxville^
132. Northern Arizona University
133t. University of Kentucky^
133t. University of Texas at El Paso
135t. Long Island University at Brooklyn
135t. University of Washington at Bothell
137. Chicago State University
138t. College of Charleston
138t. Rosemont College
140t. University of Glasgow (UK)
140t. Western Kentucky University^
142t. Brigham Young University
142t. New York University [Spanish Creative Writing]
142t. Savannah College of Art & Design
142t. University of Iowa [Spanish Creative Writing]
142t. University of Nevada at Reno
142t. University of Saskatchewan (CAN)

142t. William Paterson University
149t. California Institute of Integral Studies
149t. Creighton University
149t. Hofstra University
149t. Lindenwood University
149t. Manhattanville College
149t. Mount Saint Mary's University (CA)
149t. Our Lady of the Lake University
149t. Sam Houston State University
149t. St. Joseph's College (NY)
149t. University of Hong Kong (CHN)
149t. University of Surrey (UK)

[n = 3,121.]

^Recent data suggest this program is rising rapidly in popularity. In some cases, this is a new program that is already popular but has not been around long enough to perform well in this survey (see Chapter 18 to determine which programs are new).

Full-residency Fiction and Poetry MFA Programs: Two-Genre Five-Year Survey (2013 to 2017 Inclusive)

(ranked by number of appearances on applicants' application lists)

Top 40

1. University of Iowa [Iowa Writers' Workshop]
2. University of Michigan
3. University of Wisconsin at Madison
4. Brown University
5. Syracuse University
6. University of Texas at Austin [Michener Center]
7. Cornell University
8. University of Virginia
9. Vanderbilt University
10. Washington University at St. Louis
11. University of Minnesota
12. New York University
13. University of Alabama at Tuscaloosa
14. University of Massachusetts at Amherst

15. University of Texas at Austin [New Writers Project]
16. University of Oregon
17t. University of California at Irvine
17t. University of Mississippi
19. Indiana University
20. University of Florida
21. Ohio State University
22. Oregon State University
23. McNeese State University
24. Louisiana State University
25. Johns Hopkins University
26. University of Arizona
27. Columbia University
28. Boston University
29. University of Wyoming
30. Virginia Tech
31. University of Notre Dame
32. University of Colorado at Boulder
33. North Carolina State University
34. University of Illinois at Urbana–Champaign
35. Purdue University
36. Brooklyn College [CUNY]
37. Boise State University
38t. Hunter College [CUNY]
38t. University of Montana
40. Bowling Green State University

Second Tier

41. University of South Carolina
42t. University of California at Riverside
42t. University of Washington at Seattle
42t. Virginia Commonwealth University
45. University of Houston
46. University of Nevada at Las Vegas^
47. University of North Carolina at Greensboro
48. Portland State University
49t. Arizona State University

49t. Rutgers University at Newark^
 51. University of North Carolina at Wilmington
 52. Southern Illinois University at Carbondale
53t. Colorado State University
53t. Florida State University
55t. The New School
55t. University of California at San Diego^
 57. Texas State University
 58. Hollins University
59t. University of Arkansas at Fayetteville
59t. University of New Orleans^
61t. Georgia College
61t. Sarah Lawrence College
 63. University of Miami (FL)
64t. Eastern Washington University
64t. West Virginia University^
66t. George Mason University
66t. Rutgers University at Camden^
66t. Wichita State University
69t. San Francisco State University
69t. University of Central Florida^
69t. University of San Francisco
69t. Western Michigan University
73t. University of Massachusetts at Boston^
73t. University of New Mexico^
75t. Iowa State University
75t. Northern Michigan University^
75t. University of Alaska at Fairbanks
75t. University of Pittsburgh^
 79. University of Kansas^
80t. Columbia College Chicago
80t. Emerson College
80t. University of Maryland^

Third Tier

 83. University of New Hampshire
 84. New Mexico State University

85t. American University
85t. Old Dominion University
85t. Saint Mary's College (CA)
85t. San Diego State University
89t. Minnesota State University at Mankato
89t. School of the Art Institute of Chicago
89t. Temple University^
89t. University of Idaho
93t. Mills College
93t. Stony Brook Southampton [SUNY]
 95. Northeast Ohio Master of Fine Arts [NEOMFA]
 96. Pratt Institute
 97. University of South Florida^
98t. California Institute of the Arts [CalArts]
98t. Florida Atlantic University
98t. Queens College [CUNY]
98t. Western Washington University^
102t. City College of New York [CCNY]
102t. Florida International University
104t. Chatham University
104t. Georgia State University
104t. Kingston University (UK)
104t. Miami University (OH)^
104t. Northern Arizona University
104t. Otis College of Art and Design
104t. University of Central Arkansas
104t. University of Tennessee at Knoxville^
 112. University of Kentucky^
113t. Chapman University
113t. University of Washington at Bothell
115t. Southern Connecticut State University
115t. University of Memphis
115t. University of Utah
118t. California College of the Arts [CCA]
118t. College of Charleston
118t. Hamline University
118t. San Jose State University
118t. University of British Columbia at Vancouver (CAN)
118t. University of Missouri at Kansas City

Fourth Tier

124t. Butler University
124t. California State University at Fresno [Fresno State]
124t. California State University at San Bernardino*
124t. Naropa University
124t. Oklahoma State University
124t. University of Guelph (CAN)
124t. University of Victoria (CAN)
124t. Western Kentucky University^
132t. Brigham Young University
132t. California State University at Long Beach [Long Beach State]
132t. New York University [Spanish Creative Writing]
132t. University of Baltimore
132t. University of Iowa [Spanish Creative Writing]
132t. University of Missouri at St. Louis
132t. University of Nevada at Reno
132t. University of Texas at El Paso
140t. Adelphi University
140t. California Institute of Integral Studies
140t. The College of Saint Rose*
140t. Creighton University
140t. Hofstra University
140t. Manhattanville College
140t. Mount Saint Mary's University (CA)
140t. Our Lady of the Lake University
140t. Roosevelt University
140t. Rosemont College
140t. Sam Houston State University
140t. St. Joseph's College (NY)
140t. University of Glasgow (UK)
140t. University of Hong Kong (CHN)
140t. University of Saskatchewan (CAN)
140t. University of Surrey (UK)
140t. William Paterson University

[n = 920.]

^Recent data suggest this program is rising rapidly in popularity. In some cases, this is a new program that is already popular but has not been around long enough to perform well in this survey (see Chapter 18 to determine which programs are new).

*Program has suspended admissions as of the 2017–2018 academic year.

Full-residency Fiction MFA Programs: Nine-Year Survey (2009 to 2017 Inclusive)

(ranked by number of appearances on applicants' application lists)

1. University of Iowa [Iowa Writers' Workshop]
2. University of Michigan
3. University of Wisconsin at Madison
4. University of Texas at Austin [Michener Center]
5. Syracuse University
6. Brown University
7. Cornell University
8. University of Virginia
9. Vanderbilt University
10. University of California at Irvine
11. University of Minnesota
12. Washington University at St. Louis
13. University of Florida
14. University of Oregon
15. New York University
16. Indiana University
17. University of Alabama at Tuscaloosa
18t. Johns Hopkins University
18t. University of Massachusetts at Amherst
20. Louisiana State University
21. University of Mississippi
22. Brooklyn College [CUNY]
23. Hunter College [CUNY]
24. Ohio State University
25. University of Montana
26. Columbia University
27t. University of Texas at Austin [New Writers Project]
27t. University of Wyoming
29. Arizona State University
30. University of Arizona
31. University of Illinois at Urbana–Champaign
32. McNeese State University
33. University of Notre Dame
34. Purdue University
35. Virginia Tech
36t. Oregon State University

36t. University of Houston
38. University of Colorado at Boulder
39. The New School
40. University of North Carolina at Greensboro

41. University of North Carolina at Wilmington
42t. Boston University
42t. Southern Illinois University at Carbondale
44. Colorado State University
45t. Bowling Green State University
45t. University of Nevada at Las Vegas^
47. University of South Carolina
48t. North Carolina State University
48t. University of Arkansas at Fayetteville
50. University of California at San Diego^
51. Boise State University
52. Texas State University
53. Hollins University
54. Florida State University
55. University of California at Riverside
56t. Rutgers University at Newark^
56t. University of Miami (FL)
58. Portland State University
59. Virginia Commonwealth University
60. Sarah Lawrence College
61. University of Washington at Seattle
62. George Mason University
63. West Virginia University^
64. San Francisco State University
65. University of Kansas^
66. University of New Orleans^
67. Georgia College
68. University of New Hampshire
69. University of Maryland^
70t. University of Idaho
70t. University of Memphis
70t. University of San Francisco
70t. Western Michigan University
74. Iowa State University
75. Emerson College
76. University of New Mexico^

77. Eastern Washington University
78. Wichita State University
79. American University
80. Rutgers University at Camden^

81. University of Central Florida^
82t. San Diego State University
82t. University of Massachusetts at Boston^
84. Northern Michigan University^
85t. California Institute of the Arts [CalArts]
85t. Old Dominion University
87t. Columbia College Chicago
87t. New Mexico State University
89. University of Pittsburgh^
90t. City College of New York [CCNY]
90t. School of the Art Institute of Chicago
92. Mills College
93t. California College of the Arts [CCA]
93t. Minnesota State University at Mankato
95t. Temple University^
95t. University of Alaska at Fairbanks
97. Queens College [CUNY]
98. Northeast Ohio Master of Fine Arts [NEOMFA]
99. University of British Columbia at Vancouver (CAN)
100. Saint Mary's College (CA)
101t. California State University at Long Beach [Long Beach State]
101t. University of South Florida^
103t. Chatham University
103t. Florida Atlantic University
103t. San Jose State University
103t. Stony Brook Southampton [SUNY]
107t. Florida International University
107t. Georgia State University
109. Oklahoma State University
110. University of Missouri at Kansas City
111t. Northwestern University
111t. Otis College of Art and Design
111t. University of Guelph (CAN)
111t. University of Utah
115t. California State University at San Bernardino*
115t. University of Missouri at St. Louis

115t. Kingston University (UK)
118. Southern Connecticut State University
119t. Adelphi University
119t. Chapman University
119t. Northern Arizona University

122t. University of Kentucky^
122t. University of Tennessee at Knoxville^
122t. University of Victoria (CAN)
125t. California State University at Fresno [Fresno State]
125t. Hamline University
125t. Miami University (OH)^
125t. Naropa University
129t. Long Island University at Brooklyn
129t. University of Baltimore
129t. University of Texas at El Paso
129t. Western Washington University^
133t. Pratt Institute
133t. University of Central Arkansas
135t. College of Charleston
135t. Roosevelt University
137t. Butler University
137t. Chicago State University
137t. New York University [Spanish Creative Writing]
137t. Savannah College of Art and Design
137t. University of Glasgow (UK)
137t. University of Iowa [Spanish Creative Writing]
137t. University of Nevada at Reno
137t. University of Saskatchewan (CAN)
137t. University of Washington at Bothell
137t. Western Kentucky University^
137t. William Paterson University
148t. Brigham Young University
148t. California Institute of Integral Studies
148t. Creighton University
148t. Hofstra University
148t. Lindenwood University
148t. Manhattanville College
148t. Mount Saint Mary's University (CA)
148t. Our Lady of the Lake University
148t. Rosemont College

148t. Sam Houston State University
148t. St. Joseph's College (NY)
148t. University of Hong Kong (CHN)
148t. University of Surrey (UK)

[n = 1,711.]

^Recent data suggest this program is rising rapidly in popularity. In some cases, this is a new program that is already popular but has not been around long enough to perform well in this survey (see Chapter 18 to determine which programs are new).

*Program has suspended admissions as of the 2017–2018 academic year.

Full-residency Fiction MFA Programs: Five-Year Survey (2013 to 2017 Inclusive)

(ranked by number of appearances on applicants' application lists)

1. University of Iowa [Iowa Writers' Workshop]
2. University of Michigan
3. University of Wisconsin at Madison
4. Syracuse University
5. University of Texas at Austin [Michener Center]
6. Vanderbilt University
7. Cornell University
8. Brown University
9. University of Virginia
10. Washington University at St. Louis
11. University of Minnesota
12. New York University
13. University of Mississippi
14. University of Texas at Austin [New Writers Project]
15. University of California at Irvine
16. University of Alabama at Tuscaloosa
17. University of Florida
18. University of Oregon
19. Indiana University
20. Ohio State University
21. McNeese State University
22t. Johns Hopkins University
22t. Louisiana State University
24. Oregon State University
25. University of Massachusetts at Amherst
26. University of Arizona

27. Columbia University
28t. University of Notre Dame
28t. North Carolina State University
30t. University of Colorado at Boulder
30t. University of Wyoming
32. Boston University
33. Hunter College [CUNY]
34. Virginia Tech
35. Brooklyn College [CUNY]
36t. Purdue University
36t. University of California at Riverside
38t. Boise State University
38t. University of Illinois at Urbana–Champaign
38t. University of Montana

41. Bowling Green State University
42. University of South Carolina
43. Portland State University
44t. University of Houston
44t. University of Nevada at Las Vegas^
44t. University of North Carolina at Wilmington
44t. Virginia Commonwealth University
48. University of North Carolina at Greensboro
49. Texas State University
50. University of New Orleans^
51t. Colorado State University
51t. The New School
53t. Florida State University
53t. University of Washington at Seattle
55. Arizona State University
56. Rutgers University at Newark^
57. Southern Illinois University at Carbondale
58. Hollins University
59t. Eastern Washington University
59t. University of California at San Diego^
59t. University of Central Florida^
59t. University of Miami (FL)
63. University of Arkansas at Fayetteville
64t. Georgia College
64t. University of Kansas^
64t. West Virginia University^

67t. Western Michigan University
67t. Wichita State University
69t. Northern Michigan University^
69t. Rutgers University at Camden^
69t. Sarah Lawrence College
69t. University of New Mexico^
73t. Emerson College
73t. George Mason University
73t. Iowa State University
73t. University of Maryland^
73t. University of Massachusetts at Boston^
 78. San Francisco State University
79t. Old Dominion University
79t. University of San Francisco

81t. American University
81t. University of Alaska at Fairbanks
83t. Columbia College Chicago
83t. New Mexico State University
83t. University of Pittsburgh^
83t. University of South Florida^
87t. San Diego State University
87t. University of Idaho
89t. Florida Atlantic University
89t. Kingston University (UK)
89t. Northern Arizona University
89t. School of the Art Institute of Chicago
89t. Stony Brook Southampton [SUNY]
89t. Temple University^
89t. University of New Hampshire
96t. City College of New York [CCNY]
96t. Florida International University
96t. Georgia State University
96t. Mills College
96t. Minnesota State University at Mankato
96t. Northeast Ohio Master of Fine Arts [NEOMFA]
96t. Saint Mary's College (CA)
96t. University of Kentucky^
96t. University of Tennessee at Knoxville^
105t. Miami University (OH)^
105t. Queens College [CUNY]

107. Western Washington University^
108t. California Institute of the Arts [CalArts]
108t. Chapman University
108t. Chatham University
108t. Otis College of Art and Design
108t. Pratt Institute
108t. Southern Connecticut State University
114t. California State University at San Bernardino*
114t. College of Charleston
114t. Hamline University
114t. San Jose State University
114t. University of British Columbia at Vancouver (CAN)
114t. University of Central Arkansas
114t. University of Guelph (CAN)
114t. University of Memphis
114t. University of Missouri at Kansas City
114t. University of Utah

124t. California College of the Arts [CCA]
124t. Naropa University
124t. New York University [Spanish Creative Writing]
124t. University of Baltimore
124t. University of Iowa [Spanish Creative Writing]
124t. University of Nevada at Reno
124t. University of Texas at El Paso
124t. University of Washington at Bothell
124t. Western Kentucky University^
133t. Adelphi University
133t. Brigham Young University
133t. Butler University
133t. California Institute of Integral Studies
133t. California State University at Fresno [Fresno State]
133t. California State University at Long Beach [Long Beach State]
133t. Creighton University
133t. Hofstra University
133t. Manhattanville College
133t. Mount Saint Mary's University (CA)
133t. Our Lady of the Lake University
133t. Rosemont College
133t. Sam Houston State University
133t. St. Joseph's College (NY)

133t. University of Glasgow (UK)
133t. University of Hong Kong (CHN)
133t. University of Missouri at St. Louis
133t. University of Saskatchewan (CAN)
133t. University of Surrey (UK)
133t. University of Victoria (CAN)
133t. William Paterson University

[n = 604.]

^Recent data suggest this program is rising rapidly in popularity. In some cases, this is a new program that is already popular but has not been around long enough to perform well in this survey (see Chapter 18 to determine which programs are new).

*Program has suspended admissions as of the 2017–2018 academic year.

Full-residency Poetry MFA Programs: Nine-Year Survey (2009 to 2017 Inclusive)

(ranked by number of appearances on applicants' application lists)

1. University of Iowa [Iowa Writers' Workshop]
2. University of Michigan
3. University of Wisconsin at Madison
4. Brown University
5. Cornell University
6. University of Virginia
7. University of Massachusetts at Amherst
8. Washington University at St. Louis
9. University of Texas at Austin [Michener Center]
10. Syracuse University
11. University of Minnesota
12. Indiana University
13. Vanderbilt University
14. University of Oregon
15. University of Alabama at Tuscaloosa
16. New York University
17. University of Houston
18. Virginia Tech
19. Johns Hopkins University
20. Louisiana State University
21. Arizona State University
22. University of Illinois at Urbana–Champaign
23. University of California at Irvine
24. University of Florida

25t. Ohio State University
25t. University of Wyoming
 27. Purdue University
28t. Oregon State University
28t. University of Montana
30t. McNeese State University
30t. University of Colorado at Boulder
 32. Southern Illinois University at Carbondale
 33. University of Arkansas at Fayetteville
 34. University of North Carolina at Greensboro
 35. Virginia Commonwealth University
36t. University of Arizona
36t. University of California at San Diego^
38t. Boise State University
38t. Boston University^
 40. University of Mississippi

 41. Brooklyn College [CUNY]
 42. University of Nevada at Las Vegas^
 43. University of Notre Dame
44t. Colorado State University
44t. Hollins University
 46. Bowling Green State University
47t. University of South Carolina
47t. University of Texas at Austin [New Writers Project]
47t. University of Washington at Seattle
 50. Hunter College [CUNY]
 51. Columbia College Chicago
 52. Sarah Lawrence College
 53. George Mason University
 54. Florida State University
 55. Columbia University
 56. The New School
57t. San Diego State University
57t. University of Maryland^
 59. West Virginia University
 60. North Carolina State University
61t. University of New Hampshire
61t. University of North Carolina at Wilmington
 63. University of Pittsburgh^
 64. Rutgers University at Newark^

65t. Georgia College
65t. University of Miami (FL)^
67t. Old Dominion University
67t. Texas State University
67t. San Francisco State University
70. American University
71t. Emerson College
71t. University of California at Riverside^
71t. Western Michigan University
74t. Minnesota State University at Mankato
74t. Portland State University
76t. Iowa State University
76t. Wichita State University
78. Mills College
79t. New Mexico State University^
79t. University of Massachusetts at Boston^
79t. University of San Francisco

82t. Florida Atlantic University^
82t. Saint Mary's College (CA)
84t. University of Alaska at Fairbanks^
84t. University of Kansas^
84t. University of New Orleans^
87t. Eastern Washington University
87t. School of the Art Institute of Chicago
87t. University of Idaho
90t. California Institute of the Arts [CalArts]
90t. Temple University^
92t. Rutgers University at Camden^
92t. University of Memphis
92t. University of New Mexico^
95t. California College of the Arts [CCA]
95t. University of British Columbia at Vancouver (CAN)
97. Northern Michigan University
98t. Georgia State University
98t. University of Central Florida^
100t. Chatham University
100t. Florida International University
100t. Pratt Institute
100t. Stony Brook Southampton [SUNY]

104t. Northeast Ohio Master of Fine Arts [NEOMFA]
104t. Oklahoma State University
104t. Roosevelt University
107t. Butler University
107t. Queens College [CUNY]
107t. University of Central Arkansas
107t. University of Victoria (CAN)
111t. California State University at Fresno [Fresno State]
111t. Naropa University
111t. Otis College of Art and Design
111t. San Jose State University
111t. Western Washington University^
116t. California State University at San Bernardino*
116t. Miami University (OH)^
116t. University of Missouri at St. Louis
116t. Northwestern University
120t. University of Utah
120t. University of Washington at Bothell

122t. Chicago State University
122t. City College of New York [CCNY]
122t. University of Guelph (CAN)
122t. University of Missouri at Kansas City
122t. University of South Florida^
127t. Chapman University
127t. Hamline University
127t. Rosemont College
127t. Southern Connecticut State University
127t. University of Baltimore
127t. University of Tennessee at Knoxville^
133t. Brigham Young University
133t. California State University at Long Beach [Long Beach State]
133t. College of Charleston^
133t. The College of Saint Rose*
133t. University of Glasgow (UK)
133t. Western Kentucky University^

[n = 902.]

^Recent data suggest this program is rising rapidly in popularity. In some cases, this is a new program that is already popular but has not been around long enough to perform well in this survey (see Chapter 18 to determine which programs are new).

*Program not accepting applications as of the 2017–2018 academic year.

Full-residency Poetry MFA Programs: Five-Year Survey (2013 to 2017 Inclusive)

(ranked by number of appearances on applicants' application lists)

1. University of Michigan
2. University of Iowa [Iowa Writers' Workshop]
3. University of Wisconsin at Madison
4. Brown University
5. University of Virginia
6. University of Massachusetts at Amherst
7. Cornell University
8. Washington University at St. Louis
9. University of Texas at Austin [Michener Center]
10. Syracuse University
11t. University of Minnesota
11t. Vanderbilt University
13. New York University
14. University of Alabama at Tuscaloosa
15. University of Oregon
16. Indiana University
17. Oregon State University
18. Ohio State University
19. University of Texas at Austin [New Writers Project]
20. University of Arizona
21t. McNeese State University
21t. University of California at Irvine
21t. University of Florida
21t. Virginia Tech
25t. Boston University^
25t. Louisiana State University
27t. University of Mississippi
27t. University of Washington at Seattle
27t. University of Wyoming
30t. Johns Hopkins University
30t. University of Illinois at Urbana–Champaign
32t. Columbia University
32t. Purdue University
32t. University of Colorado at Boulder
35. Virginia Commonwealth University
36t. Boise State University

36t. University of Notre Dame
38t. Bowling Green State University
38t. Brooklyn College [CUNY]
38t. University of Houston
38t. University of South Carolina
42t. Rutgers University at Newark^
42t. University of California at San Diego^
42t. University of Montana
45t. Southern Illinois University at Carbondale
45t. University of Nevada at Las Vegas^
 47. Arizona State University
 48. University of North Carolina at Greensboro
49t. Hunter College [CUNY]
49t. North Carolina State University
49t. Sarah Lawrence College
49t. University of Arkansas at Fayetteville

53t. Colorado State University
53t. Hollins University
53t. University of California at Riverside^
53t. University of San Francisco
57t. Florida State University
57t. Georgia College
57t. University of Pittsburgh^
60t. George Mason University
60t. The New School
60t. Portland State University
60t. San Francisco State University
60t. University of Alaska at Fairbanks^
65t. Columbia College Chicago
65t. University of New Hampshire
65t. University of North Carolina at Wilmington
68t. Rutgers University at Camden^
68t. Saint Mary's College (CA)
68t. University of Massachusetts at Boston
71t. Minnesota State University at Mankato
71t. University of Miami (FL)^
71t. Wichita State University
74t. Iowa State University
74t. New Mexico State University
74t. Pratt Institute

74t. San Diego State University
74t. School of the Art Institute of Chicago
74t. Temple University
74t. Texas State University
74t. University of New Mexico^
74t. West Virginia University
74t. Western Michigan University
84t. Mills College
84t. University of Idaho
86t. American University
86t. California Institute of the Arts [CalArts]
86t. Emerson College
86t. Northeast Ohio Master of Fine Arts [NEOMFA]
86t. Northern Michigan University
86t. Stony Brook Southampton [SUNY]
86t. University of Maryland^
93t. Eastern Washington University
93t. Old Dominion University
93t. Western Washington University^
93t. University of Central Arkansas
93t. University of New Orleans^
98t. Chatham University
98t. Otis College of Art and Design
98t. Queens College [CUNY]
98t. University of Washington at Bothell

102t. Oklahoma State University
102t. University of Central Florida^
104t. Butler University
104t. California College of the Arts [CCA]
104t. California State University at Fresno [Fresno State]
104t. Chapman University
104t. City College of New York [CCNY]
104t. Florida Atlantic University^
104t. Florida International University
104t. Miami University (OH)^
104t. University of Kansas^
104t. University of Memphis
104t. University of Utah
104t. University of Victoria (CAN)
116t. Brigham Young University

116t. California State University at Long Beach [Long Beach State]
116t. College of Charleston^
116t. The College of Saint Rose*
116t. Georgia State University
116t. Hamline University
116t. Naropa University
116t. Roosevelt University
116t. San Jose State University
116t. Southern Connecticut State University
116t. University of British Columbia at Vancouver (CAN)
116t. University of Missouri at Kansas City
116t. University of Missouri at St. Louis
116t. University of South Florida^
116t. University of Tennessee at Knoxville^
116t. Western Kentucky University^

[n = 316.]

^Recent data suggest this program is rising rapidly in popularity. In some cases, this is a new program that is already popular but has not been around long enough to perform well in this survey (see Chapter 18 to determine which programs are new).
*Program not accepting applications.

Full-Residency Nonfiction MFA Programs

Well over half of terminal-degree graduate creative writing programs offer a nonfiction track. Despite this, it's only recently that nonfiction tracks have become popular—within the last fifteen years or so—so the number of nonfiction applicants nationally is still relatively low. Longstanding conventional wisdom in the creative writing applicant community, bolstered by many years of data on program applicant pools, is that for every six fiction applicants there are three poetry applicants and two nonfiction applicants. So if you're a writer applying to MFA programs and your genre is nonfiction, you and your peers in the genre make up about a quarter of the prose-applying population within the applicant community. This may help to explain why the following survey took a decade to compile; with so few nonfiction applicants, data on applicants' program preferences can be difficult to find.

One consequence of there being far fewer nonfiction programs than fiction or poetry programs, and a commensurately smaller number of applicants in the genre, is that full funding is about as difficult for nonfiction applicants to find in 2018 as it was for fiction and poetry applicants in 2003. In other words, there are fully funded programs, but you do have to hunt a bit. Right now about a third of full-residency MFA programs with fiction and poetry tracks are fully funded, and these fully funded programs make up the overwhelming majority of the forty most popular fiction and poetry programs (right now 80 percent of this latter group is fully funded, with another 10 percent or so fully funded for many admitted students). By comparison, only 40 percent of the twenty-five most popular nonfiction programs are fully funded, and many of these programs only recently became popular among applicants. There are many plausible explanations for this, including that the online-researching nonfiction applicant community is smaller and less cohesive than the fiction and poetry applicant communities, and as a result the conventional wisdom that one shouldn't go into substantial debt for a nonprofessional arts degree hasn't fully made the rounds yet among the memoirists and essayists. But another possibility is that, unlike poets and much like fiction-writers, memoirists and essayists believe they may one day be able to make a living from their writing—and are therefore willing to go into a bit more student loan debt than their peers in (at a minimum) the poetry genre.

My caution to nonfiction-writers is the same as it is to novelists and poets, however: do not expect to make a living from your work, no matter how strong you think it is and no matter how certain you are that you'll be among the less than 1 percent of creative writing MFA graduates who will earn a full-time, tenure-track job teaching nonfiction at a college or university. My dearest hope for you is that all your wishes come true, and I mean that; but at this point, as an applicant to graduate school, you must take a conservative approach and seek, to the best of your ability, a full-funding offer of admission. I promise that the overwhelming majority of you will appreciate this advice down the road. And as the rest of you will, presumably, be wealthy authors and professors, you won't feel distressed about me issuing this conventional wisdom, either.

As with the other surveys in this book, what follows is not a ranking of programs by "overall program quality." Rather, this chart merely tells you which nonfiction programs have been the most popular among online-researching applicants—the sort that form data-collection and data-sharing communities online—over the last decade. Use this chart to roughly gauge how competitive a program's admissions are, the esteem in which the program is held by the most knowledgeable applicants in your genre, and (via the symbols attached to certain programs) whether the program is seen as a rising star.

Full-residency Nonfiction and Creative Nonfiction MFA Programs: Ten-Year Survey (2008 to 2017 Inclusive)*
(ranked by number of appearances on applicants' application lists)

1. University of Iowa [Nonfiction Writing Program]
2. University of Arizona
3. University of North Carolina at Wilmington
4. University of Minnesota
5. Hollins University
6. University of Wyoming^
7. Ohio State University^
8t. Hunter College [CUNY]
8t. The New School
10. University of Alabama at Tuscaloosa^
11. Oregon State University^
12. George Mason University
13. University of Montana
14. Columbia University
15t. University of New Hampshire
15t. University of New Mexico^
17. University of Notre Dame^
18. University of Pittsburgh^
19. Sarah Lawrence College
20t. Emerson College
20t. Georgia College
22. Eastern Washington University
23. Portland State University
24. University of California at Riverside^
25. University of Idaho
26t. American University
26t. University of Colorado at Boulder
28. University of San Francisco
29t. University of Houston
29t. West Virginia University^

31t. Chatham University
31t. University of Memphis
31t. University of New Orleans^
 34. University of South Carolina^
35t. Louisiana State University^
35t. Old Dominion University
35t. Rutgers University at Camden^
35t. Rutgers University at Newark^
39t. Arizona State University
39t. California College of the Arts [CCA]
39t. University of Central Florida^
42t. Columbia College Chicago
42t. Iowa State University^
42t. Minnesota State University at Mankato
45t. Florida Atlantic University
45t. Northern Michigan University^
47t. California Institute of the Arts [CalArts]
47t. Florida International University
47t. University of South Florida^
47t. Vanderbilt University^
47t. Washington University at St. Louis^

52t. Mills College
52t. Saint Mary's College (CA)
52t. University of British Columbia at Vancouver (CAN)
55t. Florida State University
55t. School of the Art Institute of Chicago
55t. Stony Brook Southampton [SUNY]^
55t. University of Alaska at Fairbanks^
59t. San Jose State University
59t. University of Kansas^
 61. California State University at Fresno [Fresno State]
62t. Hamline University
62t. Northeast Ohio Master of Fine Arts [NEOMFA]
62t. University of Baltimore
65t. Butler University
65t. Colorado State University
65t. Pratt Institute
65t. Roosevelt University
65t. San Francisco State University
70t. Boise State University

70t. Chapman University
70t. City College of New York [CCNY]
70t. Northern Arizona University
70t. Northwestern University
70t. University of Guelph (CAN)
70t. University of Utah
70t. University of Victoria (CAN)
78t. Chicago State University
78t. Hofstra University
78t. Miami University (OH)^
78t. Naropa University
78t. Otis College of Art and Design
78t. St. Joseph's College (NY)
78t. University of Central Arkansas
78t. University of Missouri at Kansas City
78t. University of Tennessee at Knoxville^
78t. University of Texas at El Paso
78t. Vermont College of Fine Arts
78t. Western Kentucky University^
78t. Western Michigan University
78t. Western Washington University^

[n = 306.]

^Recent data suggest this program is rising rapidly in popularity. In some cases, this is a new program that is already popular but has not been around long enough to perform well in this survey (see Chapter 18 to determine which programs are new).

*During the 2008–2009, 2009–2010, and 2010–2011 admissions seasons, data were taken from the *Creative Writing MFA Handbook* website instead of the "MFA Draft" groups on Facebook. One hundred and seventy-one of the 306 applicants surveyed for this list were surveyed via this method.

Full-Residency Nonterminal MFA Programs (MA, MPW, M.St., M.Sc., MAPH and MALS)

As you've already noticed, this guidebook offers a lot of strongly worded advice. This is one of those times I'm going to go farther and suggest an absolute prescription: do not apply to a nonterminal creative writing master's degree unless you have a very, very good reason for doing so. And the number of applicants who have such a reason is vanishingly small.

Now that I've made such a strong statement, let me do my best to explain it. First, it's important to understand that the nonterminal master's degree in creative writing was developed in the 1940s as an *alternative* to the MFA the Iowa Writers' Workshop was attempting to popularize. Some of those associated with the early creative writing MA programs believed that creative writing didn't deserve its own terminal degree, and was useful only to the extent that it gave young literary artists an alternative means of preparing for doctoral study in English literature (as there were no creative writing doctoral programs back then). The problem, of course, was that doctoral programs in English literature had much the same dim view of creative writing as an academic discipline as many others in academia did and still do; even today there are many who will tell you that a master's degree in creative writing, indeed even a *terminal* master's degree in creative writing, can hurt your chances of admission to a PhD program in English literature because it casts you as an "artist" rather than a "scholar." And other than the literary studies doctoral program at the University of Wisconsin at Madison, virtually no conventional English doctorates will allow you to take more than one—and perhaps not any—creative writing workshops for credit. The wall between the discipline of creative writing and the discipline of English is still quite high, and the advent of the creative writing MA in the middle of the last century was a product of that division rather than a solution to it.

It's for this reason that the popularity of the creative writing MA has collapsed in recent years. More and more aspiring poets and writers are realizing that the creative writing MA is not an especially good preparation for an English PhD and lacks the terminality of an MFA. And the collapse of the creative writing MA has both degraded the value of that degree in professional circles and diminished the competitiveness of admissions to these programs. While a few such programs (almost all of which appear in the list that follows) are fully funded, most, being nonterminal degrees, are not. In the United States, the convention is that only terminal degrees are fully funded.

At this point in the history of creative writing, the creative writing MA remains popular among two groups of persons: (1) undergraduates who wish to remain at their current institution for a graduate degree in creative writing, and (2) postgraduates who have unsuccessfully applied to MFA programs but still wish to attend a graduate program in creative writing. As for the first group, there's not much I can say except that, in my own life, I found moving out of New England for the first time absolutely terrifying but finally immensely rewarding. So while I understand the temptation to remain at one's undergraduate institution for as long as possible, unless personal responsibilities or relationships are tethering you to a single town or city, my advice is to explore the nation the best you can—including through your choice of graduate school.

As for those who've unsuccessfully applied to creative writing MFA programs in the past, I'd say three things: (1) remember that there is no rush whatsoever to attend a graduate program in creative writing, as the median age of first-year students is 27 and the degree, being a nonprofessional degree, is not financially time-sensitive; (2) there are better ways to improve your portfolio in the hopes of reapplying to MFA programs down the line than spending tens of thousands of dollars for an entirely *separate* graduate degree; and (3) what anecdotal data we have suggest that the quality of workshops in many creative writing MA programs may not be high enough to distinguish it from an undergraduate workshop. In other words, it's not clear that MA workshops are especially good places to take a significant leap with your writing. While a fully funded MA program will give you extra time and space to work on your MFA portfolio—and if you can find such an opportunity, by all means, take it—if you're going into debt for a creative writing MA you're arguably making a financial and professional error.

Still not convinced? Then I'll offer one other piece of information: most of today's creative writing MA programs either desperately wish to, or are in the process of becoming, MFA programs. This underscores that these programs understand that they need to be offering you a terminal degree and full funding if they're going to be asking for your time and dedication. The most esteemed creative writing MA program by a fair distance—the University of California at Davis—is in fact the only creative writing MA program in the country that even registers on any of the hard-data measures you find in this book (for instance, selectivity, job placement, and fellowship placement).

One final observation I'd like to make is that these comments only apply to *American* creative writing MA programs. In the UK, the MFA degree has been almost universally rejected in favor of the MA, and so the selectivity, pedigree, and workshop quality you find at the best creative writing MA programs in the UK are commensurate with what you would expect to find at an American MFA. That said, finding a fully funded position at a British, Scottish, or Northern Irish MA borders on the impossible, so I don't know of how much value this intelligence will be.

Full-residency Nonterminal Creative Writing Master's Degrees: All-Genre Ten-Year Survey (2008 to 2017 Inclusive)*
(ranked by number of appearances on applicants' application lists)

Top 10 (United States)

    1. University of California at Davis (MA)
    2. University of Southern California (MPW)
    3. Ohio University (MA)
    4. Eastern Michigan University (MA)
    5. University of Cincinnati (MA)
  6t. Kansas State University (MA)
  6t. University of Maine at Orono (MA)
  8t. Bucknell University (MA)
  8t. DePaul University (MA)
10t. Ball State University (MA)
10t. Dartmouth College (MALS)
10t. University of Louisville (MA)
10t. University of Hawai'i at Manoa (MA)

Other US programs receiving multiple votes include Texas Tech University, University of Chicago, University of North Texas, and University of Wisconsin at Milwaukee; programs receiving a single vote include California State University at Sonoma, Carnegie Mellon University, Kennesaw State University, Mississippi State University, New York University, Northern Michigan University, Saint Louis University, San Francisco State University, University of Oklahoma, University of Rhode Island, and University of Southern Mississippi.

Top 5 (Canada)

    1. University of Toronto (MA)
    2. Concordia University (MA)
    3. University of Calgary (MA)

4t. Simon Fraser University (MA)
4t. University of New Brunswick (MA)
4t. Windsor University (MA)

Top 5 (United Kingdom)

1. University of East Anglia (MA)
2. University of Oxford (M.St.)
3t. Bath Spa University (MA)
3t. Lancaster University (MA)
3t. University of Edinburgh (M.Sc.)

Other UK programs receiving votes include University of Kent (multiple votes), University of Manchester (multiple votes), and University of Stirling (multiple votes), while one vote apiece was received by City University London, London Metropolitan University, Queen's University at Belfast, Royal Holloway at University of London, Trinity University at Dublin, University of Exeter, University of Newcastle, University of Roehampton, University of Southampton, University of Sussex, and University of Warwick.

[n = 184.]

*Includes, MA, MPW, M.St., M.Sc., MAPH, and MALS degree programs in which creative writing instruction is a primary component.

Low-Residency Creative Writing MFA Programs

It's much easier to see what makes a full-residency MFA program popular than it is a low-residency program. With full-residency programs, program size, program duration, program location, and funding are all critical measures, whereas the pedagogy at a low-residency program is oriented toward self-starting and one-on-one mentorship—and since one spends barely any time in a low-residency program's host location and can't reasonably expect much funding, one's considerations must be quite different indeed.

Certainly, a low-residency program's faculty plays an outsized role in any applicant's matriculation decision. In a low-residency program, your mentors are a much bigger part of the experience than would be the case in a full-residency program, where peers and other students daily surround you. In a sense, "pedigree" also matters more, as low-residency programs struggle to generate the same degree of gravitas as their full-residency peers, and therefore finding a low-residency MFA with high brand recognition is valuable. (If that sounds a bit cynical, consider it in different terms: such a large percentage of low-residency programs are just-founded operations at schools using this programming to raise capital that knowing your educators are connected to a time-honored curriculum and/or established pedigree is important.)

Low-residency programs are mostly identical in terms of duration—and flexibility in duration—as well as the length of the residencies. While some schools are more expensive than others, this is more a product of tuition differences than any differential in student funding. While a few programs offer hard-to-find tracks like genre or young-adult fiction, most low-residency programs are flexible enough with their criteria that writing the sort of work you want to write isn't going to be your biggest problem. A bigger concern is that you're almost certainly paying quite a bit for the degree, so you want the best teachers possible and the most valuable diploma you're able to find. Finding out the teaching abilities of individual professors can be difficult prematriculation—and as I've said throughout this guide, you can't use someone's writing ability as a proxy for quality mentorship—so it's not clear how best to make judgments about a program's pedagogy. Pedigree is rather easier to gauge, though as you can see from the list that follows many low-residency programs are at colleges and universities with a local or regional profile rather than a national one.

If I sound a bit ambivalent about providing a popularity ranking for low-residency programs, don't misunderstand me: I've been a nontraditional student at multiple graduate schools and I know the incredible value of being able to get a graduate degree without leaving your job. What concerns me is actually something quite different, and that's that the low-residency MFA market is about to change dramatically.

About a decade ago I wrote an article predicting that large public and private universities with strong brand recognition would soon begin "big-footing" the low-residency market. Now that's come to pass, with new programs being founded, in just the past decade, at

New York University, University of New Hampshire, University of
Georgia, University of California at Riverside, Miami University of
Ohio, Ithaca College, and Oregon State University. Schools within
the University of Alaska and University of Houston systems have
also initiated low-residency creative writing programs. Whither,
in that context, will less high-profile programs at (for instance)
Augsburg, Carlow, Wilkes, Converse, Ashland, Arcadia, Bloomfield,
Albertus Magnus, Cedar Crest, Pine Manor, Lindenwood, and
Seton Hill (not Seton Hall) go? If pedigree is part of what you're
paying for with a low-residency degree, how does one assess the
value of degrees from these latter institutions and others of similar
size and institutional profile?

Mind you, if you somehow discover in advance the quality
of a given low-residency faculty, and are looking for a graduate
creative writing degree not as a credential but a learning experience,
go for it. Attend any school that seems to you to meet those
requirements. But if money isn't a *major* object—as it often isn't
with low-residency programs, as students don't have to leave their
current employment—and you don't have advance knowledge of
a program faculty's mentorship skills, how do you distinguish one
low-residency fiction or poetry track from another? Certainly you
might have a sense, from the program's promotional materials, of
its "vibe," but can one really make a big life decision and a sizable
financial investment on that basis?

This is why I suspect many low-residency applicants decide
where to apply on the basis of (1) how easily they can travel to
a program's residencies, and (2) their perceptions of the quality
of the host institution. Certainly, if a program is *particularly*
expensive it'll drop off one's list, but barring that, those seem to
be the two biggest concerns. And given that, the argument that
one should wait to do a low-residency MFA program until you
can attend one that's both geographically appealing to you and at
an institution you know and respect is a compelling one. After all,
low-residency programs are growing in number at such a rate—
particularly at brand-name institutions and their affiliates—that
such a program is likely to pop up sometime in the next decade.
(Keep in mind that the average matriculation age at a low-
residency program is 37, so it would actually be unusual to seek
out such a program until one is a decade or more removed from
one's undergraduate workshops.)

Three of the programs listed in the following ranking substantially outpace all the others in name-recognition within the field of low-residency MFAs: Vermont College of Fine Arts, Warren Wilson College, and Bennington College. One could be forgiven for thinking that a large number of applicants seem to simply be applying to these three schools, and perhaps a couple others, year after year until they gain admission. And one could be forgiven for thinking that that's not, actually, such a bad application strategy. If you have some personal reason that you absolutely must do an MFA program in the next 24 months but can't leave your job, apply wherever; otherwise, thinking carefully about pedigree, logistics, and the longevity of the top low-residency programs (see "Foundation Dates" in Chapter 18) might be worth your while. And do keep tabs on the new programs forthcoming, likely with increasing regularity, at the nation's largest educational institutions.

A final note: you'll notice that the number of applicants surveyed here is rather low, and that's because low-residency applicant pools are generally very small. Meanwhile, the acceptance rates at such programs tend to be very high—with even the top programs sporting yield-exclusive acceptance rates *ten times* those of a comparably popular full-residency program. So if we'd expect a popular full-residency program to sport a yield-exclusive acceptance rate between 1 percent and 3 percent, we can expect an analogously popular low-residency program to admit between 10 percent and 30 percent of applicants before yield is taken into account. What all that leads to is (a) a much smaller data-set of applicants, as you can see here, and (b) a further reason to wait to attend a low-residency program until you're sure your writing has had to cross a high bar to gain admission. There's no sense in attending a creative writing MFA until your portfolio is really *ready* to be exposed to graduate study; you only get to do an MFA once, and you might as well do it at exactly the right time for you and your art.

Low-Residency Fiction, Poetry, and Nonfiction MFA Programs: Ten-Year Survey (2008 to 2017 Inclusive)

(ranked by number of appearances on applicants' application lists)

1. Warren Wilson College
2. Vermont College of Fine Arts

   3. Bennington College
   4. Pacific University
   5. Lesley University
   6. Antioch University at Los Angeles
   7. Queens University of Charlotte
   8. University of Southern Maine [Stonecoast]
   9. Spalding University
  10. Goddard College

  11t. Bard College
  11t. Goucher College**
  13. University of California at Riverside^
  14t. Pacific Lutheran University [Rainier]
  14t. University of Nebraska at Omaha
  16t. University of Alaska at Anchorage
  16t. University of New Orleans^
  18t. New England College
  18t. Pine Manor College
  18t. Seton Hill University

  21t. Hamline University^
  21t. Murray State University
  21t. University of British Columbia (CAN)
   24. Fairleigh Dickinson University
  25t. Hollins University
  25t. Naropa University [Main Campus]
  25t. University of Tampa^
  28t. Converse College
  28t. New York University^
  28t. Seattle Pacific University
  28t. Southern New Hampshire University^

  32t. Ashland University^
  32t. Drew University
  32t. Institute of American Indian Arts^
  32t. University of Texas at El Paso
  36t. Eastern Kentucky University
  36t. Fairfield University
  36t. Sewanee School of Letters
  36t. Wilkes University
  36t. Western Connecticut State University

41t. Carlow University
41t. Miami University (OH)^
43t. Augsburg College
43t. Cedar Crest College
43t. Chatham University
43t. Mississippi University for Women
43t. School of the Art Institute of Chicago
43t. Sierra Nevada College
43t. St. Francis College (NY)
43t. University of Houston at Victoria
43t. Whidbey Writers' Workshop****

Unranked

NR. Albertus Magnus College
NR. Antioch University at Santa Barbara
NR. Arcadia University
NR. Bloomfield College
NR. City University of Hong King (CHN)
NR. Dominican University (CA)
NR. Eastern Oregon University
NR. Full Sail University*
NR. Ithaca College
NR. Lindenwood University
NR. Naropa University [Jack Kerouac School]
NR. National University*
NR. University of New Hampshire/New Hampshire Institute of Art*****/^
NR. Oklahoma City University
NR. Oregon State University******/^
NR. Plymouth University (UK)
NR. Regis University
NR. Reinhardt University
NR. Stetson University
NR. Transart Institute
NR. University of Arkansas at Monticello*
NR. University of Georgia***
NR. University of King's College at Halifax (CAN)**
NR. West Virginia Wesleyan University
NR. Western New England University
NR. Western State College of Colorado

NR. William Paterson University

[n = 373.]

^Recent data suggest this program is rising rapidly in popularity. In some cases, this is a new program that is already popular but has not been around long enough to perform well in this survey (see Chapter 18 to determine which programs are new).

*Zero-residency program.

**Nonfiction only.

***Visual narrative only.

****Program no longer accepting applications as of the 2017–2018 academic year.

*****Program offered through the urban college of the University of New Hampshire and the New Hampshire Institute of Art, both located in Manchester, New Hampshire.

******Program offered through the Cascades campus of Oregon State University.

Creative Writing Doctoral Programs

Creative writing doctoral programs are increasingly critical pieces of the nation's creative writing infrastructure, so it's unfortunate that there's a lot of bad information going around about them. Let's set the record straight by noting that two seemingly contradictory things are happening at the same time: (1) having a creative writing PhD is quickly becoming a necessary rather than merely optional credential for securing a full-time, tenure-track teaching position in academia; and (2) there has been virtually no growth whatsoever in the number of creative writing PhD programs over the last thirty years, despite claims to the contrary. The result is that more and more MFA graduates are considering applying to these programs even as they become tougher to get into.

As we've discussed elsewhere in this guide, the creative writing MFA didn't catch on for many decades after the Iowa Writers' Workshop opened its doors in the 1930s. Some in academia believed creative writing wasn't worthy of its own terminal degree, and supported the creation of creative writing MA degrees instead; others went in the opposite direction and concluded that the *only* acceptable terminal degree for any field of study is the PhD, and therefore creative writing needed to have a number of doctoral programs as well as master's programs. This is why, of the 35 creative writing doctoral programs that follow, only ten—less than 30 percent—also offer creative writing MFA degrees. And in all but a few of these instances, insiders at the program will concede that the MFA program is overshadowed by the PhD. The reason for this is not difficult to fathom: just as MFA students tend to be a little further along with their skill development than MA students, in part because of how admissions to these programs work, PhD students selected from among the most talented MFA *graduates* in America tend to be a bit further along in their skill development than their MFA peers. This can make running a "terminal" MFA program in creative writing alongside a "terminal" PhD program in creative writing a little bit awkward.

While some creative writing MFA graduates pursue a PhD in the discipline because instead of two or three they want six or seven years studying the discipline in an institutional setting, interviews reveal that most creative writing PhD applicants are hoping to land a teaching position. Whereas about half of incoming MFA students say they hope to teach one day, and that number drops to a third by graduation, in a creative writing PhD you're likely to find that a clear majority of your classmates would seriously consider becoming a university professor. Unfortunately, per a 2010 study, creative writing PhD programs do not, as yet, have a track record of placing graduates into the nation's top fifty (magazine-ranked) college or university English departments. Rather, graduates of these programs are merely hoping to get a leg up on their peers with MFA degrees when they go on the hypercompetitive creative writing job market. And to call the market "hypercompetitive" is an understatement: only a few dozen jobs open up in each genre per year, sometimes less, and many of these jobs are at smaller regional institutions quite distant from where large literary communities have risen up.

So while those who attend a PhD program in creative writing just for the time and space to write need merely find a program that will fund them, those eyeing the academic job market have to be quite a bit more calculating. Which programs have a history of placing graduates in *any* full-time creative writing teaching jobs whatsoever? Which programs help their students hedge their bets against the possibility they can't secure a teaching position by generously funding all admittees, thereby precluding any student debt? Which programs are attached to institutions of such standing that a PhD from that institution could measurably augment any job application? (Remember that many university hiring committees have noncreative writers on them, so they'll be thinking about the institutions they're most familiar with from their own job searches.)

As you can see from the chart that follows, the small number of programs in this area and the necessity of finding a program with a strong pedigree and job-placement track record has catapulted a small number of programs well above the others in terms of applicant popularity. Of the 35 programs listed here, the top twelve most popular programs received 1,049 applications from the respondents surveyed, the next thirteen 435, and the remaining fourteen just 75. That's a pretty dramatic drop-off, but it underscores for you the highly reflexive, carefully coordinated application decisions applicants to creative writing doctoral programs are making.

As ever, if a program does not fully fund you for the entirety of your time in-program, you should seriously consider declining any offer of admission. Having gone through this process myself, I can tell you that many doctoral applicants don't even consider unfunded offers of admission to be real offers; rather, they are opportunities for you to harm your financial future for the sake of helping finance a university's English department. I recognize just how callous that sounds, but I say it here because the total cost of an unfunded doctoral program is staggering. And if that doctoral program is in a discipline that only places 1 percent of graduates in the form of employment they most covet, that sort of debt burden cannot be justified for any but the wealthy. So I hope you'll excuse my candor here—I'm hoping to paint for you a realistic picture of the costs and opportunities attached to a creative writing doctoral program.

One thing many people forget, in applying to doctoral programs in creative writing, is that you will spend somewhere between two to four times longer in such a program than you will in an MFA. That means that choosing a location you're willing to live in long-term—already a top consideration according to surveys of MFA applicants—is even more important if you're applying to a degree program beyond the MFA. The difference between living in a massive metropolitan area like Chicago (2016 population: 2.7 million), Houston (2.3 million), or Los Angeles (4 million); or a medium-size city like Denver (700,000), Milwaukee (600,000), Atlanta (500,000), or Las Vegas (650,000); or a small city like Tallahassee (200,000), Salt Lake City (200,000), or Cincinnati (300,000); or a large town like Lawrence, Kansas (95,000); or a small town like Athens, Ohio (24,000)—well, it's sizable. Some of you reading this will immediately gravitate to the idea of living in idyllic Athens, while others wouldn't find Houston acceptable if Los Angeles was in the offing. You know you better than anyone, and you must determine before applying to programs what sort of living environment you want for the next four to six years. As long as you don't mind literature courses you can probably survive the first three years of your program, but if your living environment is intolerable to you nothing else will matter.

With all that in mind, you'll note that the most popular programs listed tend to have one or more of three features: they're in a large or largish metropolitan area; they are attached to universities with a strong national profile educationally; and/ or they have a strong job-placement record. Several (for instance, Florida State University and University of Houston) benefit from having relatively popular MFA programs in creative writing, which means applicants are likely hearing about them and their benefits years before they consider applying to a PhD. Others are associated not so much with a particular type of curriculum but a particular aesthetic; experimental poets particularly admire University of Utah, for instance, and nonfiction-writers appear to have a special affinity for Ohio University. In any case, as long as you apply to a range of programs and remember that most PhD programs are as competitive in their admissions as the most selective full-residency MFA programs, you'll be fine.

Creative Writing Doctoral Programs: All-Genre Ten-Year Survey (2008 to 2017 Inclusive)

(ranked by number of appearances on applicants' application lists)

First Tier

1. University of Denver
2. University of Utah
3. University of Illinois at Chicago
4. Florida State University
5. University of Southern California
6. University of Houston
7. Ohio University

8. University of Cincinnati
9. University of Missouri at Columbia
10. University of Nebraska at Lincoln
11. University of Georgia
12t. Texas Tech University
12t. Western Michigan University

Second Tier

14. University of Wisconsin at Milwaukee
15. Georgia State University
16. University of Tennessee at Knoxville
17. State University of New York at Albany [SUNY]
18. Binghamton University
19. University of Louisiana at Lafayette
20. University of Kansas
21. University of North Texas
22. Illinois State University
23. University of Nevada at Las Vegas
24t. University of Southern Mississippi
24t. University of Wisconsin at Madison*

Third Tier

26. Oklahoma State University
27. University of Hawai'i at Manoa
28. University of North Dakota
29. University of South Dakota
30. University of Texas at Dallas
31t. Texas A&M University
31t. University of California at Santa Cruz^
33. University of Rhode Island^
34t. Goldsmiths at University of London (UK)
34t. University College Cork (IRE)
34t. University of Colorado at Boulder**/^
34t. University of Connecticut***

34t. University of Edinburgh (UK)
34t. University of New Brunswick (CAN)

Unranked

NR. Morgan State University****

[n = 346.]

^Recent data suggest this program is rising rapidly in popularity. In some cases, this is a new program that is already popular but has not been around long enough to perform well in this survey (see Chapter 18 to determine which programs are new).

*Program offers an internal minor in creative writing. Students complete a critical rather than creative dissertation, but can take up to six workshops for credit in fiction or poetry with students in the University of Wisconsin at Madison MFA program. Applicants must be admitted through the University's literary studies doctoral program. Creative portfolios may be submitted with literary studies applications.

**Program is a "PhD in Intermedia Art, Writing, and Performance."

***Creative dissertation allowed within the PhD in English program, with permission of the department. A prior creative writing MFA and/or significant creative publications are usually required.

****Internal concentration in creative writing within the English PhD.

CHAPTER SEVENTEEN

Program Rankings

Selectivity

Programs become popular among applicants for a variety of reasons: they're new, so they're getting a lot of media attention; they're old, so everyone's heard of them; they're small, so any applicant-pool spike causes their acceptance rate to plummet; they're inexpensive to apply to; they offer full funding; they're in a location many applicants want to live in, the quality of the program notwithstanding; and so on. Over the past decade we've seen substantial fluctuations in program acceptance rates from year to year, with some programs seeing rises or drops of as much as 6 percent or 7 percent from one year to the next. What I've compiled in the list that follows are the most recent publicly reported yield-exclusive acceptance rates for 100 full-residency MFA programs. While all of this data is, in the context of a graduate degree that's over eighty years old, of very recent vintage—all are taken from data-sets made available in the last 48 months—the natural cycles of the MFA-applicant community and MFA-program culture will cause some of these numbers to go up or down over time.

While the acceptance rates here are calculated to the hundredths (which is why some programs differently ranked appear to have the same acceptance rate), you should view the ranking holistically. That means that the selectivity difference between two programs ranked close to one another may, by the time you apply, be negligible or even the reverse of what you see here. But you can use this ranking to broadly assess (a) how competitive MFA admissions are, and

(b) how two or more programs appearing in dramatically different spots in this listing may compare in terms of selectivity. For while programs may routinely fluctuate 2 percent to 3 percent from what appears here, and on extremely rare occasions, as I mentioned, temporarily spike or plummet by 6 percent or 7 percent, this ranking gives a rather good indication of the selectivity "neighborhood" in which we expect to find each program. The exceptions to this are noted with a "∧" or "∨"; these symbols denote programs which, because of publicly announced funding increases or (relative-to-field) decreases, are likely to now be positioned in a higher or lower selectivity "tier" than they appear in here. Programs with acceptance rates lower than the final ranked program appearing here should be considered, relative to the rest of the graduate programs in the discipline, nonselective.

As ever, this data includes only those programs willing to make their critical admissions data public—as programs in other disciplines do. Programs that guard this data (an increasingly small number, as you can see here) do not appear in this listing. Because no programs release "yield" data as part of their promotional materials, the acceptance rates here are yield-exclusive. Want to figure out a program's yield-*inclusive* acceptance rate? A good rule of thumb is that "very selective" and "selective" programs will see between 50 percent and 100 percent of their acceptances say "yes." So if we take, merely as a hypothetical, a school like Vanderbilt University, whose MFA has an annual incoming cohort of six, a 100 percent yield means six people were offered admission and all accepted (in which case the acceptance rate that follows is also a "yield-inclusive" acceptance rate). If the program's yield were instead 50 percent, it would mean that one person declined to enroll for every person who said yes—so the school had to accept *twice* its annual incoming cohort size (twelve instead of six) to fill its class. In that case, its yield-inclusive acceptance rate would be exactly double what you see here, or 1.8 percent. On the other end of the spectrum, in a recent year the graduate creative writing program at The New School reported to *Peterson's* that it had 365 applicants and accepted 277 of them (75 percent). Because only 81 (29 percent) of the admitted students accepted the program's offer of admission and matriculated, the program's yield-exclusive acceptance rate for that particular admissions cycle would be 81 divided by 365, or 22 percent. You can see that, in this case, the yield-inclusive acceptance rate (75 percent) is well over three times as high as the program's yield-exclusive acceptance rate (22 percent). Programs that appear here in the "less selective" category are likely to have yields similar to those at The New School, so you may have to multiply the acceptance rates you see here by three or more to estimate a yield-inclusive acceptance rate. (Obviously the yield-exclusive acceptance rate we're reporting for The New School here, 37.3 percent, can't—by the basic rules of percentages—be tripled, so we must assume that in the most recent year data was available, The New School enjoyed a yield higher than the 29 percent it previously reported to *Peterson's*.)

Because single-track yield-exclusive acceptance rates are more volatile than all-track yield-exclusive acceptance rates, in a given year a program's yield in your genre of application could range well above (or below) what we might expect based on the overall selectivity of the program. Keep that in mind as you use the data shown here as a very rough sketch of the odds faced by applicants to graduate creative writing programs.

Full-Residency Fiction and Poetry MFA Programs: Very Selective

(with the most recent publicly available yield-exclusive acceptance rates in parentheses)

1. Vanderbilt University (0.9%)
2. Cornell University (1.2%)
3. Brown University (1.3%)
4. University of Wisconsin at Madison (1.4%)
5. University of Texas at Austin [Michener Center] (1.7%)
6. University of Oregon (1.7%)
7. University of California at Irvine (1.8%)
8. Syracuse University (1.9%)
9. University of Virginia (1.9%)
10. Washington University at St. Louis (2%)
11. University of Michigan (2.2%)
12. University of Florida (2.4%)
13. Johns Hopkins University (2.6%)
14. University of Minnesota (2.6%)
15. Boise State University (2.6%)
16. University of Wyoming (2.8%)
17. Indiana University (2.9%)
18. University of Mississippi (3.0%)

19. University of Iowa [Iowa Writers' Workshop] (3.5%)*
20. University of Massachusetts at Amherst (3.5%)
21. Oregon State University (3.5%)
22. Virginia Tech (3.5%)
23. University of Alabama at Tuscaloosa (3.7%)
24. University of California at San Diego (3.7%)
25. Brooklyn College [CUNY] (3.8%)
26. Purdue University (4.0%)
27. University of Arkansas at Fayetteville (4.0%)
28. University of Arizona (4.0%)
29. Hunter College [CUNY] (4.0%)
30. Colorado State University (4.0%)∨
31. New York University (4.2%)
32. University of North Carolina at Greensboro (4.3%)
33. McNeese State University (4.4%)
34. West Virginia University (4.7%)
35. University of Nevada at Las Vegas (4.8%)
36. Louisiana State University (5.0%)
37. University of Notre Dame (5.0%)
38. Hollins University (5.0%)
39. Arizona State University (5.1%)
40. University of Houston (5.4%)
41. Southern Illinois University at Carbondale (5.5%)
42. Ohio State University (5.7%)
43. University of Illinois at Urbana–Champaign (5.7%)
44. Boston University (5.9%)
45. University of Washington at Seattle (5.9%)∨
46. University of South Carolina (6.0%)
47. University of Miami (FL) (6.7%)
48. North Carolina State University (6.7%)
49. University of New Mexico (6.7%)
50. University of Colorado at Boulder (6.7%)

Full-Residency Fiction and Poetry MFA Programs: Selective
(with the most recent publicly available yield-exclusive acceptance rates in parentheses)

51. University of Guelph (CAN) (8.0%)∨
52. Virginia Commonwealth University (8.3%)∧
53. Georgia College (8.4%)

54. Bowling Green State University (8.7%)
55. University of Maryland (9.4%)∧
56. New Mexico State University (9.8%)
57. University of Texas at Austin [New Writers Project] (9.9%)∧
58. University of Massachusetts at Boston (10.1%)∧
59. Portland State University (10.7%)
60. University of Montana (11.0%)
61. Texas State University (11.0%)
62. University of North Carolina at Wilmington (11.2%)
63. Wichita State University (11.4%)
64. University of New Hampshire (11.6%)∨
65. George Mason University (11.7%)
66. University of New Orleans (12.0%)
67. Northern Michigan University (12.5%)
68. University of San Francisco (12.8%)
69. Saint Mary's College (CA) (13.1%)
70. University of British Columbia at Vancouver (CAN) (13.5%)
71. American University (13.6%)
72. Old Dominion University (13.6%)
73. CalArts (15.1%)
74. Rutgers University at Newark (15.8%)∧
75. Butler University (15.8%)∨

Full-Residency Fiction and Poetry MFA Programs: Less Selective
(with the most recent publicly available yield-exclusive acceptance
rates in parentheses)

76. Sarah Lawrence College (16.6%)
77. University of Idaho (17.3%)
78. University of Missouri at St. Louis (17.5%)
79. University of California at Riverside (17.9%)∧
80. University of South Florida (20.0%)∧
81. Temple University (20.5%)
82. Queens College [CUNY] (20.5%)
83. Florida State University (21.0%)
84. Emerson College (21.1%)
85. Rutgers University at Camden (21.4%)∧
86. Savannah College of Art and Design (22.7%)
87. Otis College of Art and Design (22.9%)
88. Iowa State University (23.8%)∧

89. University of Pittsburgh (24.1%)∧
90. School of the Art Institute of Chicago (24.3%)
91. Eastern Washington University (25.0%)
92. University of Missouri at Kansas City (25.0%)
93. San Francisco State University (25.4%)
94. Long Island University at Brooklyn (25.7%)
95. Columbia University (26.1%)
96. California College of Arts [CCA] (32.4%)
97. University of Central Florida (32.7%)∧
98. The New School (37.3%)
99. Hofstra University (43.2%)
100. Chapman University (55.0%)

∧Programs believed, based on recent applicant polling, to have become *more* selective since the last time their selectivity data was publicly available.

∨Programs believed, based on recent applicant polling, to have become *less* selective since the last time their selectivity data was publicly available.

*The Nonfiction Writing Program at the University of Iowa last had a reported yield-exclusive acceptance rate of 4.0%.

Full-Residency MFA Programs: Fiction Tracks Only*

(with most recent publicly available yield-exclusive acceptance rates in parentheses)

1. Cornell University (0.7%)
2. University of Virginia (0.8%)
3. Brown University (0.9%)
4. University of Wisconsin at Madison (1.0%)
5. University of Wyoming (1.0%)∨
6. Syracuse University (1.1%)
7. University of Texas at Austin (1.1%)
8. University of Oregon (1.1%)
9. University of Michigan (1.2%)
10. University of California at Irvine (1.3%)
11. Washington University at St. Louis (1.5%)
12. Boise State University (1.5%)∨
13. Hunter College [CUNY] (1.6%)
14. University of Florida (1.6%)
15. Louisiana State University (1.6%)
16. Ohio State University (2.0%)
17. University of Mississippi (2.0%)

18. Johns Hopkins University (2.1%)
19. University of Iowa [Iowa Writers' Workshop] (2.7%)
20. Oregon State University (2.9%) ∨
21. University of Alabama at Tuscaloosa (3.0%)
22. University of Washington at Seattle (3.0%)∨
23. Virginia Tech (3.0%)
24. University of Illinois at Urbana–Champaign (3.3%)
25. Arizona State University (3.5%)
26. University of Massachusetts at Amherst (3.6%)
27. University of New Mexico (3.6%)
28. Brooklyn College [CUNY] (3.7%)
29. Purdue University (4.0%)
30. University of North Carolina at Greensboro (4.6%)
31. Colorado State University (4.9%)∨
32. Boston University (5.0%)
33. Southern Illinois University at Carbondale (5.0%)
34. New York University (5.6%)
35. University of Idaho (6.0%)
36. North Carolina State University (6.4%)
37. University of Maryland (7.1%)
38. University of South Carolina (7.9%)
39. McNeese State University (8.3%)
40. Portland State University (9.1%)
41. Texas State University (10.0%)
42. University of Missouri at St. Louis (12%)
43. Wichita State University (12.1%)
44. Florida International University (13.3%)
45. San Francisco State University (15.6%)
46. University of Missouri at Kansas City (16.7%)
47. Rutgers University at Camden (19.9%)∧
48. Columbia University (20.0%)
49. Eastern Washington University (20.0%)
50. University of New Hampshire (24.2%)∨

*The expectation that programs will release track-specific selectivity data is understandably much less than that they will release overall acceptance rates in the way other types of graduate programs do. For this reason, the ranking that follows should be read as a compilation and ordering of the most recent data available from the programs with available data from the last eight application cycles. For additional context on this listing, see the introduction to the "overall" ranking just given. Two key differences between this listing and that one, however, are that: (a) fluctuations in single-track data can be twice that of overall admissions figures; and (b) the "∧" or "∨" symbols are here used—because this is not a tiered ranking—simply to indicate that applicant polling suggests a program's fiction-track acceptance rate has notably risen or dropped since its most recent data release.

Full-Residency MFA Programs: Poetry Tracks Only*

(with the most recent publicly available yield-exclusive acceptance rates in parentheses)

1. University of Texas at Austin [Michener Center] (1.2%)
2. Vanderbilt University (1.5%)
3. Brown University (1.8%)
4. Cornell University (2.0%)
5. University of Wisconsin at Madison (2.3%)
6. Washington University at St. Louis (2.4%)
7. University of Oregon (2.8%)
8. University of Virginia (2.9%)
9. Louisiana State University (3.3%)
10. Oregon State University (3.3%)∨
11. University of California at Irvine (3.3%)
12. Arizona State University (3.7%)
13. Syracuse University (3.8%)
14. University of Michigan (3.9%)
15. Virginia Tech (4.0%)
16. University of Florida (4.6%)
17. Johns Hopkins University (4.9%)
18. Colorado State University (5.0%)∨
19. Purdue University (5.1%)
20. University of Alabama at Tuscaloosa (5.3%)
21. University of Iowa [Iowa Writers' Workshop] (5.5%)
22. University of Mississippi (5.7%)
23. North Carolina State University (6.3%)
24. University of Illinois at Urbana–Champaign (6.7%)
25. Ohio State University (6.7%)
26. New York University (6.8%)
27. University of Wyoming (6.8%)
28. University of North Carolina at Greensboro (7.1%)
29. Brooklyn College [CUNY] (8.3%)
30. Boston University (8.9%)
31. University of Massachusetts at Amherst (9.5%)
32. Wichita State University (9.5%)

33. University of Maryland (10.0%)
34. Rutgers University at Camden (12.1%)∧
35. University of New Mexico (13.6%)∧
36. McNeese State University (16.7%)
37. University of Missouri at St. Louis (17.5%)
38. San Francisco State University (20.0%)
39. Florida International University (20.0%)
40. Portland State University (31.6%)

*These rankings are subject to all the considerations already mentioned for the fiction-track and overall selectivity rankings, with the additional caveat that because poetry applicant pool sizes are much smaller than fiction-track pools, acceptance rates will vary even more widely from year to year.

Program Size

Some applicants will prefer large programs, while others will search for smaller ones. A small program might give you more access to professors, let you get to know the work of your peers more intimately, and be better able to respond to unexpected circumstances (financial or otherwise) that befall an individual student. On the other hand, a large program might have a more vibrant social scene, comprise a greater diversity of aesthetic styles and student demographics, and have a much larger alumni network. Which type of program is right for you is entirely up to you. To the extent this is a "ranking," it is *not* an assessment of quality. If you want a small program, begin reading this ranking from the number-one program end; if you want a large program, reverse the order and start reading from the bottom of the ranking. It's as simple as that.

Full-Residency MFA Programs: Small Incoming Cohort (1–10)
(61 programs; 35.9% of full-residency MFAs)

1. Long Island University at Brooklyn (3)
2t. University of California at San Diego (4)
2t. University of Utah (4)**
4t. Boise State University (5)
4t. Chatham University (5)*
4t. University of Kansas (5)

 4t. University of Victoria (CAN) (5)
 8t. Louisiana State University (6)
 8t. Northern Michigan University (6)
 8t. Sam Houston State University (6)
 8t. University of Alaska at Fairbanks (6)
 8t. University of Illinois at Urbana–Champaign (6)
 8t. University of Miami (FL) (6)
 8t. University of Wisconsin at Madison (6)
 8t. Vanderbilt University (6)
 8t. Western Kentucky University (6)
 8t. William Paterson University (6)
18t. Pratt Institute (7)
18t. University of Central Arkansas (7)
18t. University of Mississippi (7)
18t. University of New Mexico (7)
18t. University of Texas at Austin [New Writers Project] (7)
23t. Cornell University (8)
23t. Hofstra University (8)
23t. Indiana University (8)
23t. Johns Hopkins University (8)
23t. McNeese State University (8)
23t. New Mexico State University (8)
23t. Otis College of Art and Design (8)
23t. Purdue University (8)
23t. University of Colorado at Boulder (8)
23t. University of Houston (8)**
23t. University of Maryland (8)
23t. University of Nevada at Reno (8)
23t. University of South Carolina (8)
23t. University of South Florida (8)
23t. Virginia Tech (8)
38t. Chicago State University (9)
38t. Manhattanville College (9)
38t. Southern Illinois University at Carbondale (9)
38t. University of Idaho (9)
38t. University of Memphis (9)
38t. University of Notre Dame (9)
38t. University of San Francisco (9)
38t. University of Wyoming (9)
38t. Virginia Commonwealth University (9)

38t. Western Michigan University (9)
38t. Wichita State University (9)
49t. Arizona State University (10)
49t. Bowling Green State University (10)
49t. Brigham Young University (10)
49t. Florida Atlantic University (10)
49t. Florida International University (10)
49t. Georgia College (10)
49t. Iowa State University (10)
49t. Old Dominion University (10)
49t. University of Massachusetts at Boston (10)
49t. University of Missouri at St. Louis (10)
49t. University of Oregon (10)
49t. University of Virginia (10)
49t. West Virginia University (10)

*Full-residency cohort only.

**MFA only (does not include creative writing doctoral students).

Full-Residency MFA Programs: Medium-Size Incoming Cohort (11–20)

(62 programs; 36.5% of full-residency MFAs)

62t. Brown University (11)
62t. California Institute of Integral Studies (11)
62t. Colorado State University (11)
62t. University of Iowa [Nonfiction Writing Program] (11)
62t. University of Minnesota (11)
62t. University of Missouri at Kansas City (11)
62t. University of North Carolina at Greensboro (11)
62t. University of Washington at Seattle (11)
70t. Adelphi University (12)
70t. California State University at Long Beach [Long Beach State] (12)
70t. College of Charleston (12)
70t. Creighton University (12)
70t. Hollins University (12)
70t. Kingston University (UK) (12)
70t. Northern Arizona University (12)
70t. Queens College [CUNY] (12)
70t. Roosevelt University (12)

70t. Southern Connecticut State University (12)
70t. Syracuse University (12)
70t. University of Arizona (12)
70t. University of California at Irvine (12)
70t. University of Florida (12)
70t. University of Texas at Austin [Michener Center] (12)
70t. University of Texas at El Paso (12)
70t. University of Texas at Rio Grande Valley (12)
87t. Georgia State University (13)
87t. North Carolina State University (13)
87t. Northwestern University (13)
87t. Oklahoma State University (13)*
87t. Temple University (13)
87t. University of Central Florida (13)
87t. University of Kentucky (13)
94t. California State University at Fresno [Fresno State] (14)
94t. Oregon State University (14)
94t. Rutgers University at Newark (14)
94t. St. Joseph's College (NY) (14)
94t. University of Washington at Bothell (14)
94t. Washington University at St. Louis (14)
100t. Butler University (15)
100t. Ohio State University (15)
100t. Rutgers University at Camden (15)
100t. University of Arkansas at Fayetteville (15)
100t. University of Baltimore (15)
100t. University of Nevada at Las Vegas (15)
100t. University of New Hampshire (15)
100t. University of Tennessee at Knoxville (15)*
108t. University of Pittsburgh (16)
108t. Western Washington University (16)
110t. Boston University (18)
110t. California Institute of the Arts [CalArts] (18)
110t. Hunter College [CUNY] (18)
110t. Minnesota State University at Mankato (18)
110t. Naropa University (18)
110t. University of Alabama at Tuscaloosa (18)
110t. University of California at Riverside (18)
117t. American University (20)
117t. Mount St. Mary's University (CA) (20)

117t. Northeast Ohio Master of Fine Arts [NEOMFA] (20)
117t. San Diego State University (20)
117t. Stony Brook Southampton [SUNY] (20)
117t. Texas State University (20)
117t. University of Massachusetts at Amherst (20)

*Figure includes creative writing doctoral students.

Full-Residency MFA Programs: Large Incoming Cohort (21–30)
(14 programs; 8.2% of full-residency MFAs)

124t. Chapman University (22)
124t. University of Michigan (22)
124t. University of Montana (22)
127t. Portland State University (23)
127t. School of the Art Institute of Chicago (23)
127t. University of British Columbia at Vancouver (CAN) (23)
127t. University of North Carolina at Wilmington (23)
 131. Saint Mary's College (CA) (24)
132t. Brooklyn College [CUNY] (25)
132t. Eastern Washington University (25)
 134. University of New Orleans (26)
135t. Hamline University (30)
135t. San Francisco State University (30)
135t. Savannah College of Art and Design (30)*

*Savannah location only. Figure includes half the program's online students.

Full-Residency MFA Programs: Very Large Incoming Cohort (31–50)
(11 programs; 6.5% of full-residency MFAs)

 138. California College of the Arts (33)
 139. Rosemont College (35)
 140. Columbia College Chicago (36)
 141. George Mason University (38)
 142. Lindenwood University (40)
 143. New York University (42)
 144. San Jose State University (43)
 145. Florida State University (45)*
 146. Emerson College (49)
147t. Mills College (50)

147t. University of Iowa [Iowa Writers' Workshop] (50)

*Figure includes creative writing doctoral students.

Full-Residency MFA Programs: Ultra-Large Incoming Cohort (50+)
(4 programs; 2.4% of full-residency MFAs)

148. Sarah Lawrence College (63)
149. The New School (95)
150. Columbia University (100)
151. City College of New York [CCNY] (102)

Full-Residency MFA Programs: Cohort Size Unknown
(16 programs; 9.4% of full-residency MFAs)

NR. Birkbeck—University of London (UK)
NR. CALMAT
NR. The College of New Rochelle
NR. De La Salle University (PHI)
NR. Fudan University (CHN)
NR. Our Lady of the Lake University
NR. Shanghai University (CHN)
NR. Universidad Nacional de Colombia (COL)
NR. University College Dublin (IRE)
NR. University of British Columbia at Okanagan (CAN)
NR. University of Glasgow (UK)
NR. University of Guelph (CAN)
NR. University of Hong Kong (CHN)
NR. University of Iowa [Spanish Creative Writing]
NR. University of Saskatchewan (CAN)
NR. University of Surrey (UK)

Funding

Ranking program funding is an inexact science because most programs release incomplete data, cost-of-living assessments change year to year, and some programs fund incoming students unequally—making it difficult to determine the median ("all things being equal") funding package at a given program. Some programs release so little data that interpretation must be applied to vague terminology like "limited" and "highly competitive," though the fact that so many programs use such language suggests they consider it a sort of common parlance. Do not use this ranking to make fine distinctions, but rather to define broad tiers; the difference in funding between two programs three spots apart in this ranking may, in a given year, be zero, though two programs ten or more spots apart can reliably be considered to have discernible differences in funding. Given the chief admonition you've found in this guide—"Don't go into substantial debt for a nonprofessional arts degree"—ranking the programs as I have here should give you enough indication of where you will find substantial future student loan debt and where you will not. By the same token, independently wealthy applicants or those who, for whatever reason, have decided to take on heavy student loan debt, can expect to find not just that but also easier admission (by dint of less competition) at programs ranked lower in this listing. So some reading this will want to use it top-to-bottom, and others, perhaps, bottom-to-top.

A final note: most of the programs listed here would fund all students if they could; only some unfunded programs disguise their lack of funding online or make little effort to remedy it. So programs ranked lower in this listing are not being impugned, merely accurately detailed for the sake of their future applicants.

Fully Funded Programs (Ranked by Annual Funding Package Value) *

1. Rutgers University at Camden
2. Cornell University
3. Washington University at St. Louis
4. University of Texas at Austin [Michener Center]
5. University of Houston
6. Rutgers University at Newark
7. Vanderbilt University
8. University of Illinois at Urbana–Champaign
9. Ohio State University
10. University of Wisconsin at Madison
11. University of Pittsburgh
12. Syracuse University
13. Iowa State University
14. University of Virginia
15. Louisiana State University
16. Brown University
17. University of Michigan

18. Purdue University
19. University of Notre Dame
20. University of Arizona
21. University of Oregon
22. University of Tennessee at Knoxville
23. Virginia Tech
24. University of Florida
25. West Virginia University
26. University of Iowa [Iowa Writers' Workshop]
27. University of Iowa [Nonfiction Writing Program]
28. Arizona State University
29. University of Alabama at Tuscaloosa
30. University of Nevada at Las Vegas
31. University of Maryland
32. University of Arkansas at Fayetteville
33. University of Wyoming
34. University of South Carolina
35. University of Miami (FL)
36. Indiana University
37. Hollins University
38. University of Mississippi
39. University of California at Riverside
40. University of California at San Diego
41. Boise State University
42. Johns Hopkins University
43. Miami University (OH)
44. North Carolina State University
45. University of California at Irvine
46. Northwestern University
47. Boston University
48. University of South Florida
49. University of Minnesota
50. University of Texas at Austin [New Writers Project]
51. Southern Illinois University at Carbondale
52. Oregon State University

Nearly Fully Funded Programs (Ranked by Annual Funding Package Value)

53. Georgia College
54. Western Kentucky University

55. Florida Atlantic University
56. University of Massachusetts at Boston
57. Virginia Commonwealth University
58. University of New Mexico
59. University of North Carolina at Greensboro
60. Wichita State University
61. University of Massachusetts at Amherst
62. University of Iowa [Spanish Creative Writing]
63. Western Michigan University
64. McNeese State University
65. Oklahoma State University
66. Florida State University
67. University of Kansas
68. University of Kentucky

Well-Funded Programs (Ranked by Availability of Funding)

69. Northern Michigan University
70. Minnesota State University at Mankato
71. University of Idaho
72. Bowling Green State University
73. University of Colorado at Boulder
74. University of Alaska at Fairbanks
75. University of Utah
76. University of North Carolina at Wilmington
77. University of Montana
78. New Mexico State University

Moderately Funded Programs (Ranked by Availability of Funding)

79. University of Central Florida
80. University of Missouri at Kansas City
81. Temple University
82. College of Charleston
83. Western Washington University
84t. Brigham Young University
84t. Colorado State University
84t. George Mason University
84t. Old Dominion University
84t. San Diego State University
84t. Texas State University
84t. University of Memphis
84t. University of Missouri at St. Louis

84t. University of New Orleans
84t. University of Texas at El Paso
94t. American University
94t. Eastern Washington University
94t. Emerson College
94t. Florida International University
94t. Hunter College [CUNY]
94t. University of New Hampshire
94t. University of San Francisco
94t. University of Victoria (CAN)
94t. University of Washington in Seattle
103t. Brooklyn College [CUNY]
103t. Georgia State University
103t. Sam Houston State University
103t. Creighton University
103t. William Paterson University
103t. Stony Brook Southampton [SUNY]
103t. Southern Connecticut State University
103t. San Jose State University
103t. Long Island University in Brooklyn
103t. California State University at Fresno [Fresno State]
103t. University of British Columbia at Vancouver (CAN)
103t. Northeast Ohio Master of Fine Arts [NEOMFA]
103t. University of Texas at Rio Grande Valley
103t. University of Nevada at Reno
103t. Rosemont College
118t. California College of the Arts [CCA]
118t. University of Guelph (CAN)

Poorly Funded Programs (Ranked by Availability of Funding)

120. Roosevelt University
121. New York University
122t. Hofstra University
122t. Otis College of Art and Design
124. University of Central Arkansas
125. Chapman University
126t. Northern Arizona University
126t. Portland State University
128. Chatham University

129. St. Joseph's College (NY)
130. Adelphi University
131t. Queens College [CUNY]
131t. University of Baltimore
133. City College of New York [CCNY]
134t. Chicago State University
134t. Columbia University
134t. Mills College
134t. Naropa University
134t. Saint Mary's College (CA)
134t. The New School
140t. California State University at Long Beach [Long Beach State]
140t. Hamline University
140t. San Francisco State University
140t. School of the Art Institute of Chicago
144t. Butler University
144t. Vermont College of Fine Arts
144t. Manhattanville College
144t. Mount St. Mary's University (CA)
144t. Sarah Lawrence College
144t. Savannah College of Art and Design
144t. University College Dublin (IRE)
144t. University of Washington in Bothell
144t. University of Surrey (UK)
153. Lindenwood University

Unfunded Programs

154t. California Institute of the Arts [CalArts]
154t. California Institute of Integral Studies
154t. California University of Management and Technology [CALMAT]
154t. Columbia College Chicago
154t. Kingston University (UK)
154t. Pratt Institute
154t. University of British Columbia at Okanagan (CAN)
154t. University of Glasgow (UK)
154t. University of Saskatchewan (CAN)

New and Unassessed Programs

NR. Birkbeck—University of London (UK)
NR. The College of New Rochelle
NR. De La Salle University (PHI)
NR. Fudan University (CHN)
NR. Our Lady of the Lake University
NR. Shanghai University (CHN)
NR. Universidad Nacional de Colombia (COL)
NR. University of Hong Kong (CHN)

(A Partial List of) Programs With Some Postgraduate Funding**

Cornell University
Florida State University
Louisiana State University
University of California at Riverside
University of Iowa [Iowa Writers' Workshop]
University of Kentucky
University of Miami
University of Michigan
University of Nevada in Las Vegas

*Programs with a single unfunded position reported (out of all members of each incoming cohort) are still eligible for the "fully funded" list. All stipends have been adjusted for the cost of living in the program's host location. Programs that do not specify healthcare or fees coverage have had national-average, cost-of-living-adjusted amounts for both of these student expenses deducted from their stipends. Topping-up funds, minor scholarships, and minor fellowships with amounts unspecified are added to stipends using a national average figure. The duration of a program's funding is not considered for one important reason—not every applicant prefers three years of graduate school to two, or four to three, and so on. If you prefer a longer program to a shorter one, check the duration of each program and adjust their ranking here accordingly. All programs in the "fully funded" category are "fully funded" by virtue of offering, once tuition, healthcare, and student fees are paid, a nine-month stipend that is above the federal poverty level. Programs that do not announce a stipend have their stipend automatically set at 10 percent over the nine-month federal poverty level.

"Nearly fully funded" programs either (a) fully fund all students at an average rate (when all costs and cost-of-living adjustments are considered) below the federal poverty line, or (b) fully fund above that line between 75 percent and 90 percent of incoming students.

"Well-funded" programs meet the same standards as qualification "(b)" for "nearly fully funded" programs, but for between 50 percent and 75 percent of incoming students. As with all of the funding assessments here, programs that explicitly state their stipends, healthcare and fee coverages, and the percent of the class covered by any awards listed have a strong advantage over programs that do not provide this data and therefore take on national average figures for these measures.

"Moderately funded" programs are assessed just as "well-funded" programs are, with the exception that the former offer qualifying aid to 25 percent to 50 percent of incoming students. One exception to this rule is that programs that waive tuition for all or nearly all students but offer few or no teaching assistantships (and therefore no stipend, healthcare coverage, or fees coverage for students) are eligible to be ranked in this category. Programs that have previously achieved full funding in a single (or more) year over the last five years receive a bump of approximately ten positions in this category, as present, funding data may not fully reflect the program's capacity to fully fund students in the future.

"Poorly funded" programs offer scattershot funding. A large number of students may get some form of tuition or stipend assistance, but much of it is minimal given the costs of attendance and there is no clear indication that even 25 percent of students are fully funded.

An "unfunded" program is one whose marketing materials give no indication that any funding is offered at all. Any funding opportunities available at these schools have been kept private in the ten years since *Poets & Writers* notified programs that their funding packages would be adjudicated on the basis of their websites.

**Some programs offer a percentage of recent graduates additional, postgraduate funding. Because not all programs advertise these opportunities—for good reason, as doing so might build up unreasonable expectations among the applicant class— what follows is a list of programs that do advertise the possibility of such funding.

Student-Faculty Ratio

Some of the best teachers in higher education are adjunct professors, lecturers, instructors, and visiting professors. But what "student-faculty ratios" measure is not the teaching ability of any given faculty member, but the chances, all things being equal, that you will be able to access your program's core—"permanent"—faculty during your time in-program.

Adjunct professors may be working at multiple colleges simultaneously; visiting professors may well be gone by the time an applicant excited to work with them gets to campus; lecturers and instructors are often on short-term contracts that could see them moving on to other employment in the near term. MFA students already have to navigate their full-time, tenure-track creative writing professors unexpectedly being on sabbaticals, book tours, or visiting-faculty jaunts elsewhere; a student-faculty ratio that registers temporary faculty—or faculty whose primary assignment is in a different academic department altogether from the MFA program you're looking at—isn't much help to an applicant. And certainly the many programs that list former, emeritus, or on-leave faculty in their promotional materials cannot be permitted to have applicants thinking these teachers will be available to them if they matriculate.

With that in mind, the ranking that follows takes into account only full-time, tenure-track creative writing professors who are part of a program's "core" or "permanent" faculty. It does not reward programs simply for having a long faculty roster full of people you will never see in-program, or whose presence long-term on-campus you can't rely upon in advance. It also, unlike some other listings of program faculty, doesn't reward programs that overuse adjuncts or brief on-campus appearances by well-known alumni in order to associate as many luminaries with the program as possible.

This is, in other words, a student-faculty ratio ranking that is rigorous and thoroughly *real*—accurately anticipating (all things being equal) the quantity if not the quality of student-faculty interactions you might expect should you attend any of the programs listed. Should it differ from the more promising faculty data that a program quite understandably wants you to see, and therefore features on its website, keep that in mind. Note too that programs very close to one another in this ranking are likely indistinguishable in student-faculty ratio, as the programs' ratios are determined down to the hundredths.

Student-Faculty Ratios for Full-Residency MFA Programs*
(with the number of students per full-time, tenure-track creative writing faculty member in parentheses)

1. Long Island University at Brooklyn (1.20)
2. University of Victoria (CAN) (1.25)
3. William Paterson University (1.33)
4. Vanderbilt University (1.71)
5t. Cornell University (1.78)
5t. Johns Hopkins University (1.78)
7. University of Miami (FL) (1.83)
8. Pratt Institute (1.88)
9t. Louisiana State University (2.00)
9t. University of Wisconsin at Madison (2.00)

11. Brown University (2.20)
12. University of Virginia (2.22)
13. University of California at Riverside (2.25)
14. University of Maryland (2.29)
15t. University of Central Arkansas (2.33)
15t. University of New Mexico (2.33)
17. Western Kentucky University (2.40)
18. University of Notre Dame (2.43)
19t. Chatham University (2.50)
19t. Colorado State University (2.50)
19t. Brigham Young University (2.50)
19t. University of Kansas (2.50)
23. St. Joseph's College (NY) (2.55)
24t. Boston University (2.57)
24t. University of Wyoming (2.57)
26. University of South Carolina (2.67)
27. University of Texas at Rio Grande Valley (2.73)
28. Sam Houston State University (2.75)
29. University of San Francisco (2.88)
30. University of Kentucky (2.89)
31t. New Mexico State University (3.00)
31t. University of California at San Diego (3.00)
31t. University of Mississippi (3.00)
31t. Virginia Tech (3.00)
35t. Northern Michigan University (3.13)
35t. University of Idaho (3.13)
37. University of North Carolina at Greensboro (3.14)
38. Rutgers University at Newark (3.18)
39t. University of Illinois at Urbana–Champaign (3.20)
39t. University of Minnesota (3.20)
41. University of Arizona (3.27)
42t. Adelphi University (3.29)
42t. University of South Florida (3.29)
44. University of Central Florida (3.33)
45. Virginia Commonwealth University (3.38)
46t. California State University at Long Beach [Long Beach State] (3.43)
46t. Northern Arizona University (3.43)
46t. University of Colorado at Boulder (3.43)
49. Northwestern University (3.50)

50. Columbia College Chicago (3.60)
51t. University of Missouri at Kansas City (3.67)
51t. University of Oregon (3.67)
53. North Carolina State University (3.71)
54t. Arizona State University (3.75)
54t. Boise State University (3.75)
54t. West Virginia University (3.75)
57. University of Texas at El Paso (3.89)
58t. Creighton University (4.00)
58t. Hollins University (4.00)
58t. Hunter College [CUNY] (4.00)
58t. Indiana University (4.00)
58t. Oregon State University (4.00)
58t. Otis College of Art and Design (4.00)
58t. University of Pittsburgh (4.00)
65. University of Iowa [Nonfiction Writing Program] (4.13)
66. Temple University (4.17)
67. University of British Columbia at Vancouver (CAN) (4.18)
68t. University of Texas at Austin [The Michener Center] (4.22)
68t. University of Texas at Austin [New Writers Project] (4.22)
70t. Florida Atlantic University (4.29)
70t. Florida International University (4.29)
70t. Old Dominion University (4.29)
70t. Queens College [CUNY] (4.29)
74. Purdue University (4.40)
75t. Rutgers University at Camden (4.50)
75t. Syracuse University (4.50)
75t. University of Alaska at Fairbanks (4.50)
78. Western Washington University (4.57)
79t. Chicago State University (4.60)
79t. School of the Art Institute of Chicago (4.60)
79t. University of Washington at Seattle (4.60)
82. Northeast Ohio Master of Fine Arts [NEOMFA] (4.62)
83t. College of Charleston (4.80)
83t. University of Nevada at Reno (4.80)
85t. Bowling Green State University (5.00)
85t. Hofstra University (5.00)
85t. Iowa State University (5.00)
88t. California Institute of the Arts [CalArts] (5.14)
88t. University of Florida (5.14)

90t. Southern Illinois University at Carbondale (5.40)
90t. University of Washington at Bothell (5.40)
90t. Western Michigan University (5.40)
 93. University of North Carolina at Wilmington (5.42)
 94. University of Michigan (5.50)
 95. University of Utah (5.57)
 96. University of Montana (5.63)
 97. McNeese State University (5.75)
 98. Georgia College (5.80)
99t. California College of the Arts [CCA] (6.00)
99t. Naropa University (6.00)
99t. Southern Connecticut State University (6.00)
99t. Texas State University (6.00)
103. University of Alabama at Tuscaloosa (6.20)
104t. Eastern Washington University (6.25)
104t. University of Missouri at St. Louis (6.25)
106. Chapman University (6.28)
107. University of Houston (6.30)
108. Butler University (6.33)
109t. Minnesota State University at Mankato (6.43)
109t. University of Nevada at Las Vegas (6.43)
111. Emerson College (6.47)
112. Lindenwood University (6.67)
113t. University of New Hampshire (7.00)
113t. Washington University at St. Louis (7.00)
115. Brooklyn College [CUNY] (7.14)
116t. University of Arkansas at Fayetteville (7.50)
116t. University of California at Irvine (7.50)
116t. University of Massachusetts at Boston (7.50)
119. Portland State University (7.67)
120t. Kingston University (UK) (8.00)
120t. Mount St. Mary's University (CA) (8.00)
122. San Francisco State University (8.18)
123. California State University at Fresno [Fresno State] (8.40)
124. University of Massachusetts at Amherst (8.57)
125. University of New Orleans (8.67)
126. Rosemont College (8.75)
127. George Mason University (8.77)
128t. Manhattanville College (9.00)
128t. Ohio State University (9.00)

128t. Roosevelt University (9.00)
128t. Sarah Lawrence College (9.00)
128t. University of Baltimore (9.00)
128t. Wichita State University (9.00)
134. California Institute of Integral Studies (9.33)
135t. Columbia University (10.00)
135t. Oklahoma State University (10.00)
135t. San Diego State University (10.00)
135t. Savannah College of Art and Design (10.00)
135t. Stony Brook Southhampton [SUNY] (10.00)
135t. University of Tennessee at Knoxville (10.00)
141. Georgia State University (10.50)
142. University of Iowa [Iowa Writers' Workshop] (11.00)
143t. American University (12.00)
143t. Saint Mary's College (CA) (12.00)
145. Florida State University (13.00)
146. University of Memphis (13.50)
147. Hamline University (15.00)
148. New York University (19.00)
149. Mills College (20.83)
150. San Jose State University (21.50)
151. City College of New York [CCNY] (31.88)
152. The New School (38.00)

*Programs whose cohort size is unknown could not be included here. Programs without known student-faculty ratios include Birkbeck—University of London (UK), CALMAT, The College of New Rochelle, De La Salle University (PHI), Fudan University (CHN), Our Lady of the Lake University, Shanghai University (CHN), Universidad Nacional de Colombia (COL), University College Dublin (IRE), University of British Columbia at Okanagan (CAN), University of Glasgow (UK), University of Guelph (CAN), University of Hong Kong (CHN), University of Iowa [Spanish Creative Writing], University of Saskatchewan (CAN), and University of Surrey (UK).

Fellowship Placement

One type of data that helps us understand the role of academic-institutional creative writing in the lifetimes of creative writers is postgraduate placement data. As has been noted, a full-time creative writing teaching position is available, at the university level, for less than 1 percent of annual graduates of creative writing MFA programs. This begs the question of what career and artistic paths degreed poets and writers are taking upon graduation from their MFA programs.

Between 2003 and 2018, all known creative writing fellowships specifically designed for post-MFA poets and writers, 40 in all, were surveyed to determine the alma maters of those poets and writers who received such fellowships. Around 1,500 fellowship-placement "events" were catalogued, during a timespan in which more than 75,000 poets and writers graduated from terminal-degree creative writing programs. This suggests that less than 2 percent of the annual graduates of MFA programs are receiving further institutional support post-MFA via creative writing fellowships.

In the chart that follows, each listed institution has been assigned a placement "score" via the following equation: the number of placement events involving individuals from a given MFA program divided by the annual cohort size of that program in fiction and poetry. Creative nonfiction graduates and creative writing doctorate-holders were not considered for the main placement assessment, and where two programs received the same score the tie was broken in favor of the program with more total placements. Programs without extant graduating classes for the entirety of the assessment period receive pro-rated scores based on the performance of their eligible graduating cohorts.

The following forty creative writing fellowships were considered for this assessment: The Akademie Schloss Solitude Fellowship Program in Stuttgart, Germany; The Axton Fellowship at University of Louisville in Kentucky; the Bard Fiction Prize and Residency at Bard College in Annandale-on-Hudson, New York; the Bennett Fellowship and Writer-in-Residence Program at Phillips Exeter Academy in Exeter, New Hampshire; the Gaius Charles Bolin Fellowship at Williams College in Williamstown, Massachusetts; the Bread Loaf Writers' Conference Fellowships ("Waiterships") at Middlebury College in Vermont; the Amy Clampitt Residency Award at the Amy Clampitt House in Lenox, Massachusetts; the Eva Jane Coombe Writer-in-Residence Program at Seven Hills School in Cincinnati, Ohio; the Daehler Fellowship/Writer-in-Residence Program at Colorado College in Colorado Springs; the Emory Creative Writing Fellowship in Atlanta, Georgia; the Fine Arts Work Center Fellowship in Provincetown, Massachusetts; the

Gettysburg Emerging Writer Lectureship at Gettysburg College in Pennsylvania; the Hodder Fellowship at Princeton University in New Jersey; the Hugo House Writer-in-Residence Program at the Richard Hugo House in Seattle, Washington; the HUB-BUB Artist-in-Residence Program in Spartansburg, South Carolina; the Jack Kerouac House Residency in Orlando, Florida; the Kelly Writers House ArtsEdge Residency at the University of Pennsylvania in Philadelphia; the Kenan Visiting Writer Program at the University of North Carolina in Chapel Hill; the Kenyon Review Fellowships at Kenyon College in Ohio; the Herbert W. Martin Postgraduate Fellowship in Creative Writing and Diversity at Dayton University in Ohio; the James Merrill Writer-in-Residence Program at the James Merrill House in Stonington, Connecticut; the Jenny McKean Moore Writer-in-Residence Program at George Washington University in Washington, DC; the Moseley Fellowship in Creative Writing at Pomona College in California; the Olive B. O'Connor Fellowship at Colgate University in Hamilton, New York; the Dobie Paisano Fellowship Program at the University of Texas in Austin; the Charles Pick Fellowships at the University of East Anglia in Norwich, UK; the Madeleine P. Plonsker Emerging Writer's Residency Prize at Lake Forest College in Illinois; the Ruth Lilly Poetry Fellowships from the Poetry Foundation in Chicago, Illinois; the Philip Roth Residency at Bucknell University in Lewisburg, Pennsylvania; the Writer-in-Residence Program at The Saint Albans School in Washington, DC; the Southern Review Resident Scholar Program at Louisiana State University in Baton Rouge; the Stadler Fellowship at Bucknell University in Lewisburg, Pennsylvania; the Steinbeck Fellowship for Fiction Writers at the Center for Steinbeck Studies at San Jose State University in California; the Stegner Fellowship at Stanford University in Palo Alto, California; the Elma Stuckey Liberal Arts and Sciences Emerging Poet-in-Residence Program at Columbia College in Chicago; the Tickner Fellowship at The Gilman School in Baltimore, Maryland; the Vermont Studio Center Fellowships at the Vermont Studio Center in Johnson; the Wisconsin Creative Writing Institute Fellowship at the University of Wisconsin in Madison; the David T. K. Wong Fiction Fellowships at the University of East Anglia in Norwich, UK; and the Writer-in-Residence Fellowships at the Kimmel Harding Nelson Center for the Arts in Nebraska City, Nebraska.

Fellowship Placement Ranking for Full-Residency Fiction and Poetry MFA Programs: Two-Genre Fifteen-Year Survey (2003 to 2017 Inclusive)

Top 25

1. University of Wisconsin at Madison
2. University of Virginia
3. University of Texas at Austin [Michener Center]
4. Cornell University
5. University of Iowa [Iowa Writers' Workshop]
6. University of Michigan
7. Washington University at St. Louis
8. University of Houston
9. University of Oregon
10. University of Maryland
11. Vanderbilt University
12. Johns Hopkins University
13. University of Illinois at Urbana–Champaign
14t. Indiana University
14t. University of Minnesota
16. Ohio State University
17. University of Washington at Seattle
18. Purdue University
19t. Hunter College [CUNY]
19t. Syracuse University
21. University of Montana
22. University of Arkansas
23. University of Arizona
24. Brown University
25. Boston University

Second Tier

26. University of Massachusetts at Amherst
27. University of North Carolina at Greensboro
28. Arizona State University

29. University of Notre Dame
30t. University of South Florida
30t. University of Wyoming
32. Northern Michigan University
33. Rutgers University at Newark
34. University of Pittsburgh
35. Louisiana State University
36. University of California at Irvine
37. New York University
38. University of North Carolina at Wilmington
39. Columbia University
40. University of Florida
41. University of Miami (FL)
42. University of Massachusetts at Boston
43. Emerson College
44. University of California at San Diego
45. George Mason University
46t. Bowling Green State University
46t. University of Alabama at Tuscaloosa
48. Old Dominion University
49t. Florida State University
49t. University of New Hampshire

Third Tier

51. Virginia Commonwealth University
52. Colorado State University
53. McNeese State University
54t. Boise State University
54t. Rutgers University at Camden
54t. University of Alaska at Fairbanks
57. Portland State University
58. Mills College
59. Hollins University
60. University of Texas at Austin [New Writers Project]
61. Sarah Lawrence College
62. The New School
63. American University
64. Southern Illinois University at Carbondale

65t. Iowa State University
65t. University of San Francisco
 67. University of New Mexico
 68. Georgia College
 69. Brooklyn College [CUNY]
 70. North Carolina State University
 71. San Francisco State University
 72. University of Utah
 73. Saint Mary's College (CA)
74t. Florida International University
74t. University of Mississippi

Fourth Tier

 76. California Institute of the Arts [CalArts]
 77. Minnesota State University at Mankato
 78. University of Kansas
 79. Oregon State University
 80. Florida Atlantic University
 81. Texas State University
82t. California State University at Fresno [Fresno State]
82t. Western Michigan University
84t. California Institute of Integral Studies
84t. University of Missouri at Kansas City
 86. University of California at Riverside
 87. Virginia Tech
 88. University of Central Florida
 89. West Virginia University
90t. University of Idaho
90t. University of Memphis
 92. Adelphi University
 93. University of New Orleans
 94. Butler University
 95. New Mexico State University
 96. University of Nevada at Las Vegas
97t. Eastern Washington University
97t. School of the Art Institute of Chicago
97t. University of British Columbia (CAN)
100. Chicago State University

101. Hamline University
102. University of Missouri at St. Louis
103. California State University at Long Beach [Long Beach State]
104. Stony Brook Southampton [SUNY]
105. San Diego State University
106. City College of New York [CCNY]
107. California College of the Arts [CCA]
108. San Jose State University

[n = 1,523 eligible placement events across all degree programs.]

*Ties broken by program with more total placements. Scores pro-rated for programs not extant for the entirety of the assessment period.

Fellowship Placement Ranking for Low-Residency Fiction and Poetry MFA Programs: Two-Genre Fifteen-Year Survey (2003 to 2017 Inclusive)

Top 20

1. Warren Wilson College
2. Vermont College of Fine Arts
3. Bennington College
4. University of Nebraska at Omaha
5. University of New Orleans
6. New York University
7. University of Southern Maine [Stonecoast]
8. Pine Manor College
9. Drew University
10. Pacific Lutheran University
11. Ashland University
12. University of Alaska at Anchorage
13. Queens University of Charlotte
14. Spalding University
15. Bard College
16. Naropa University
17. Lesley University
18. Goddard College
19. Antioch University
20. Pacific University

[n = 1,523 eligible placement events across all degree programs.]

Fellowship Placement Ranking for Full-Residency Fiction and Poetry PhD Programs: Two-Genre Fifteen-Year Survey (2003 to 2017 Inclusive)

Top 20

1. University of Houston
2. Western Michigan University
3. Florida State University
4. University of Southern California
5t. University of Denver
5t. University of Tennessee at Knoxville
7. University of Nebraska at Lincoln
8. University of Georgia
9. Georgia State University
10. Texas Tech University
11. University of Southern Mississippi
12. University of Nevada at Las Vegas
13. University of Utah
14. University of Missouri at Columbia
15. University of Cincinnati
16. University of Illinois at Chicago
17. Ohio University
18t. University of North Texas
18t. University of Wisconsin at Milwaukee
20t. Illinois State University
20t. University of Louisiana at Lafayette

[n = 1,523 eligible placement events across all degree programs.]

Job Placement

Less than 1 percent of MFA program graduates in fiction, poetry, and creative nonfiction can expect to be hired into a full-time, tenure-track job teaching creative writing at the university level. This underscores not only that a graduate creative writing program is *not* vocational training, but also that we must do much more research on MFA program graduates' postgraduate outcomes—as right now more than 99 percent of graduates are not ending up in the academy long-term. While artists and literary critics sometimes discuss the MFA as a "professionalizing" degree, we have no hard data to back up that claim; as the research undergirding the data in this guide confirms, even the creative writing MFA programs most successful at placing their graduates in full-time, tenure-track university teaching positions are in fact sending only the smallest fraction of their alumni into long-term employment in academia. By way of example, the Iowa Writers' Workshop has graduated approximately 500 poets and writers in the last decade, but publicly available data only records 13 percent of Workshop graduates earning tenured positions in creative writing over this time-period—and since not all of those newly minted assistant professors graduated from the University of Iowa over the last decade, the chance that a 2018 Workshop graduate will end up in a tenure-track position teaching creative writing is likely around 10 percent. And the University of Iowa ranks second out of the nation's approximately 250 MFA programs in this critical measure of postgraduate outcomes.

In the chart that follows, each MFA program was assigned a job-placement score by dividing the number of reported full-time university hires of that program's alumni between 2008 and 2017 (inclusive) and the size of the program's annual matriculating class. Data for the chart was taken from the highest-traffic online data archive for academic hiring in creative writing in the United States, *The Academic Jobs Wiki*. During the period this data archive was surveyed, nearly 500 job-placement events recorded the name of the job recipient. These 464 events constitute around two-thirds of all available tenure-track creative writing job openings during this period; data on the recipients of the remaining positions were not publicly available.

Just under half of all full-residency programs (84) had at least one placement over the last ten job-application cycles; just under a third of all such programs (55) had multiple placements. That's worth thinking about for a moment: it means that half of all MFA programs have no public record of placing *any* graduates in a full-time, tenure-track teaching position in poetry, fiction, or creative nonfiction in the last decade. And two-thirds of all full-residency programs didn't have that happen (per the available public records) more than once over this period. And for what it's worth, the job-placement history of today's low-residency programs lags behind even this spotty record.

Job Placement Ranking for Full-Residency Fiction and Poetry MFA Programs: Two-Genre Ten-Year Survey (2008 to 2017 Inclusive)

The Top 25

1. University of Virginia
2. University of Iowa [Iowa Writers' Workshop]
3. University of Houston
4t. Indiana University
4t. Johns Hopkins University
6. Ohio State University
7. University of Texas at Austin [Michener Center]
8. University of Arkansas at Fayetteville
9. University of Maryland
10t. University of Notre Dame
10t. University of Wisconsin at Madison
12. University of California at Irvine
13t. University of Pittsburgh
13t. Washington University at St. Louis
15. Cornell University
16. University of Oregon
17. University of Florida
18. University of Arizona
19. Brown University
20t. Bowling Green State University
20t. University of Alabama at Tuscaloosa
22. Syracuse University
23. University of Massachusetts at Amherst
24. Southern Illinois University at Carbondale
25t. Boston University
25t. University of Minnesota

Second Tier

27. University of Washington at Seattle
28. University of Michigan
29. New Mexico State University

30t. Virginia Commonwealth University
30t. West Virginia University
30t. Western Michigan University
 33. Eastern Washington University
 34. New York University
 35. George Mason University
 36. University of Mississippi
 37. University of Montana
 38. Colorado State University
 39. Purdue University
40t. Northern Michigan University
40t. University of Alaska at Fairbanks
40t. University of Kansas
 43. Wichita State University
44t. Arizona State University
44t. California Institute of the Arts [CalArts]
 46. University of New Mexico
47t. Emerson College
47t. University of North Carolina at Wilmington
 49. Minnesota State University at Mankato
50t. University of Colorado at Boulder
50t. University of Idaho
50t. University of Illinois at Urbana–Champaign
50t. University of Memphis
50t. University of Miami (FL)
50t. University of San Francisco
50t. University of South Carolina
50t. University of Wyoming
50t. Vanderbilt University

Third Tier

 59. Brooklyn College [CUNY]
 60. University of New Orleans
 61. American University
62t. Georgia College
62t. Old Dominion University
 64. Columbia University

65t. Hollins University
65t. McNeese State University
65t. Queens College [CUNY]
65t. Virginia Tech
 69. University of Central Florida
70t. San Francisco State University
70t. Texas State University
 72. Sarah Lawrence College
73t. Florida State University
73t. University of North Carolina at Greensboro
 75. Stony Brook Southampton [SUNY]

Fourth Tier

76. School of the Art Institute of Chicago
77. Mills College
78. San Diego State University
79. Saint Mary's College (CA)
80. The New School

[n = 464.]

Job Placement Ranking for Full-Residency Nonfiction and Creative Nonfiction MFA Programs: One-Genre Ten-Year Survey (2008 to 2017 Inclusive)

Top 10

1. University Iowa [Iowa Writers' Workshop]
2. University of Montana
3. West Virginia University
4. Ohio State University
5t. Old Dominion University
5t. University of Minnesota
5t. University of Wyoming
8t. University of Alabama at Tuscaloosa
8t. University of New Orleans

8t. University of Pittsburgh
8t. University of Washington at Seattle

Second Tier

12. Eastern Washington University
13. Columbia University
14. Hunter College [CUNY]
15. Chatham University

[n = 44.]

Job Placement Ranking for Full-Residency Fiction and Poetry PhD Programs: Two-Genre Ten-Year Survey (2008 to 2017 Inclusive)

Top 10

1. University of Utah
2. Western Michigan University
3. University of Houston
4. Florida State University
5. University of Denver
6. University of Nevada at Las Vegas
7. University of Missouri at Columbia
8. University of Nebraska at Lincoln
9. University of Southern California
10. University of Cincinnati

Second Tier

11t. University of Kansas
11t. University of Louisiana at Lafayette
13. University of Tennessee at Knoxville
14. University of Illinois at Chicago
15. Texas Tech University
16. University of Georgia

17t. Oklahoma State University
17t. University of South Dakota
 19. Ohio University
 20. Texas A&M University

Third Tier

21t. University of Southern Mississippi
21t. State University of New York at Albany [SUNY]
 23. Binghamton University
 24. University of Wisconsin at Milwaukee
 25. University of North Texas

[n = 163.]

Job Placement Ranking for Full-Residency Nonfiction and Creative Nonfiction PhD Programs: One-Genre Ten-Year Survey (2008 to 2017 Inclusive)

Top 5

 1t. University of Denver
 1t. University of Houston
  3. University of Missouri at Columbia
 4t. Ohio University
 4t. University of Illinois at Chicago
 4t. University of Nebraska at Lincoln

[n = 11.]

Job Placement Ranking for Low-Residency Fiction, Poetry, and Nonfiction/Creative Nonfiction MFA Programs: Three-Genre Ten-Year Survey (2008 to 2017 Inclusive)

Top 10

 1. University of New Orleans
 2. Vermont College of Fine Arts

3. Bennington College
4. University of California at Riverside
5t. Naropa University
5t. University of Southern Maine [Stonecoast]
7. Ashland University
8. Bard College
9. Warren Wilson College
10. Goddard College

[n = 21.]

CHAPTER EIGHTEEN

Program Features

Before you make a rough draft of your application list—that is, a list of the graduate creative writing programs you intend to apply to—you should ask yourself some questions to determine which programs are even *eligible* to be on your list. Narrowing down your options this way is essential, given that there are 250 creative writing MFA programs to choose from. So, are you only looking at full-residency programs, or would you consider a low-residency program? Are you angling for a two-year program or a three-year program? Would you like a well-established program, or a relatively new one? How important is it that the program you choose offers a nonfiction track? Are you willing to take the GRE? Do you need to attend your program part-time, at night, or on the weekends? This chapter will help you figure out which programs meet your needs based upon these and other key questions.

The data in this chapter is taken from programs' promotional materials, and like any program features it may change over time. Use this information as a reliable guide that must nevertheless be followed up with additional research. If you're interested in a program, check their website to be certain you have up-to-the-second data on their program features.

Full-Residency MFA Program Foundation Dates

1930s. (1; 100% of new MFA programs this decade were full-residency)

   1. University of Iowa [Iowa Writers' Workshop] (1936)

1940s. (0)

1950s. (0)

1960s. (11; 100% of new MFA programs this decade were full-residency)

  2t. University of Massachusetts at Amherst (1964)
  2t. University of North Carolina at Greensboro (1964)
  2t. University of Oregon (1964)
  5t. University of Arkansas at Fayetteville (1965)
  5t. University of British Columbia (CAN) (1965)
   7. University of Alaska at Fairbanks (1966)
  8t. Cornell University (1967)
  8t. University of Montana (1967)
 10t. Bowling Green State University (1968)
 10t. Columbia University (1968)
  12. Sarah Lawrence College (1969)

1970s. (9; 82% of new MFA programs this decade were full-residency)

  13. University of California at Irvine (1970)
  14. University of Arizona (1972)
  15. University of Alabama at Tuscaloosa (1973)
 16t. Brooklyn College [CUNY] (1974)
 16t. Naropa University [Jack Kerouac School] (1974)
  18. Wichita State University (1977)
  19. Washington University at St. Louis (1978)
 20t. University of Florida (1979)
 20t. University of Houston (1979)

1980s. (26; 93% of new MFA programs this decade were full-residency)

 22t. American University (1980)

22t. George Mason University (1980)
22t. Indiana University (1980)
22t. New College of California (1980)*
26t. Eastern Washington University (1981)
26t. Emerson College (1981)
26t. McNeese State University (1981)
26t. University of Virginia (1981)
26t. Western Michigan University (1981)
31t. University of Michigan (1982)
31t. University of Pittsburgh (1982)
31t. University of Utah (1982)
 34. Virginia Commonwealth University (1983)
35t. Arizona State University (1985)
35t. Colorado State University (1985)
35t. De La Salle University (PHI) (1985)
38t. Pennsylvania State University (1986)*
38t. University of Iowa [Nonfiction Writing Program] (1986)
38t. University of San Francisco (1986)
41t. Louisiana State University (1987)
41t. Purdue University (1987)
41t. University of Washington at Seattle (1987)
44t. Florida International University (1989)
44t. Georgia State University (1989)
44t. San Diego State University (1989)
44t. University of Memphis (1989)

1990s. (35; 90% of new MFA programs this decade were full-residency)

48t. Brown University (1990)
48t. University of Maryland (1990)
50t. San Francisco State University (1991)
50t. Texas State University at San Marcos (1991)
50t. University of Miami (FL) (1991)
50t. University of New Orleans (1991)
50t. University of South Carolina (1991)
55t. Ohio State University (1992)
55t. Syracuse University (1992)
55t. University of Texas at El Paso (1992)
 58. University of Texas at Austin [Michener Center] (1993)
59t. Hamline University (1994)

59t. Old Dominion University (1994)
59t. University of Notre Dame (1994)
62t. California Institute of the Arts [CalArts] (1995)
62t. California State University at Long Beach [Long Beach State] (1995)
62t. Saint Mary's College (CA) (1995)
62t. Minnesota State University at Mankato (1995)
62t. Minnesota State University at Moorhead (1995)*
67t. The New School (1996)
67t. New York University (1996)
67t. Southern Illinois University at Carbondale (1996)
67t. University of Idaho (1996)
67t. University of Minnesota (1996)
67t. University of North Carolina at Wilmington (1996)
73t. California State University at Fresno [Fresno State] (1997)
73t. School of the Art Institute of Chicago (1997)
73t. University of Nevada at Las Vegas (1997)
76t. California State University at Chico (1998)*
76t. Roosevelt University (1998)
76t. Stony Brook Southampton [SUNY] (1998)
76t. University of Missouri at St. Louis (1998)
80t. Boise State University (1999)
80t. Chapman University (1999)
80t. Hunter College [CUNY] (1999)

2000s. (65; 66% of new MFA programs this decade were full-residency)

83t. California College of the Arts [CCA] (2000)
83t. Otis College of Art and Design (2000)
85t. Chicago State University (2001)
85t. San Jose State University (2001)
85t. University of Mississippi (2001)
85t. West Virginia University (2001)
89t. Chatham University (2002)
89t. Georgia College (2002)
89t. New Mexico State University (2002)
89t. Oregon State University (2002)
89t. University of California at Riverside (2002)
89t. University of Illinois at Urbana–Champaign (2002)
89t. University of Wisconsin at Madison (2002)

96t. Hollins University (2003)
96t. Lindenwood University (2003)
98t. Adelphi University (2004)
98t. Florida Atlantic University (2004)
98t. Johns Hopkins University (2004)
98t. Rosemont College (2004)
98t. University of Baltimore (2004)
103t. City College of New York [CCNY] (2005)
103t. Florida State University (2005)
103t. Northeast Ohio Master of Fine Arts [NEOMFA] (2005)
103t. North Carolina State University (2005)
103t. Savannah College of Art and Design (2005)
103t. University of Kansas (2005)
103t. University of New Mexico (2005)
103t. University of Wyoming (2005)
103t. Vanderbilt University (2005)
103t. Virginia Tech (2005)
113t. Boston University (2006)
113t. University of Central Florida (2006)
113t. Columbia College Chicago (2006)
113t. Iowa State University (2006)
113t. Long Island University at Brooklyn (2006)
113t. University of Colorado at Boulder (2006)
113t. University of Georgia (2006)**
113t. University of Guelph (CAN) (2006)
113t. University of Texas at Rio Grande Valley (2006)
122t. Queens College [CUNY] (2007)
122t. Rutgers University at Newark (2007)
122t. University College Dublin (IRE) (2007)
122t. University of Massachusetts at Boston (2007)
122t. University of Texas at Pan American (2007)
122t. Universidad Nacional de Colombia at Bogotá (COL) (2007)
122t. University of New Hampshire (2007)
129t. Butler University (2008)
129t. California Institute of Integral Studies (2008)
129t. Goldsmiths—University of London (UK) (2008)*
129t. Mills College (2008)
129t. Northwestern University (2008)
129t. Rutgers University at Camden (2008)

129t.   Southern Connecticut State University (2008)
129t.   University of Central Oklahoma (2008)*
129t.   University of Glasgow (UK) (2008)
129t.   University of Missouri at Kansas City (2008)
129t.   University of South Florida (2008)
140t.   California State University at San Bernardino (2009)*
140t.   Kingston University (UK) (2009)
140t.   Oklahoma State University (2009)
140t.   Portland State University (2009)
140t.   University of British Columbia at Okanagan (2009)
140t.   University of California at San Diego (2009)
140t.   University of Victoria (CAN) (2009)
140t.   William Paterson University (2009)

2010s. (35, 48% of new MFA programs this decade
are full-residency)

148t.   Brigham Young University (2010)
148t.   Fudan University (CHN) (2010)
148t.   Northern Michigan University (2010)
148t.   Temple University (2010)
148t.   University of Texas at Austin [New Writers Project] (2010)
153t.   California University of Management and Technology
        [CALMAT] (2011)
153t.   Hofstra University (2011)
153t.   Shanghai University (CHN) (2011)
153t.   University of Central Arkansas (2011)
153t.   University of Hong Kong (CHN) (2011)
153t.   University of Saskatchewan (CAN) (2011)
159t.   Manhattanville College (2012)
159t.   Northern Arizona University (2012)
159t.   Sam Houston State University (2012)
159t.   University of Canterbury (NZ) (2012)*
159t.   University of Iowa [Spanish Creative Writing] (2012)
159t.   University of Washington at Bothell (2012)
165t.   The College of Saint Rose (2013)*
165t.   Creighton University (2013)
165t.   St. Joseph's College (NY) (2013)
165t.   Western Washington University (2013)
169t.   University of Kentucky (2014)
169t.   University of Tennessee at Knoxville (2014)
169t.   Falmouth University (UK) (2014)*

169t.   Mount St. Mary's University (CA) (2014)
169t.   Our Lady of the Lake University (2014)
169t.   Pratt Institute (2014)
169t.   University of Nevada at Reno (2014)
169t.   University of Surrey (UK) (2014)
177t.   College of New Rochelle (2015)***
177t.   University of St. Andrews (UK) (2015)
177t.   Western Kentucky University (2015)
180t.   Birkbeck—University of London (UK) (2016)***
180t.   Miami University (OH) (2016)
180t.   New York University [Spanish Creative Writing] (2016)
180t.   Vermont College of Fine Arts (2016)****
180t.   College of Charleston (2016)
185.   Southern Illinois University at Edwardsville (2018)

*Program discontinued.

**While the full-residency MFA has been discontinued, the university continues to offer a creative writing doctoral program and a low-residency MFA.

***No poetry track offered.

****Full-residency program in writing and publishing.

Low-Residency MFA Program Foundation Dates

1970s. (2; 18% of new MFA programs this decade were low-residency)

1t.   Goddard College (1976)
1t.   Warren Wilson College (1976)

1980s. (2; 7% of new MFA programs this decade were low-residency)

3t.   Bard College (1981)
3t.   Vermont College of Fine Arts (1981)

1990s. (4; 10% of new MFA programs this decade were low-residency)

5.   Bennington College (1995)
6t.   Antioch University (1997)
6t.   Goucher College (1997)***
8.   Fairleigh Dickinson University (1998)

2000s. (34; 34% of new MFA programs this decade were low-residency)

   9. University of New Orleans (2000)
10t. Queens University of Charlotte (2001)
10t. Spalding University (2001)
12t. New England College (2002)
12t. University of Southern Maine [Stonecoast] (2002)
12t. University of Texas at El Paso (2002)**
15t. Lesley University (2003)
15t. Naropa University [Main Campus] (2003)
15t. Wilkes University (2003)
18t. Carlow University (2004)
18t. National University (2004)**
18t. Pacific Lutheran University [Rainier] (2004)
18t. Pacific University (2004)
18t. Western Connecticut State University (2004)
18t. Transart Institute (2004)
24t. Murray State University (2005)
24t. Plymouth University (UK) (2005)
24t. Seattle Pacific University (2005)
24t. Southern New Hampshire University (2005)
24t. University of British Columbia at Vancouver (CAN) (2005)
24t. University of Nebraska at Omaha (2005)
24t. Whidbey Writers' Workshop (2005)*
31t. Pine Manor College (2006)
31t. Sewanee: University of the South (2006)
33t. Ashland University (2007)
33t. Hamline University (2007)
35t. Eastern Kentucky University (2008)
35t. Seton Hill University (2008)
35t. University of Alaska at Anchorage (2008)
35t. University of California at Riverside (2008)
39t. Chatham University (2009)
39t. Converse College (2009)
39t. Drew University (2009)
39t. Fairfield University (2009)

2010s. (38; 52% of new MFA programs this decade are low-residency)

43t. City University of Hong Kong (CHN) (2010)

43t. Full Sail University (2010)**
45t. Albertus Magnus College (2011)
45t. Arcadia University (2011)
45t. Oklahoma City University (2011)
45t. West Virginia Wesleyan University (2011)
45t. Western State College of Colorado (2011)
50t. Augsburg College (2012)
50t. Cedar Crest College (2012)
50t. Eastern Oregon University (2012)
50t. Institute of American Indian Arts (2012)
50t. New York University (2012)
50t. Sierra Nevada College (2012)
50t. University of Tampa (2012)
57t. New Hampshire Institute of Art (2013)
57t. Oregon State University (2013)*****
57t. University of Arkansas at Monticello (2013)**
57t. University of King's College, Halifax (CAN) (2013)***
61t. Miami University (Ohio) (2014)
61t. Regis University (2014)
61t. School of the Art Institute of Chicago (2014)
61t. University of Georgia (2014)****
61t. University of Houston at Victoria (2014)
61t. Western New England University (2014)
67t. Mississippi University for Women (2015)
67t. Stetson University (2015)
69t. Emerson College (2016)^
69t. Miami University (OH) (2016)
69t. Naropa University [Jack Kerouac School] (2016)
69t. Reinhardt University (2016)
73t. Antioch University at Santa Barbara (2017)
73t. Bloomfield College (2017)
73t. Ithaca College (2017)
73t. St. Francis College (NY) (2017)
73t. Dominican University (CA) (2017)
78t. Bay Path University (2018)**/***
78t. Randolph College (2018)
78t. Salve Regina University [Newport] (2018)
78t. University of New Hampshire/New Hampshire Institute of Art (2018)
82. Hawai'i Pacific University (2019)

*Program discontinued.

**Zero-residency program.

***Nonfiction only.

****Visual narrative only.

*****Program offered at Cascades campus of Oregon State University.

^ Program in Popular Fiction.

Program Admission and Graduation Requirements

Programs That Require the GRE for Admission (54; 32% of full-residency MFA programs)

Bowling Green State University

Brigham Young University

College of Charleston

Creighton University*

Eastern Washington University

Emerson College

Florida International University

Florida State University

Hofstra University

Indiana University

Iowa State University

Johns Hopkins University

Louisiana State University

North Carolina State University

Old Dominion University

Our Lady of the Lake University

Purdue University

Rutgers University at Newark

Sam Houston State University

San Diego State University**

Southern Illinois University at Carbondale

Temple University***

Texas State University****

University of Alaska at Fairbanks

University of Arkansas

University of Central Arkansas

University of Colorado at Boulder
University of Florida
University of Houston
University of Idaho
University of Illinois at Urbana–Champaign
University of Memphis
University of Miami (FL)
University of Mississippi
University of Missouri at Kansas City
University of Missouri at St. Louis***
University of Nevada at Reno
University of North Carolina at Greensboro
University of Notre Dame
University of Pittsburgh
University of South Carolina
University of South Florida
University of Tennessee at Knoxville
University of Texas at Austin [New Writers Project]
University of Texas at Austin [Michener Center]
University of Utah
University of Washington at Seattle
University of Wyoming
Vanderbilt University
Washington University at St. Louis
West Virginia University
Western Kentucky University
Western Michigan University
Western Washington University

*Not required in initial application, but the program may request it of some applicants.

**Students with low GPAs may be asked for GRE scores.

***Required only for applicants who wish to be considered for funding.

****GRE requirement unclear—contact the program coordinator if you're seeking funding.

*Programs That Require Foreign Language Proficiency (7; 4.1% of full-residency MFA programs)**

Boston University
Florida State University
Johns Hopkins University
University of Colorado at Boulder

University of Houston
University of Kansas
University of Tennessee at Knoxville

*Proficiency is required for graduation, not admission.

Program Curricula

*Full-Residency Programs That Expressly Permit Cross-Genre Study (119; 70% of programs)**

Adelphi University
American University
Boise State University
Brooklyn College [CUNY]
Brown University
Butler University
California College of the Arts [CCA]
California Institute of the Arts [CalArts]
California Institute of Integral Studies
California State University at Fresno [Fresno State]
California State University at Long Beach [Long Beach State]
Chapman University
Chatham University
Chicago State University
College of Charleston
The College of New Rochelle
Colorado State University
Eastern Washington University
Emerson College
Florida Atlantic University
Florida International University
Florida State University
George Mason University
Georgia College
Hamline University
Hofstra University
Hollins University
Indiana University
Iowa State University
Lindenwood University

Long Island University at Brooklyn
Louisiana State University
Manhattanville College
Mills College
Minnesota State University at Mankato
Mount St. Mary's University (CA)
Naropa University [Jack Kerouac School]
Northeast Ohio Master of Fine Arts [NEOMFA]
New Mexico State University
North Carolina State University
Northern Arizona University
Northern Michigan University
Northwestern University
Ohio State University
Oklahoma State University
Old Dominion University
Otis College of Art and Design
Our Lady of the Lake University
Portland State University
Pratt Institute
Purdue University
Queens College [CUNY]
Roosevelt University
Rosemont College
Rutgers University at Camden
Rutgers University at Newark
St. Joseph's College (NY)
Saint Mary's College (CA)
Sam Houston State University
San Diego State University
San Francisco State University
San Jose State University
Sarah Lawrence College
School of the Art Institute of Chicago
Southern Connecticut State University
Southern Illinois University at Carbondale
Stony Brook Southampton [SUNY]
University of Alabama at Tuscaloosa
University of Alaska at Fairbanks
University of Arizona
University of Arkansas

University of Baltimore
University of British Columbia at Okanagan (CAN)
University of British Columbia at Vancouver (CAN)
University of California at Riverside
University of California at San Diego
University of Central Arkansas
University of Central Florida
University of Colorado at Boulder
University of Florida
University of Guelph (CAN)
University of Houston
University of Kansas
University of Massachusetts at Amherst
University of Memphis
University of Miami (FL)
University of Minnesota
University of Missouri at Kansas City
University of Missouri at St. Louis
University of Montana
University of Nevada at Las Vegas
University of New Hampshire
University of New Mexico
University of New Orleans
University of North Carolina at Wilmington
University of Notre Dame
University of Pittsburgh
University of San Francisco
University of Saskatchewan (CAN)
University of South Florida
University of Surrey (UK)
University of Tennessee at Knoxville
University of Texas at Austin [Michener Center]
University of Texas at El Paso
University of Texas at Rio Grande Valley
University of Victoria (CAN)
University of Washington at Bothell
University of Washington at Seattle
University of Wisconsin at Madison
University of Wyoming
Vanderbilt University
Virginia Commonwealth University

Virginia Tech
West Virginia University
Western Kentucky University
Western Michigan University
Western Washington University
Wichita State University
William Paterson University

*This is a nonexhaustive list based on programs' promotional materials. Programs that permit or even require cross-genre study are included here; programs that only allow cross-genre study with the permission of the program are not (as permission cannot be counted upon in advance). This list also excludes programs that (a) allow narrow cross-genre work but forbid poets to write prose and vice versa, or (b) leave their degree requirements ambiguous on the topic of cross-genre study— usually by way of appearing to forbid it without stating so expressly. Cross-genre study is such an important component of graduate creative writing education that applicants interested in working across genres should not risk being kept from doing so. If you have questions about a given program's policies, contact the program coordinator directly.

Programs That Can Be Attended Part-Time*

Adelphi University
City College of New York [CCNY]
The College of New Rochelle
Emerson College
Hamline University
Kingston University (UK)
Lindenwood University
Northwestern University
Portland State University
Southern Connecticut State University
University of Hong Kong (CHN)
University of Texas at Rio Grande Valley
University of Washington at Bothell**

*Assessment is based on programs' promotional materials. Other programs may offer this option as well.

**Students can elect not to be in residence on campus in their second year of the program.

Programs That Can Be Attended on Nights and/or Weekends*

California Institute of Integral Studies
Hofstra University
Hunter College [CUNY]

Lindenwood University
Manhattanville College
St. Joseph's College (NY)
University of Missouri at St. Louis
University of San Francisco
William Paterson University

*Assessment is based on programs' promotional materials. Other programs may offer this option as well.

Programs with Nonfiction Tracks (102; 59.7% of full-residency MFA programs)

Adelphi University
American University
Boise State University*
Brigham Young University
Butler University
California College of the Arts [CCA]
California Institute of the Arts [CalArts]
California Institute of Integral Studies
California State University at Fresno [Fresno State]
Chapman University
Chatham University
Chicago State University
City College of New York [CCNY]
The College of New Rochelle
Columbia University
Creighton University
De La Salle University (PHI)
Eastern Washington University
Emerson College
Florida Atlantic University
Florida International University
Florida State University
George Mason University
Georgia College
Hamline University
Hofstra University
Hollins University
Hunter College [CUNY]
Iowa State University

Lindenwood University
Long Island University at Brooklyn
Louisiana State University
Miami University (OH)
Minnesota State University at Mankato
Mount St. Mary's University (CA)
Northeast Ohio Master of Fine Arts [NEOMFA]
The New School
Northern Arizona University
Northern Michigan University
Northwestern University
Ohio State University
Oklahoma State University
Old Dominion University
Oregon State University
Otis College of Art and Design
Portland State University
Pratt Institute
Queens College [CUNY]
Roosevelt University
Rosemont College
Rutgers University at Camden
Sam Houston State University
San Francisco State University
San Jose State University
Sarah Lawrence College
Savannah College of Art and Design
School of the Art Institute of Chicago
St. Joseph's College (NY)
Stony Brook Southampton [SUNY]
University of Alabama
University of Alaska at Fairbanks
University of Arizona
University of Baltimore
University of British Columbia at Vancouver (CAN)
University of British Columbia at Okanagan (CAN)
University of California at Riverside
University of Central Arkansas
University of Central Florida
University of Colorado at Boulder**
University of Guelph (CAN)

University of Hong Kong (CHN)
University of Houston
University of Idaho
University of Iowa [Nonfiction Writing Program]
University of Kansas
University of Minnesota
University of Missouri at Kansas City
University of Montana
University of Nevada at Las Vegas
University of New Hampshire
University of New Mexico
University of New Orleans
University of North Carolina at Wilmington
University of Notre Dame
University of Pittsburgh
University of San Francisco
University of Saskatchewan (CAN)
University of South Carolina
University of South Florida
University of St. Andrews (UK)
University of Tennessee at Knoxville
University of Texas at El Paso
University of Texas at Rio Grande Valley
University of Victoria (CAN)
University of Wyoming
Washington University at St. Louis
Vermont College of Fine Arts***
West Virginia University
Western Kentucky University
Western Michigan University
Western Washington University
William Paterson University

*Unfunded track.
**Students must customize their own course of study.
***Full-residency writing and publishing MFA program.

*Programs with Tracks Other Than Fiction, Nonfiction, Poetry, Playwriting, or Screenwriting**

Brown University (Digital Language Arts, Cross-disciplinary)
Chapman University (Digital Modes)

Chatham University (Children's Writing, Dual Genre)
Emerson College (Popular Fiction Writing and Publishing)
Lindenwood University (Genre Fiction)
Long Island University at Brooklyn (Cross-Genre)
Manhattanville College (Cross-Genre)
Mills College (Book Arts)
The New School (Writing for Children and Young Adults)
Queens College [CUNY] (Literary Translation)
Rosemont College (Publishing, Young Adult Fiction)
Saint Mary's College (CA) (Dual Fiction/Poetry Concentration)**
Sarah Lawrence College (Speculative Fiction)
Simmons College (Writing for Children)***
University of Alabama at Tuscaloosa (Cross-Genre)
University of Arkansas at Fayetteville (Literary Translation)
University of Baltimore (Publishing Arts)
University of British Columbia at Vancouver (CAN) (Multi-Genre)
University of Guelph (CAN) (Mixed/Hybrid Genre)
University of Miami (FL) (Cross-Genre)
Western Washington University (Cross-Genre)
William Paterson University (Cross-Genre)

*This is a nonexhaustive list, taken from programs' promotional materials.

**Requires an additional year of study.

***Because this program has no other tracks but this one, it is not discussed in detail in this guide.

Programs With a Themed Curriculum

Chatham University (Travel, Nature, Social Outreach)
Chicago State University (African American Literature/Art)
Iowa State University (Environment)
Our Lady of the Lake University (Social Justice)
Pratt Institute (Contemporary Politics)
University of Washington at Bothell (Poetics)

Programs Open to Experimental Writing (13; 7.7% of full-residency MFA programs)*

Brown University
California Institute of the Arts [CalArts]
California College of the Arts [CCA]
Chapman University
Mills College

Naropa University
Otis College of Art and Design
Pratt Institute
Rutgers University at Camden
Rutgers University at Newark
School of the Art Institute of Chicago
Temple University
University of California at San Diego
University of Arizona
University of Notre Dame
University of Utah
University of Washington at Bothell

*Graduate creative writing programs have a (somewhat deserved) reputation for being *most* welcoming to conventional poetry, fiction, and nonfiction. Every year, creative writers of a more experimental bent wonder whether they will be able to find a program whose faculty and students are as interested in challenging form, genre, and audience expectations as they are. This is a nonexhaustive list of full-residency MFA programs that answer to that description. This list draws primarily from programs' promotional materials. Just because a program does not appear here does not mean its faculty is hostile to innovative writing; it simply means any such openness has not been emphasized in the program's marketing materials. That said, if you are a literary artist whose works challenge conventional writing modes, be aware that your work may find a slightly less welcoming response from writing program admissions committees.

Programs That Have Dual-Degree Options (6; 3.6% of full-residency MFA programs)

Chapman University (MA/MFA)
Cornell University (MFA/JD)
McNeese State University (MA/MFA)
Our Lady of the Lake University (MA/MFA)
Rosemont College (MA/MFA)
University of Alaska at Fairbanks (MA/MFA)

Program Duration

One-Year Programs (3; 1.8% of full-residency MFA programs)

Boston University
Birkbeck—University of London (UK)*
University College Dublin (IRE)

*Applicant must have MA at time of application.

One- to Two-Year Programs (2; 1.2% of full-residency MFA programs)*

Lindenwood University
Rosemont College

*Duration depends on the curricular choices of students.

Two-Year Programs (73; 43.2% of full-residency MFA programs)

Adelphi University
Bowling Green State University
Brigham Young University
Brooklyn College
Brown University
California College of the Arts [CCA]
California Institute of the Arts [CalArts]
California State University in Long Beach [Long Beach State]
Chapman University
Chatham University
College of Charleston
The College of New Rochelle
Columbia College Chicago
Columbia University
Cornell University
Creighton University
De La Salle University (PHI)
Hollins University
Hunter College [CUNY]
Johns Hopkins University
Kingston University (UK)
Long Island University at Brooklyn
Manhattanville College
Mount St. Mary's University (CA)
Naropa University
The New School
New York University
North Carolina State University
Northern Arizona University
Oregon State University
Otis College of Art and Design

Portland State University
Pratt Institute
St. Joseph's College (NY)
Saint Mary's College (CA)
San Jose State University
Sarah Lawrence College
Savannah College of Art and Design
School of the Art Institute of Chicago
Southern Connecticut State University
Stony Brook Southampton [SUNY]
Temple University
University of British Columbia at Vancouver (CAN)
University of California at Riverside
University of Guelph (CAN)
University of Hong Kong (CHN)
University of Iowa [Iowa Writers' Workshop]
University of Kentucky
University of Maryland
University of Miami (FL)
University of Michigan
University of Missouri at Kansas City
University of Montana
University of North Carolina at Greensboro
University of Notre Dame
University of Oregon
University of Saskatchewan (CAN)
University of St. Andrews (UK)
University of Surrey (UK)
University of Tennessee at Knoxville
University of Texas at Austin [New Writers Project]
University of Utah
University of Victoria (CAN)
University of Virginia
University of Washington at Bothell
University of Washington at Seattle
University of Wisconsin at Madison
University of Wyoming
Vanderbilt University
Washington University at St. Louis
Western Kentucky University

Western Washington University
William Paterson University

Two- to Three-Year Programs (22; 13% of full-residency MFA programs)*

Butler University
California Institute of Integral Studies
Chicago State University
City College of New York [CCNY]
Colorado State University
Eastern Washington University
Emerson College**
Hofstra University
Mills College
Minnesota State University at Mankato
Northwestern University
Queens College [CUNY]
Rutgers University at Camden
Rutgers University at Newark
Sam Houston State University***
University of California at Irvine
University of California at San Diego
University of Central Florida
University of Missouri at St. Louis
University of New Hampshire
University of San Francisco**
University of Texas at Rio Grande Valley**

*Duration depends on the curricular choices of students.
**Program is two and a half years.
***Two-year program with an optional additional six months.

Three-Year Programs (58; 34.3% of full-residency MFA programs)

American University
Arizona State University
Boise State University
California State University at Fresno [Fresno State]
Florida Atlantic University
Florida International University
Florida State University

George Mason University
Georgia College
Hamline University
Indiana University
Iowa State University
Louisiana State University
McNeese State University
Northeast Ohio Master of Fine Arts [NEOMFA]
New Mexico State University
Northern Michigan University
Ohio State University
Oklahoma State University
Old Dominion University
Our Lady of the Lake University
Purdue University
Roosevelt University
San Diego State University
San Francisco State University
Southern Illinois University at Carbondale
Syracuse University
Texas State University
University of Arizona
University of Baltimore
University of Central Arkansas
University of Colorado at Boulder
University of Florida
University of Houston
University of Idaho
University of Illinois at Urbana–Champaign
University of Iowa [Nonfiction Writing Program]
University of Kansas
University of Massachusetts at Amherst
University of Massachusetts at Boston
University of Memphis
University of Minnesota
University of Mississippi
University of Nevada at Las Vegas
University of Nevada at Reno
University of New Mexico
University of New Orleans
University of North Carolina at Wilmington

University of Pittsburgh
University of South Carolina
University of South Florida
University of Texas at Austin [Michener Center]
University of Texas at El Paso
Virginia Commonwealth University
Virginia Tech
West Virginia University
Western Michigan University
Wichita State University

Three- to Four-Year Programs (2; 1.2% of full-residency MFA programs)

Georgia State University
University of Alabama at Tuscaloosa

Four-Year Programs (1; 0.6% of full-residency MFA programs)

University of Arkansas at Fayetteville

Programs of Unknown Duration (8; 4.7% of full-residency MFA programs)

California University of Management and Technology [CALMAT]
Fudan University (CHN)
Shanghai University (CHN)
Universidad Nacional de Colombia at Bogotá (COL)
University College Dublin (IRE)
University of British Columbia at Okanagan (CAN)
University of Glasgow (UK)
University of Iowa [Spanish Creative Writing]

Creative Writing Doctoral Programs

Programs in the United States (35; 35% of total creative writing doctoral programs)

Binghamton University
Florida State University
Georgia State University
Illinois State University

Morgan State University*
Ohio University
Oklahoma State University
State University of New York at Albany [SUNY]
Texas A&M University
Texas Tech University
University of Cincinnati
University of Colorado at Boulder**
University of Connecticut***
University of Denver
University of Georgia
University of Hawai'i
University of Houston
University of Illinois at Chicago
University of Kansas
University of Louisiana at Lafayette
University of Missouri at Columbia
University of Nebraska at Lincoln
University of Nevada at Las Vegas
University of North Dakota
University of North Texas
University of Rhode Island
University of South Dakota
University of Southern California
University of Southern Mississippi
University of Tennessee at Knoxville
University of Texas at Dallas
University of Utah
University of Wisconsin at Madison****
University of Wisconsin at Milwaukee
Western Michigan University

*Internal concentration in creative writing within the English PhD program.

**Program is a "PhD in Intermedia Art, Writing, and Performance."

***Admission to English PhD and department permission required for creative dissertation.

****Admission to literary studies PhD and critical dissertation required (internal minor in creative writing is selected upon matriculation).

*Programs in the United Kingdom (47; 49% of total program list)**

Anglia Ruskin University
Bath Spa University

Brunel University at West London
Cardiff University
Edge Hill University
De Montfort University at Leicester
Essex University
Kingston University at London
Lancaster University
Loughborough University
Manchester Metropolitan University
Middlesex University
Newcastle University
Northumbria University
Nottingham Trent University
The Open University
Queen's University at Belfast
Roehampton University
Saint Mary's University College at Twickenham
Swansea University
University of Bedfordshire
University of Bolton
University of Bradford
University of Chester
University of Chichester
University of East Anglia
University of Edinburgh
University of Exeter
University of Glasgow
University of Gloucestershire
University of Kent
University of Leeds
University of London (Goldsmiths)
University of London (Royal Holloway)
University of Manchester
University of Nottingham
University of Plymouth
University of Reading
University of Saint Andrews
University of Salford
University of Southampton
University of Sussex

University of Wales at Aberystwyth
University of Wales at Bangor
University of Wales at Lampeter
University of Winchester
Warnborough College

*In the UK, the term "creative writing PhD" means something quite different than it does in the United States. In the United States, creative writing doctoral students complete the same course of study their peers in the graduate English program do, with the exception that they can take a number of creative writing workshops for credit; after taking a similar preliminary examination as their peers, however, creative writing PhD students in the United States are permitted to write a creative rather than critical dissertation in fulfillment of their requirements for the degree. By comparison, creative writing PhD students in the UK do very little—often no—coursework at all, receiving their doctorate after a two- or three-year course of study in which their only academic requirement is regular meetings with an academic advisor. Arguably, the creative writing doctorate in the United Kingdom is more analogous to a creative writing fellowship in the United States, with the added (and not insubstantial) value of granting a doctoral degree.

Programs in Australia and New Zealand (13; 14% of total program list)

Deakin University
Flinders University
Monash University
Royal Melbourne Institute of Technology
Swinburne University of Technology
University of Adelaide
University of Melbourne
University of New South Wales
University of Queensland
University of Western Australia
University of Wollongong
Victoria University
Victoria University of Wellington

Programs in Canada (2; 1% of total program list)

University of Calgary
University of New Brunswick

Programs in the Philippines (1; 1% of total program list)

University of the Philippines at Diliman

PROGRAM INDEX

North America

Alabama

Full-Residency MFA Programs
   University of Alabama at Tuscaloosa

Alaska

Full-Residency MFA Programs
   University of Alaska at Fairbanks

Low-Residency MFA Programs
   University of Alaska at Anchorage

Arizona

Full-Residency MFA Programs
   Arizona State University
   Northern Arizona University
   University of Arizona

Arkansas

Full-Residency MFA Programs
   University of Arkansas at Fayetteville
   University of Central Arkansas

Low-Residency MFA Programs
  University of Arkansas at Monticello

California

Full-Residency MFA Programs
  California College of the Arts [CCA]
  California Institute of the Arts [CalArts]
  California Institute of Integral Studies
  California State University at Fresno [Fresno State]
  California State University at Long Beach [Long Beach State]
  California University of Management & Technology [CALMAT]
  Chapman University
  Mills College
  Mount St. Mary's University (CA)
  Otis College of Art & Design
  Saint Mary's College (CA)
  San Diego State University
  San Francisco State University
  San Jose State University
  University of California at Irvine
  University of California at Riverside
  University of California at San Diego
  University of San Francisco

Low-Residency MFA Programs
  Antioch University at Los Angeles
  Antioch University at Santa Barbara
  Dominican University
  National University
  University of California at Riverside

Creative Writing Doctoral Programs
  University of Southern California

Colorado

Full-Residency MFA Programs
  Colorado State University
  Naropa University [Jack Kerouac School]
  University of Colorado at Boulder

Stetson University
University of Tampa

Creative Writing Doctoral Programs
Florida State University

Georgia

Full-Residency MFA Programs
Georgia College
Georgia State University
Savannah College of Art & Design

Low-Residency MFA Programs
Reinhardt University
University of Georgia

Creative Writing Doctoral Programs
Georgia State University
University of Georgia

Hawaii

Low-Residency MFA Programs
Hawai'i Pacific University

Creative Writing Doctoral Programs
University of Hawai'i

Idaho

Full-Residency MFA Programs
Boise State University
University of Idaho

Illinois

Full-Residency MFA Programs
Chicago State University
Columbia College Chicago

Kentucky

Full-Residency MFA Programs
  University of Kentucky
  Western Kentucky University

Low-Residency MFA Programs
  Eastern Kentucky University
  Murray State University
  Spalding University

Louisiana

Full-Residency MFA Programs
  Louisiana State University
  McNeese State University
  University of New Orleans

Low-Residency MFA Programs
  University of New Orleans

Creative Writing Doctoral Programs
  University of Louisiana at Lafayette

Maine

Low-Residency MFA Programs
  University of Southern Maine [Stonecoast]

Maryland

Full-Residency MFA Programs
  Johns Hopkins University
  University of Baltimore
  University of Maryland

Low-Residency MFA Programs
  Goucher College

Creative Writing Doctoral Programs
  Morgan State University

Massachusetts

Full-Residency MFA Programs
Boston University
Emerson College
University of Massachusetts at Amherst
University of Massachusetts at Boston

Low-Residency MFA Programs
Bay Path University
Emerson College
Lesley University
Pine Manor College
Western New England University

Michigan

Full-Residency MFA Programs
University of Michigan
Northern Michigan University
Western Michigan University

Creative Writing Doctoral Programs
Western Michigan University

Minnesota

Full-Residency MFA Programs
Hamline University
Minnesota State University at Mankato
University of Minnesota

Low-Residency MFA Programs
Augsburg College
Hamline University

Mississippi

Full-Residency MFA Programs
University of Mississippi

Brooklyn College [CUNY]
City College of New York [CCNY]
College of New Rochelle
Columbia University
Cornell University
Hofstra University
Hunter College [CUNY]
Long Island University at Brooklyn
Manhattanville College
The New School
New York University
Pratt Institute
Queens College [CUNY]
Sarah Lawrence College
St. Joseph's College (NY)
Stony Brook Southampton
Syracuse University

Low-Residency MFA Programs
Bard College
Ithaca College
New York University
St. Francis College
Transart Institute

Creative Writing Doctoral Programs
Binghamton University
State University of New York at Albany [SUNY]

North Carolina

Full-Residency MFA Programs
North Carolina State University
University of North Carolina at Greensboro
University of North Carolina at Wilmington

Low-Residency MFA Programs
Queens University of Charlotte
Warren Wilson College

North Dakota

Creative Writing Doctoral Programs
University of North Dakota

Ohio

Full-Residency MFA Programs
Bowling Green State University
Miami University
NEOMFA
Ohio State University

Low-Residency MFA Programs
Ashland University
Miami University

Creative Writing Doctoral Programs
Ohio University
University of Cincinnati

Oklahoma

Full-Residency MFA Programs
Oklahoma State University

Low-Residency MFA Programs
Oklahoma City University

Creative Writing Doctoral Programs
Oklahoma State University

Oregon

Full-Residency MFA Programs
Oregon State University
Portland State University
University of Oregon

Low-Residency MFA Programs
    Eastern Oregon University
    Oregon State University
    Pacific University

Pennsylvania

Full-Residency MFA Programs
    Chatham University
    Rosemont College
    Temple University
    University of Pittsburgh

Low-Residency MFA Programs
    Arcadia University
    Carlow University
    Cedar Crest College
    Seton Hill University
    Chatham University
    Wilkes University

Rhode Island

Full-Residency MFA Programs
    Brown University

Low-Residency MFA Programs
    Salve Regina University [Newport]

Creative Writing Doctoral Programs
    University of Rhode Island

South Carolina

Full-Residency MFA Programs
    College of Charleston
    University of South Carolina

Texas Tech University
University of Houston
University of North Texas
University of Texas at Dallas

Utah

Full-Residency MFA Programs
Brigham Young University
University of Utah

Creative Writing Doctoral Programs
University of Utah

Vermont

Full-Residency MFA Programs
Vermont College of Fine Arts

Low-Residency MFA Programs
Bennington College
Goddard College
Vermont College of Fine Arts

Virginia

Full-Residency MFA Programs
George Mason University
Hollins University
Old Dominion University
University of Virginia
Virginia Commonwealth University
Virginia Tech

Low-Residency MFA Programs
Randolph College

Washington

Full-Residency MFA Programs
Eastern Washington University
University of Washington at Bothell
University of Washington at Seattle
Western Washington University

Low-Residency MFA Programs
Pacific Lutheran University [Rainier]
Seattle Pacific University

West Virginia

Full-Residency MFA Programs
West Virginia University

Low-Residency MFA Programs
West Virginia Wesleyan University

Wisconsin

Full-Residency MFA Programs
University of Wisconsin at Madison

Creative Writing Doctoral Programs
University of Wisconsin at Madison
University of Wisconsin at Milwaukee

Wyoming

Full-Residency MFA Programs
University of Wyoming

Canada: Alberta

Creative Writing Doctoral Programs
University of Calgary

Canada: British Columbia

Full-Residency MFA Programs
   University of British Columbia at Okanagan
   University of British Columbia at Vancouver
   University of Victoria

Low-Residency MFA Programs
   University of British Columbia at Vancouver

Canada: New Brunswick

Creative Writing Doctoral Programs
   University of New Brunswick

Canada: Nova Scotia

Low-Residency MFA Programs
   University of King's College, Halifax

Canada: Ontario

Full-Residency MFA Programs
   University of Guelph

Canada: Saskatchewan

Full-Residency MFA Programs
   University of Saskatchewan

Beyond North America

Australia and New Zealand

Creative Writing Doctoral Programs
   Deakin University
   Flinders University
   Monash University

Royal Melbourne Institute of Technology
Swinburne University of Technology
University of Adelaide
University of Melbourne
University of New South Wales
University of Queensland
University of Western Australia
University of Wollongong
Victoria University
Victoria University of Wellington

China

Full-Residency MFA Programs
Fudan University
Shanghai University
University of Hong Kong

Low-Residency MFA Programs
City University of Hong Kong

Colombia

Full-Residency MFA Programs
Universidad Nacional de Colombia in Bogotá

Ireland

Full-Residency MFA Programs
University College Dublin

Creative Writing Doctoral Programs
University College Cork

The Philippines

Full-Residency MFA Programs
De La Salle University

Creative Writing Doctoral Programs
   University of the Philippines at Diliman

United Kingdom

Full-Residency MFA Programs
   Birkbeck—University of London
   Kingston University
   Goldsmiths—University of London
   University of Glasgow
   University of Surrey
   University of St. Andrews

Low-Residency MFA Programs
   Plymouth University

Creative Writing Doctoral Programs
   Anglia Ruskin University
   Bath Spa University
   Brunel University at West London
   Cardiff University
   Edge Hill University
   De Montfort University at Leicester
   Essex University
   Kingston University at London
   Lancaster University
   Loughborough University
   Manchester Metropolitan University
   Middlesex University
   Newcastle University
   Northumbria University
   Nottingham Trent University
   The Open University
   Queen's University at Belfast
   Roehampton University
   Saint Mary's University College at Twickenham
   Swansea University
   University of Bedfordshire
   University of Bolton
   University of Bradford

INDEX